Socialism: The Failed Idea That Never Dies

SOCIALISM: THE FAILED IDEA
THAT NEVER DIES

KRISTIAN NIEMIETZ

Institute of
Economic Affairs

First published in Great Britain in 2019 by
The Institute of Economic Affairs
2 Lord North Street
Westminster
London SW1P 3LB
in association with London Publishing Partnership Ltd
www.londonpublishingpartnership.co.uk

The mission of the Institute of Economic Affairs is to improve understanding
of the fundamental institutions of a free society by analysing and expounding
the role of markets in solving economic and social problems.

A CIP catalogue record for this book is available from the British Library.

ISBN 978-0-255-36770-7

Many IEA publications are translated into languages other
than English or are reprinted. Permission to translate or to reprint
should be sought from the Director General at the address above.

Typeset in Kepler by T&T Productions Ltd
www.tandtproductions.com

Printed and bound in Great Britain by Hobbs the Printers Ltd

The red flag of international Socialism waves from the palace and from all the public buildings of Berlin. [...] [O]ur long years of toil and battling for the righteous cause of the people are now crowned with success. The old rotten regime, with its [...] system of plundering the working classes, has crumbled to pieces. And for the benefit of my children, and children's children, I intend to set down, in a humble way, some little account of the beginning of this new reign of brotherhood and universal philanthropy.

Eugen Richter
Pictures of the Socialistic Future (1893: Chapter 1)

An order has just been issued to reduce the bread rations of the entire population by one half, and to do away with the meat rations altogether. [...] I find I shall henceforth be no longer able to give the same full account of events as they happen. The twelve hours day comes into force tomorrow, so I shall then not have much time for writing. [...] I notice that I am regarded with such increasing suspicion that a search might be made, and my papers confiscated at any moment.

Eugen Richter
Pictures of the Socialistic Future (1893: Chapter 32)

CONTENTS

ABOUT THE AUTHOR

Dr Kristian Niemietz is Head of Political Economy at the Institute of Economic Affairs. He studied economics at the Humboldt University Berlin and the University of Salamanca, and political economy at King's College London. Kristian previously worked at the Berlin-based Institute for Free Enterprise (IUF) and taught economics at King's College London. He is the author of the books *A New Understanding of Poverty* (2011), *Redefining the Poverty Debate* (2012) and *Universal Healthcare Without the NHS* (2016).

SUMMARY

Socialism is popular in the UK – not just among students, but also among people in their 30s and 40s. This is confirmed by survey after survey. Surveys also show that support for socialism in general terms is matched by support for a broad range of individual policies that could reasonably be described as socialist.

Curiously, support for socialism in the abstract is *not* matched by positive perceptions of any actual example, contemporary or historical, of a socialist system in action. People with a rose-tinted view of, for example, the former Warsaw Pact countries, of Maoist China, of North Vietnam or North Korea are a small minority in Britain today. Socialists have successfully distanced themselves from the over two dozen failed attempts to build a socialist society. Their claim that these systems were never 'really' socialist, but represented a distortion of the socialist ideal, has become conventional wisdom. Today, holding the failures of, for example, the former Soviet Union against a contemporary socialist is considered crass and boorish.

Yet while socialists distance themselves from contemporary and historical examples of socialism, they usually struggle to explain what exactly they would do differently. Socialists tend to escape into abstraction, and talk about lofty aspirations rather than tangible institutional characteristics. Those aspirations (for example, 'democratising the economy'), however, are nothing new. They are the same aspirations that motivated earlier socialist projects. Socialism has never fulfilled those aspirations, but this is not for a lack of trying.

The not-*real*-socialism defence is only ever invoked retrospectively, namely, when a socialist experiment has already been widely discredited. As long as a socialist experiment is in its prime, almost nobody disputes its socialist credentials. On the contrary: practically all socialist regimes have gone through honeymoon periods, during which they were enthusiastically praised and held up as role models by plenty of prominent Western intellectuals. It is only after the event (i.e. once they have become an embarrassment for the socialist cause) that their version of socialism is retroactively redefined as 'unreal'.

This pattern started in the 1930s, when thousands of Western intellectuals went on political pilgrimages to the Soviet Union. Even though the atrocities of that regime were widely known – or at least know*able* – in the West, the Soviet Union was widely held up to be a worker-run grassroots democracy in the making. When 'Stalin-mania' later fell out of fashion, most of Stalin's Western admirers did not officially renounce their position, but simply fell silent on the issue.

In the 1960s, the same thing happened again, except that this time, Cuba, North Vietnam, and above all, Maoist China, became the utopias *du jour*. Echoing the earlier wave of pilgrimages to the Soviet Union, Western intellectuals flocked to these places in large numbers and returned full of praise. The new utopias were presented as an alternative to Western capitalism on the one hand, but also to the discredited socialism of the Soviet Union and its allies on the other hand. The 'this-time-is-completely-different' is not remotely new: since the 1960s, Western intellectuals have explicitly defined all new socialist experiments in opposition to earlier, failed attempts.

When Cuba, Vietnam and Maoist China fell out of fashion in the 1970s, Albania and Cambodia took their place. The scale of the pilgrimages was tiny this time, but the basic pattern was the same: Western admirers claimed that while earlier socialist experiments had been corrupted, this time, a genuine workers' and peasants' democracy would emerge. Due to their extreme isolationism, these countries were not tainted by associations with discredited versions of socialism.

The two most obvious natural experiments of socialism are the splitting of Korea and Germany into a socialist and a broadly capitalist part. It is clear today that these experiments have produced conclusive results – but this was not always so clear, and, as long as the jury was out, plenty of Western intellectuals sympathised with the socialist rather than the capitalist parts of these countries.

The most recent example of the above-described pattern – enthusiastic endorsement, followed by retroactive disowning – is Venezuela. 'Venezuela-mania' started around 2005, and once again the central claim was that this time would be completely different: '21st century socialism' would be a democratic bottom-up socialism, which had nothing in common with the authoritarian top-down socialism of yesteryear. Venezuela soon found itself swamped by Western pilgrims. With Venezuela's descent into economic chaos, political unrest and authoritarianism, Venezuela-mania began to fade not long after Chávez's death. After a period of silence, Western socialists began to explicitly dispute the socialist credentials of *Chavismo*. Venezuela is joining a long list of countries that were never 'really' socialist.

Despite its long list of failures, socialism remains far more popular than capitalism. The research of Jonathan Haidt, which shows that most political and moral reasoning is about finding post-hoc justifications for an initial intuitive judgement, goes a long way towards explaining why this is the case. The case for capitalism is counterintuitive: to most of us, capitalism simply *feels* wrong. Socialism, in contrast, chimes with our moral intuitions. Socialism simply *feels* right. Being a socialist is a 'default opinion', which comes easily and naturally to us. Appreciating the benefits of a market economy, in contrast, takes some intellectual self-discipline. Even prominent free-market intellectuals, such as Milton Friedman and F. A. Hayek, did not start their careers as free marketeers.

We can't concede the end of communism. Communism hasn't been tried on a society-wide basis.

Professor Stephen Resnick, University of Massachusetts

There hasn't been a shred of socialism in the Soviet Union. [...] It's got nothing to do with socialism.

Professor Noam Chomsky (n. d.)

Socialism is a good idea, which has just been badly implemented.

From a 2002 survey in east Germany;
82 per cent of respondents agreed.

A socialist society [...] doesn't exist yet, but one day it must.

Owen Jones (2016)

The primary lesson here is not about [...] 'socialism' or even 'communism' since Castro, Mao, Stalin, and Lenin did not actually attempt to implement [...] those ideas.

Nathan Robinson (*Current Affairs*) (2017)

Socialism has never been tried.

The Socialist Party of Great Britain (1999)

The struggle between communism and capitalism never happened. The Soviets didn't establish communism.

Professor Richard Wolff, University of Massachusetts

China and Cuba, like the former Soviet Union and Eastern Bloc, have nothing to do with socialism.

The International Socialist Organization (n.d.)

Socialism [...] has not failed, because it has not begun yet.

United Left [East German opposition group] (1990)

The Stalinist bureaucracy of [East Germany] [...] discredited the idea of socialism. We, the Spartacists, say: Socialism, under the real leadership of the working class, has not even begun yet.

Spartakist-Arbeiterpartei Deutschlands
[East German opposition party] (1990)

[T]here is no country in the world today that I would describe as socialist.

Eric Ruder, *Socialist Worker* (2010)

[W]hy do we blame socialism? It is not the ideology that is at work here [in Venezuela], just like socialism wasn't practiced during the Soviet Union [...] If Maduro and his government truly fulfilled the stated values of egalitarian democratic socialism, people wouldn't be starving.

Ryan Beitler (2017)

[A]fter seventy years of experience with socialism, it is safe to say that most intellectuals [...] remain [...] unwilling to wonder whether there might not be a reason why socialism, as often as it is attempted, never seems to work out as its intellectual leaders intended. The intellectuals' vain search for a truly socialist community [...] results in the idealisation of, and then disillusionment with, a seemingly endless string of 'utopias' – the Soviet Union, then Cuba, China, Yugoslavia, Vietnam, Tanzania, Nicaragua.

F. A. Hayek (1988)

TABLES AND FIGURES

1 THE ENDURING APPEAL OF SOCIALISM

Introduction: socialism is popular

Support for socialism in the abstract

Socialism is popular in Britain. Not just among millennials, but also among people in their 30s and 40s. According to a YouGov (2016a) survey, two in five British people aged between 18 and 50 years have a favourable opinion of socialism. Another two in five are not sure, leaving only one in five with an unfavourable opinion. Capitalism, meanwhile, has far more critics than supporters in the same age group; in fact, it has more critics than supporters across *all* age groups.[1]

In a similar survey, 43 per cent of respondents said that having 'a genuinely socialist government' would make the UK 'a better place to live' (YouGov 2017a). One in five respondents were indifferent or unsure, leaving only 36 per cent who thought that it would make the UK 'a worse place to live'.

---

[1] Disapproval of one system does not automatically mean approval of the other. It is possible to be opposed to both, either as a form of nihilism ('all systems are bad'), or combined with advocacy of something else entirely. Among those over the age of 65, there is net disapproval of both socialism *and* capitalism.

In a complementary survey, only 29 per cent of people between the ages of 18 and 50 agreed with the statement 'Competition among private-sector companies increases living standards for the great majority of people, as it leads to new and better goods and services, creates extra jobs and keeps down prices' (YouGov 2017b). But as many as 37 per cent agreed with the opposite statement, namely 'Competition among private-sector companies reduces the living standards of millions of people, because it helps mainly the rich, leads to poverty wages for many workers, and often results in shoddy goods and services.' (The remainder answered 'Don't know'.)

Those findings are corroborated by a recent Populus survey, which asked respondents about their main associations with capitalism, socialism and various other -isms. Common associations with capitalism include 'greedy', 'selfish', 'corrupt' and 'divisive' (but also 'innovative'). Common associations with socialism include 'For the greater good', 'Delivers most for most people' and 'Fair', terms that almost nobody in Britain associates with capitalism (Legatum Institute 2017). The most common negative association with socialism is 'naïve', a trait which is not really all that negative, and which some may actually find endearing.[2]

---

2 Curiously, while the survey shows positive associations with the term 'socialism', it also shows negative associations with the term 'communism'. If we take the dictionary meaning of those terms at face value, this makes no sense: you cannot logically combine a positive view of socialism with a negative view of communism. In Marxist theory, 'communism' is simply the hypothetical final stage of socialism, the stage that is reached when socialism is so advanced that it no longer requires a state apparatus. Presumably,

Support for socialist policies

Terms like 'socialism' and 'capitalism' may mean different things to different people. But support for socialism in the abstract is also matched by support for individual policies that could reasonably be described as 'socialist', perhaps not on their own, but at least as a bundle.

Figure 1   Support for public ownership by sector (in %)

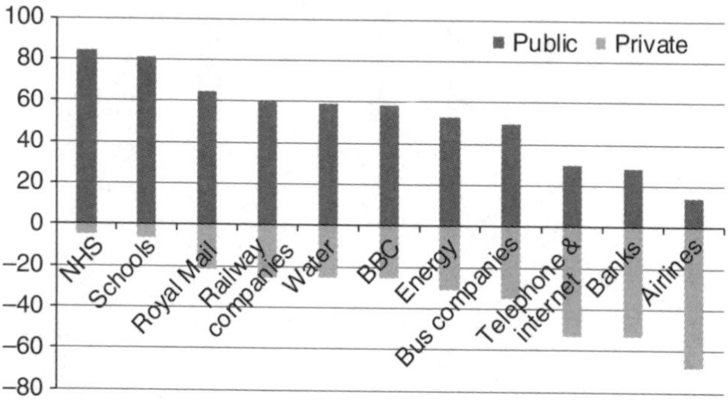

Source: Based on YouGov (2017c).

Industry nationalisations, for example, enjoy widespread popular support. A majority of people favour the (re-)nationalisation of bus companies, energy providers, water companies, the railways and Royal Mail (see Figure 1). Where a sector is already nationalised, such as primary/secondary education and healthcare, there is

most survey participants associate the term 'communism' with the kind of socialism that actually existed in Eastern Europe and elsewhere, and the term 'socialism' with the ideal, which, in the minds of many, has not been tainted by its messy real-world applications.

virtually nobody in the country who wants to change that (YouGov 2017c).[3] Earlier, similar surveys show even larger pro-nationalisation majorities for even more industries (YouGov 2016b, 2015a, 2013).

Figure 2 Support for public ownership by sector (in %)

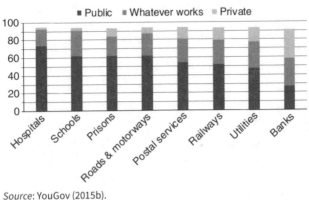

Source: YouGov (2015b).

Another survey finds that one in four respondents want to nationalise car companies and travel agents, while one in three want to nationalise food retailing (Legatum Institute 2017).[4] Ian Dunt, the editor of Politics.co.uk, was right

---

3   Five per cent of respondents say that they want to privatise the NHS. While clearly a minority, this is, on the face of it, a lot more than 'virtually nobody'. However, it is an idiosyncrasy of surveys that every option that is available will normally be chosen by at least *some* respondents. Scott Alexander (2013) calls this phenomenon the 'Lizardman's Constant', a reference to a US survey where people were asked whether they believe that the world is run by intelligent lizardmen from outer space. Four per cent replied yes.

4   The numbers are not directly comparable to the YouGov surveys, because the Populus survey does not include a 'Don't know' option.

when he said that 'the public hardly believe in the private running of anything' (Dunt 2015).

For most industries, the pro-nationalisation majority remains intact even when surveys include an additional, pragmatic-sounding response option such as 'whatever works best' (see Figure 2). This suggests that for most supporters of public ownership this is a matter of principle rather than a belief in the superior efficiency of the public sector.

Figure 3   Support for price controls by sector (in %)

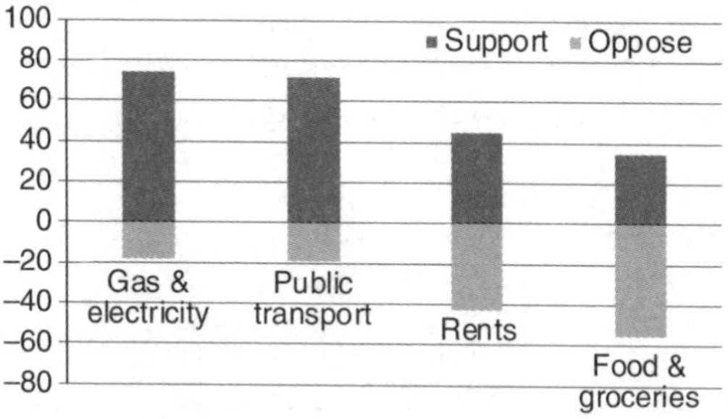

Source: YouGov (2013).

Price controls are also a very popular policy, albeit with a lot of variation between sectors (see Figure 3). More than seven out of ten respondents support price caps for energy and public transport, with fewer than one in five opposing. In this particular survey, supporters and opponents of rent controls roughly balance each other, but more recent, similarly worded surveys on the same subject find large majorities favouring rent controls (see Hilton 2016). There is no overall support for

Venezuela-style price controls for food and groceries, but a significant minority – more than one in three respondents – are in favour of that as well.

Government regulation and interference with business decisions are also popular, both in the abstract and when specific examples are mentioned (see Table 1).

Table 1   Support for regulation

Dominant view	Minority view	Margin
'The pay of senior execs should be capped.'	'Businesses should pay their senior execs what they see fit.'	56%
'Government needs to do more to regulate how businesses behave.'	'Government regulates businesses too much.'	32%
'Zero hours contracts should be abolished.'	'Zero hours contracts offer useful work.'	22%
'Companies have a responsibility to ensure they have a decent number of workers at board level.'	'It doesn't matter if there aren't any workers on boards.'	15%
'Link people's pay to the value their jobs contribute to broader society.'	'Allow people to get what their employers/customers are willing to pay.'	8%

Legatum Institute (2017).

A relative majority also supports a larger state, as opposed to the status quo or a smaller state (see Figure 4). The margin vis-à-vis the status quo is not huge, and it is not consistent over the years. But it is a consistent finding that virtually nobody in Britain wants the state to be any smaller than it currently is.

Most of these policies are not exceptionally radical on their own. A nationalised railway industry or capped bus fares would not turn Britain into North Korea. We can find plenty of prosperous market economies which have implemented one or more of those policies (although none that have implemented the whole package).

Figure 4   Support for a larger state (in %)

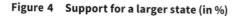

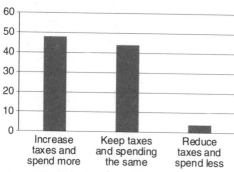

Source: NatCen Social Research (2017).

But what such results do show is that the often-heard claim that Britain is in the grip of a 'neoliberal hegemony' is the exact opposite of the truth. In the economic sphere, the zeitgeist is statist and interventionist. Support for free markets is an exotic and unpopular fringe opinion. As Allister Heath, the editor of the *Sunday Telegraph*, puts it (2017):

> Spend more, regulate more, tax more: it's UK politics' stultifying new orthodoxy. Its proponents [...] set the parameters of our increasingly narrow national conversation. [...] There is no longer a debate: merely a relentless assault on capitalism [...] amplified by 'centrists' who keep conceding to the Left.

The anti-capitalist mainstream

Surveys provide a glimpse into the mood among the general population. Among the politically most active sections of society, socialist – or at least anti-capitalist – ideas have long been predominant, and highly fashionable. For example, all high-profile protest movements in recent decades – be it anti-austerity, Occupy or anti-globalisation – were explicitly anti-capitalist.[5] In 2011, a small 'Rally Against Debt' in Westminster attracted considerable media coverage, although it was, according to the *New Statesman*, only attended by about 200 people.[6] This was because it was so counterintuitive. We are so used to the idea that protest must be left-wing and anti-capitalist that the idea of a protest against government largesse feels jarring.

Last but not least, the politics/economics sections of high street book stores are also invariably dominated by anti-capitalist literature. The books of Naomi Klein, Noam Chomsky, Slavoj Žižek, Yanis Varoufakis, Owen Jones, Ha-Joon Chang, Paul Mason, Russell Brand, etc., are bestsellers within their genre; pro-market books are a rarity. Writers such as Joseph Stiglitz, Paul Krugman or Thomas

---

5   This is, at least, the situation in the UK and the rest of Europe. In the US, the Tea Party could be considered a protest movement against government largesse, although it is really a broader coalition in which the social conservatism probably outweighs the anti-statism.

6   Rally Against Debt? It was more of a long queue, *New Statesman*, 15 May 2011 (http://www.newstatesman.com/blogs/the-staggers/2011/05/rally-cuts-debt-event-lisa-low).

Piketty are clearly politically on the centre-left, but in relative terms their books are often the most 'neoliberal' ones one can find in a typical high street bookstore. If this constitutes a 'neoliberal hegemony', one wonders what a left-wing hegemony would look like.

After the 2017 General Election, the *Financial Times* claimed that 'Jeremy Corbyn has staged an unprecedented socialist revival'.[7] He has done no such thing. One cannot revive what has never been dead. Socialism has never been away; it has just not always been at the immediate forefront of day-to-day politics. It may have returned there with 'Corbyn-mania', but the appeal of socialism was never about any one particular political candidate, party or movement.

Some readers will probably find it odd that although this book is partly about socialism in Britain, it has next to nothing to say on 'Corbyn-mania', Corbynomics, Momentum, etc. But this follows logically from the recognition that 'Corbynistas' are not the radical insurgents they think themselves to be. They do not, and indeed could not, challenge 'the prevailing orthodoxy' because in many ways their ideas *are* the prevailing orthodoxy. They are just a political manifestation of a widespread antipathy to the market economy, which long predates them, and which will outlive them, in whatever form. When Hayek dedicated his book *The Road to Serfdom* to the socialists

---

7   Jeremy Corbyn has staged an unprecedented socialist revival, *Financial Times*, 9 June 2017 (https://www.ft.com/content/05f8abe0-4d03-11e7-a3f4 -c742b9791d43).

of *all* parties, he knew what he was doing. Today, he would probably dedicate it to the socialists of all parties, protest movements, campaign groups, charities, universities, religious organisations, media outlets and social media platforms.

The pervasiveness of socialist assumptions

What is perhaps more important than support for any specific socialist policy or set of policies is the fact that socialist *assumptions* about economic life permeate our whole economic policy discourse. These assumptions are rarely spelt out explicitly, and most people would probably not even regard them as 'socialist' – just as 'common sense'.

Take the above-mentioned support for nationalising industries, such as energy or train operators: this need not, in itself, be a socialist position. One can take the view that market competition is *generally* beneficial, but that some sectors are just not amenable to it (say, due to natural monopoly elements). This is not a socialist argument. But it is *not* the argument that is usually made.

The conventional argument is that 'profiteering corporations' are 'ripping off the public', and must therefore be nationalised in order to make them work for 'the common good'. They must be made accountable to the public rather than to private shareholders.[8] Very few people will regard

---

8   For example: Rail privatisation: legalised larceny, *The Guardian*, 4 November 2013 (https://www.theguardian.com/commentisfree/2013/nov/04/rail -privatisation-train-operators-profit). For Tories, privatisation is still a

this sentiment as 'socialist'. But for at least four reasons, it very much is.

Firstly, average profit margins in the sectors where support for nationalisation is strongest are only about 3–4 per cent.[9] This suggests that the argument for nationalisation is not an economic argument at all, but a moralistic impulse – a knee-jerk condemnation of the profit motive. This anti-profit moralism is part of a socialist mindset.

Secondly, the argument rests on the assumption that the public sector is driven by altruistic motives, and that therefore, whatever is done by the state is done with 'the common good' in mind. This is a quintessentially socialist assumption. It is also, to say the least, debatable. As economists of the Public Choice School have demonstrated time and again, self-interested behaviour exists in the public/political sphere as much as anywhere else: senior civil servants trying to expand their budgets and their remit in order to improve their prestige; rent seeking by special interest groups; political clientelism; 'jobs for the boys' tendencies, etc. (see, for example, Tullock 2006 [1976]).

---

matter of dogmatic faith, *Independent*, 14 July 2013 (http://www.indepen dent.co.uk/voices/comment/owen-jones-for-tories-privatisation-is-still-a -matter-of-dogmatic-faith-8708021.html).

9   The government's 'temporary' energy price cap is bad economics, IEA blog, 19 October 2017 (https://iea.org.uk/the-governments-temporary-en ergy-price-cap-is-bad-economics/). Even these margins could not simply be passed on to consumers after nationalisation, because a nationalised industry still needs to raise capital in some way, and it will not obtain it for free. See: Do train operating companies earn 'massive' profits? *Full Fact*, 14 November 2013 (https://fullfact.org/news/do -train-operating-companies-earn-massive-profits/).

Thirdly, there is the assumption that there must be a conflict between the aim of satisfying people's needs and the aim of earning a profit. But under conditions of voluntary exchange within the rule of law, how else can a company make a profit other than by supplying what people want, at a price they are prepared to pay? How could it be profitable to ignore people's needs?

Fourthly, there is the idea that nationalisation brings an industry 'under democratic control' and makes it 'accountable to the public'.[10] This, too, is a socialist assumption, and a very dubious one at that. As Seldon (2004 [1990]: 179) explained:

> [T]he notion that 'society as a whole' can control 'its productive resources' is common in socialist writing but is patently unrealistic. The machinery of social control has never been devised. There is no conceivable way in which the British citizen can control the controllers of 'his' state railway or NHS, except so indirectly that it is in effect inoperative.

And elsewhere (ibid.: 210):

> What belongs nominally to everyone on paper belongs in effect to no-one in practice. Coalfields, railways, schools and hospitals that are owned 'by the people' are in real life owned by phantoms. No nominal owner can sell, hire,

---

10 See, for example: Reality Check: Why does Labour want to control National Grid?, *BBC News*, 11 May 2017 (http://www.bbc.co.uk/news/business-39884416).

lend, bequeath or give them to family, friends or good causes. Public ownership is a myth and a mirage. It is the false promise and the Achilles' heel of socialism. The effort required to 'care' for the 50-millionth individual share of a hospital or school owned by 50 million people, even if identifiable, would far outweigh the benefit; so it is not made, even if it could be. The task is deputed to public servants answerable to politicians who in turn are in socialist mythology answerable to the people. In this long line of communication the citizen is often in effect disenfranchised.

We can also see a quasi-socialist mindset in populist rhetoric which frames practically all social conflicts as conflicts between 'the people' (also known as 'working people' or 'ordinary people') and 'the elites', or some variation thereof, such as 'the 99 per cent' versus 'the 1 per cent'. This is a watered-down version of Marxist class theory, in which social classes, not individuals or more specific groups, form the main unit of analysis. In this mindset, 'The People' are a homogeneous group with common, and easily identifiable, economic interests and preferences. There is therefore a very easy solution to most of our economic and social problems: get rid of The Elites, and replace them with champions of The People.

But the People-versus-Elites template is a very poor guide to the political conflicts we actually observe. Of course, our personal preferences and economic interests sometimes correlate with social class – just as they sometimes correlate with age, gender, region, family status, ethnicity, tenure, occupational status, religion, nationality or health status. But social class is just one dividing line among many. On virtually all the high-profile issues of our time (Brexit, immigration, the housing crisis, 'austerity', welfare reform, etc.), the dividing lines run across social classes, not between them.[11] Socialists sometimes acknowledge this, but they put it down to a form of 'false consciousness' deliberately created by The Elites in order to distract and divide The People.[12]

This is because socialist mythology treats The People as a romanticised abstraction, which has little to do with actual people. As Terry Pratchett writes in one of his novels:

> Some [...] were on the side of what they called 'the people'. Vimes had spent his life on the streets, and had met

---

11 See, for example: Trump and Brexit: why it's again NOT the economy, stupid, *Politics and Policy* blog, 9 November 2016 (http://blogs.lse.ac.uk/politics andpolicy/trump-and-brexit-why-its-again-not-the-economy-stupid/); The Corbynistas are wrong: there's no such thing as 'The People', IEA blog, 5 May 2017 (https://iea.org.uk/the-corbynistas-are-wrong-theres-no-such -thing-as-the-people/).

12 For example: Don't let Trump fool you: rightwing populism is the new normal, *The Guardian*, video, 6 January 2016 (https://www.theguardian.com/ commentisfree/video/2016/jan/06/dont-let-trump-fool-you-rightwing -populism-is-the-new-normal-video); We'll never stop Brexit or Trump until we address the anger fuelling both, *The Guardian*, 10 November 2017 (https://www.theguardian.com/global/commentisfree/2017/nov/10/ never-stop-brexit-trump-address-anger-impeachment-second-referen dum); Naomi Klein on neoliberalism and the fightback against Donald Trump, *The Guardian*, books podcast, 4 July 2017 (https://www.the guardian.com/books/audio/2017/jul/04/naomi-klein-trump-neoliberal ism-left-failed-books-podcast); The rise of Europe's far right will only be halted by a populism of the left, *The Guardian*, 14 May 2014 (https:// www.theguardian.com/commentisfree/2014/may/14/rise-of-europe -far-right-only-halted-by-populism-of-left).

decent men and fools and people who'd steal a penny from a blind beggar and people who performed silent miracles [...], but he'd never met The People.

People on the side of The People always ended up disappointed, in any case. They found that The People tended not to be grateful or appreciative or forward-thinking or obedient.[13]

Socialist assumptions can also be found in the unconditionally sympathetic coverage of industry strikes in the 'progressive' press.[14] Most economists, whatever their political persuasion, would argue that the main determinant of pay levels is productivity. Industrial action may well often be justified, but it is a sideshow: if we want to see wage increases, then we must, first and foremost, support measures that facilitate productivity growth. Economists disagree profoundly over what those measures are, but not on the fundamental point.

---

13 *Night Watch* (2002), quoted at https://www.goodreads.com/quotes/373774 -there-were-plotters-there-was-no-doubt-about-it-some.

14 For example: Junior doctors are striking for us all – to save the NHS and to make a stand, *The Guardian*, 12 January 2016 (https://www.theguardian. com/commentisfree/2016/jan/12/junior-doctor-strike-save-nhs-stand -up-government); Celebrate the strikers this week – they are fighting for us all, *The Guardian*, 6 July 2014 (https://www.theguardian.com/comment isfree/2014/jul/06/celebrate-strikers-media-opposed-trade-unions); Five reasons public service workers are right to strike, *The Guardian*, 28 November 2011 (https://www.theguardian.com/commentisfree/2011/nov/28/pub lic-service-workers-strike); Power or productivity? Why we disagree over tube strikes, IEA blog, 10 July 2015 (https://iea.org.uk/blog/power -or-productivity-why-we-disagree-over-tube-strikes).

Contemporary socialists, however, see living standards primarily as the result of power struggles. Living standards of ordinary people rise when they organise and fight for it, and stagnate or fall when they cease to organise and fight for it. In this mindset, the focus is almost exclusively on the distribution of wealth, not on its generation.

Finally, plenty of controversial causes become a lot more popular as soon as they are cloaked in anti-capitalist rhetoric. For example, Snowdon (2017: 75–80) shows that while 'nanny state' measures (i.e. paternalistic lifestyle regulations) are not particularly popular in Britain, they become so as soon as they are presented as anti-industry measures. The difference is, of course, illusory. It is impossible to make it harder for a company to *sell* a product without also making it harder for customers to *buy* that product. Nonetheless, shifting the emphasis from consumers to producers is an effective strategy, because it taps into popular anti-capitalist sentiments.

We can see the same strategy at work when 'NIMBY' (i.e. anti-housebuilding) protesters present housing development as an activity that merely lines the pockets of developers, but fulfils no useful social purpose otherwise (see Niemietz 2015: 17). We can also see it when anti-aviation/anti-tourism activists claim that they only want to hit airlines and airport operators, not tourists (see Niemietz 2013: 41).

We could go on. It is, above all, in this sense that socialism is alive and well in Britain. Socialism in Britain is not primarily a political programme, but a set of assumptions that are widely held, but rarely explicitly spelt out, and therefore rarely questioned.

Socialism and social democracy

Before wading into a discussion about socialism, a note of clarification regarding terminology is required. The general definition of 'socialism' is straightforward enough: according to the Merriam-Webster dictionary, it is 'any of various economic and political theories advocating collective or governmental ownership and administration of the means of production and distribution of goods'. Yet in practice, at least in the UK and the US, the term is also sometimes used in reference to countries with strong social democratic traditions, such as the Nordic countries. So is the apparent popularity of socialism really just a semantic confusion? Are self-described socialists really just Nordic-style social democrats with a penchant for socialist rhetoric?

The short answer is no. It is not that self-described socialists are not 'really' socialists. Rather, many self-described admirers of the Nordic model are not really admirers of the Nordic model.

What is 'the Nordic model'? On the British left, the term is often used in the sense of 'a heavily interventionist, state-dominated economy, which stops just short of being fully socialist'. For example, journalist Abi Wilkinson writes:

> Despite massive differences between the countries, some [...] argue that a leftwards shift [in the UK] would result in political and economic collapse similar to [...] Venezuela. In reality, the Nordic states are a much better point

of comparison. More mixed economies and comprehensive welfare states lead them to outperform the UK.[15]

This is not true. The Nordic economies are not 'more mixed economies'. The difference between them and Venezuela is not a difference in degree. It is a qualitative difference, namely the difference between a *large* state and an *interventionist* state. The Nordic states are large, but they are not particularly interventionist. The Nordic economies are characterised by high taxes and high levels of public spending, but they are otherwise relatively liberal market economies.

The Nordic countries generally score very highly on indices such as the Economic Freedom Index or the Ease of Doing Business Index – *except* in those subcategories that are specifically related to the tax burden (Fraser Institute 2017; World Bank 2017). On the latter index, Denmark and Norway rank higher than the UK and the US, with Sweden just one place behind. On the former index, the UK and the US rank above the Nordic countries, but the difference is solely due to the latter's low scores in the 'Size of Government' subcategory. In the other subcategories, Denmark, Finland and Sweden rank above the UK and the US, with Norway ranking between them (see Figure 5).

This means that relative to most other developed economies, the Nordic economies are not heavily regulated,

---

15 I'm not buying this sudden surge of compassionate Conservatism, *Total Politics*, 11 August 2017 (https://www.totalpolitics.com/articles/opinion/abi-wilkinson-im-not-buying-sudden-surge-compassionate-conserva tism).

the state is not an active participant in economic life, and it does not try to direct economic activity. Nordic governments do not interfere heavily in wage and price setting processes, and they do not engage in an activist industrial policy. They privatised many formerly state-owned enterprises long ago. Even in the provision of public services, they often rely on market-like mechanisms, while also allowing private sector participation. Local authorities are, to a large extent, responsible for their own spending, which they must fund through locally raised taxes (OECD n.d.).

Figure 5   Economic Freedom scores

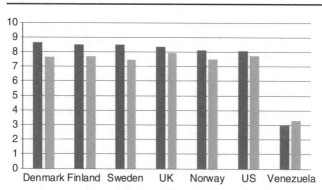

■ Excluding 'Size of Government' category
■ Including 'Size of Government' category

Source: Fraser Institute (2017).

British admirers of the Nordic model – or rather, of what they *perceive* to be the 'Nordic model' – never mention those liberal aspects of the Nordic economies. They only focus on their high taxes and high levels of welfare spending, and otherwise project what they want to see into those countries.

But most of the socialist policies which are popular in Britain – nationalisations, wage and price controls, industrial policy,[16] a rejection of market mechanisms and private sector involvement in public services, etc. – do not have much of a counterpart in the Nordic countries. At the same time, UK policies which do have a close Nordic equivalent are controversial in the UK, and tend to be opposed by socialists.

For example, the UK's free schools were explicitly modelled on the Swedish *friskolor*. The creation of an internal market within the NHS has also been, if not directly inspired by, then at least mirrored by a similar agenda in Sweden. The socialist left in the UK has opposed those changes right from the start, and continues to advocate their abolition.

The difference between socialism and social democracy is perhaps clearer in countries such as the Netherlands, Germany and Sweden, which have (or used to have) a major social democratic party and a major socialist party side by side. There, a socialist party would not simply be the more radical version of a social democratic party. Rather, such parties might have similar positions on taxation and welfare spending, while differing sharply on issues such as nationalisation, price controls, allowing the profit motive, and so on.

The combination of relatively liberal economic policies on the one hand, and generously funded public/social services on the other hand, is, of course, not unheard of

---

16 For example: Owen Jones's 'Agenda for Hope': We want a fairer society – and here's how we can achieve it, 26 January 2014, *Independent* (http://www.independent.co.uk/voices/comment/owen-joness-agenda-for-hope-we-want-a-fairer-society-and-here-s-how-we-can-achieve-it-9086440.html).

in the UK. This is more or less what the 'Third Way', a leit-motif of the New Labour government's domestic policies, was about. To what extent it became a political reality is a matter of debate, but at least in terms of their political ideas, it is the Third Way advocates – *not* the socialist left – who can be reasonably described as Nordic-style social democrats. 'Blairite', of course, has long become a term of abuse on the socialist left, a synonym for traitor and sell-out.

Support for socialism, then, really is what it says on the tin. It is *not* support for Nordic-style social democracy, or for its continental cousins, i.e. Dutch or German social democracy. A rhetorical embrace of 'the Nordic model' counts for little if it is coupled with a rejection of all the features that make the Nordic model work.

A lazy straw man?

Over the past hundred years, there have been more than two dozen attempts to build a socialist society. It has been tried in the Soviet Union, Yugoslavia, Albania, Poland, Vietnam, Bulgaria, Romania, Czechoslovakia, North Korea, Hungary, China, East Germany, Cuba, Tanzania, Benin, Laos, Algeria, South Yemen, Somalia, the Congo, Ethiopia, Cambodia, Mozambique, Angola, Nicaragua and Venezuela, among other countries. All of these attempts have ended in varying degrees of failure. How can an idea which has failed so many times, in so many different variants and so many radically different settings, still be so popular?

Part of the reason has to be that socialists have long been very effective at distancing themselves from real-world examples of socialism in action. Today, holding the failures of, for example, the Soviet Union against a self-described socialist is considered a cheap shot, not an intellectually respectable argument. Bringing up a real-world example of socialism guarantees scoffing and eye-rolling; it is seen as boorish, low-brow and ignorant.

Contemporary socialists take it as given that contemporary or historic examples of socialist states were never *really* socialist. These represent a perverted version of socialism, which bears so little resemblance to what contemporary socialists have in mind that there is no value in bringing them up at all.

For Noam Chomsky, calling the Soviet Union 'socialist' is just 'a way to defame socialism':

> [T]here hasn't been a shred of socialism in the Soviet Union. Now, of course, they *called* it socialism. But they also called it democracy. They were 'people's democracies' [...] So if you think that the fall of the Soviet Union is a blow to socialism, you'll also think [...] that it's a blow to democracy. After all, they called themselves democracies, too. So why isn't it a blow to democracy? Makes as much sense. [...]
>
> It had nothing to do with socialism. [...] What [socialism] always meant [...] was that [...] working people take control of production [...] [Soviet] Russia is about the most anti-socialist place you can imagine [...] [It] had no element of workers' control, or involvement, or

participation. It's got nothing to do with socialism. It's the exact opposite on every point.[17]

According to Richard Wolff, a professor of economics at the University of Massachusetts, Amherst, 'The struggle between communism and capitalism never happened. The Soviets didn't establish communism'.[18]

Stephen Resnick, a professor of economics at the same university, believes that 'We can't concede the end of communism. Communism hasn't been tried on a society-wide basis. It's a boastful notion that communism has been vanquished'.[19]

Nathan Robinson, the editor of *Current Affairs*, writes:

When anyone points me to the Soviet Union or Castro's Cuba and says 'Well, there's your socialism,' my answer [...] [is] that these regimes bear absolutely no relationship to the principle for which I am fighting. [...] The primary lesson here is not about [...] 'socialism' or even 'communism' since Castro, Mao, Stalin, and Lenin did not actually attempt to implement any of those ideas.[20]

---

17 The Soviet Union vs. Socialism (https://www.youtube.com/watch?v=06-Xc AiswY4&feature=youtu.be). See also Chomsky (1986).

18 USSR strayed from communism, say economics professors, *The Campus Chronicle*, 11 October 2002 (https://www.umass.edu/pubaffs/chronicle/ archives/02/10-11/economics.html).

19 Ibid.

20 How to be a socialist without being an apologist for the atrocities of communist regimes, *Current Affairs*, 25 October 2017 (https://www.current affairs.org/2017/10/how-to-be-a-socialist-without-being-an-apologist-for -the-atrocities-of-communist-regimes).

Washington Post columnist Elizabeth Bruenig reacted with indignation when, in response to her article 'It's time to give socialism a try', some of her critics brought up actual examples of socialism:

> I knew there would be [...] disagreement. And I knew that most [...] of it would unfold in bad faith. [...]
>
> In the case of my column, this meant many interlocutors taking socialism to mean something along the lines of Soviet communism or the Venezuelan system [...] I don't think anybody actually believes I'm rooting for totalitarian forms of socialism, nor for its most devastatingly ill-managed variants: I said I wasn't, after all.[21]

Closer to home, in a BBC *Daily Politics* programme, *Guardian* columnist Zoe Williams said:

> I do think there's something almost superstitious about the way nobody can even hear the word 'Marx' without saying [...] 'we're all gonna die, we're all going to be put into a Gulag.' [...] China [referring to Maoist China] is not any more a manifestation of Marxism than Norway is. I mean, this man [Karl Marx] was an economist [...] [T]he fact that some people used his name to start revolutions [...] is nothing to do with Marx.[22]

21 Let's have a good-faith argument about socialism, *Washington Post*, 11 March 2018 (https://www.washingtonpost.com/opinions/lets-have-a-good-faith -argument-about-socialism/2018/03/11/96d66720-23e4-11e8-86f6-54bfff 693d2b_story.html?utm_term=.51fc1c5003a6).

22 Daily Politics Show, *BBC Politics*, 1 November 2013 (https://www.facebook .com/BBCPolitics/videos/758283277521866/).

Shortly after the death of Fidel Castro, journalist Owen Jones claimed that Cuba was not 'really' socialist – and nor was any other country:

> Socialism without democracy [...] isn't socialism. [...] Socialism means socialising wealth and power – but how can power be socialised if it's concentrated in the hands of an unaccountable elite? [...]
>
> A socialist society [...] doesn't exist yet, but one day it must.[23]

Thus, contemporary socialists believe that their brand of socialism is so fundamentally different from anything that has gone by that name in the past that it makes all comparisons meaningless. Historical evidence of socialism in action can therefore hold no relevant lessons. It can be safely ignored.

Escape into the abstract, leaps of faith

Despite the vehemence with which contemporary socialists reject comparisons with any variant of socialism that has so far been tried, they usually struggle to explain what exactly they would do differently. What is the difference between 'real socialism' and 'unreal socialism'? What is it about the versions of socialism practised in the Warsaw Pact countries, Maoist China, North Vietnam, North Korea, etc., that makes them all 'unreal'? What would they have had to change in order to move into the 'real socialism' category?

---

23 My thoughts on Cuba, *Medium*, 29 November 2016 (https://medium.com/@ OwenJones84/my-thoughts-on-cuba-32280774222f).

This is where contemporary socialists usually become evasive and talk about lofty ambitions rather than tangible institutional characteristics. Real socialism, they claim, is a democratic socialism from below, a socialism which democratises economic life, and ensures that wealth and power are evenly shared. Real socialism puts ordinary working people – not technocrats, dictators or party elites – in charge.

Apart from its vagueness, this description contains two gigantic leaps of faith.

1. Contemporary socialists assume that the autocratic, stratified character of previous (and remaining) socialist regimes was deliberate. Socialist politicians *could* have established worker-run grassroots democracies, but *chose* not to do so. They *could* have established systems in which power would be vested in the hands of ordinary workers, but they did not want to. Establishing an authentic workers' democracy, then, is merely a matter of political will.[24]

2. Contemporary socialists appear to assume that a democratised, participatory version of socialism would not just be more humane, but also *economically* more successful. Autocratic socialism failed, but *democratic* socialism would have worked just fine, in terms of economic performance.[25]

---

24 In previous decades, it was more common to blame circumstances of history, economic underdevelopment, Western hostility, 'capitalist encirclement' and/or the 'false consciousness' of the masses.

25 This assumption is never explicitly spelt out, but, as we will see, it follows implicitly from socialists' refusal to debate the economic failures of

An example which illustrates these tendencies – an escape into abstraction, coupled with the two aforementioned leaps of faith – is Noam Chomsky's (1986) article 'The Soviet Union Versus Socialism'. For Chomsky, socialism, properly understood, means:

> the liberation of working people from exploitation. As the Marxist theoretician Anton Pannekoek observed, 'this goal is not reached and cannot be reached by a new directing and governing class substituting itself for the bourgeoisie,' but can only be 'realized by the workers themselves being master over production'.

Real socialism means:

> to convert the means of production into the property of freely associated producers and thus the social property of people who have liberated themselves from exploitation by their master, as a fundamental step towards a broader realm of human freedom.

These are nice aspirations. But they are also highly abstract aspirations. Which set of institutions would deliver them? How would those institutions work? How would we monitor whether they deliver what they ought to deliver, and how would we correct them if they do not? These are questions Chomsky does not bother to address.

---

socialist countries. Socialists will merely point out that these countries were not democratic, ergo, they were not really socialist, ergo, their experience is not relevant, and there is nothing to be learned from them.

And while Chomsky denounces the USSR's 'Red Bureaucracy', its 'new class' and its 'state priests' at great length, he does not have a single word to say on the Soviet Union's *economic* deficiencies. Apparently, he sees it as self-evident that if the workers of the Soviet Union had thrown out the Red Bureaucrats, and run the economy themselves, the country's economic problems would have disappeared.

Another example is Owen Jones's article on the future of Cuba, written shortly after Fidel Castro's death. Jones explains how Cuba's current 'unreal' socialism could yet become 'the real thing':

> Cuba could democratise and grant political freedoms currently denied as well as defending [...] the gains of the revolution. [...] [T]his is the next stage of the revolution. [...] The only future for socialism [...] is through democracy. That doesn't just mean standing in elections [...] It means organising a movement rooted in people's communities and workplaces. It means arguing for a system that extends democracy to the workplace and the economy. That's socialism: the democratisation of every aspect of society.[26]

So again, instead of providing at least a rough outline of how a 'real' socialist system might work, Jones escapes into abstract aspirations. 'Extending democracy to the

---

26 My thoughts on Cuba, *Medium*, 29 November 2016 (https://medium.com/@OwenJones84/my-thoughts-on-cuba-32280774222f).

economy' and 'democratising every aspect of society' are nice soundbites, but what does this mean in practice? What would an institutional framework which fulfils those aspirations look like?

And while Jones talks a lot about the need for political reform, he never hints at economic reform. He seems to assume that political democratisation would also, somehow, sort out the country's economic underdevelopment.

A third example is the *New York Times* article 'Socialism's future may be its past' by Bhaskar Sunkara, the founder of *Jacobin* magazine.[27] Sunkara believes that a century after the October Revolution, it is time to give socialism another try. But this time will be different:

> This time, people get to vote. Well, debate and deliberate and then vote — and have faith that people can organize together to chart new destinations for humanity. Stripped down to its essence, and returned to its roots, socialism is an ideology of radical democracy. [...] [I]t seeks to empower civil society to allow participation in the decisions that affect our lives. A huge state bureaucracy [...] can be just as alienating and undemocratic as corporate boardrooms, so we need to think hard about the new forms that social ownership could take.

The same pattern of escaping into lofty ambitions, and the same leaps of faith, are in evidence. Enabling people to

---

27 Socialism's future may be its past, *New York Times*, 26 June 2017 (https://www.nytimes.com/2017/06/26/opinion/finland-station-communism-socialism.html).

'organise together to chart new destinations for humanity', 'empowering civil society' and 'allowing participation in the decisions that affect our lives' are fine aspirations, but they are just that. Apart from 'people get to vote', Sunkara tells us nothing about how a system which delivers that might work in practice.

Like Chomsky and Jones, Sunkara seems to believe that this is simply a matter of willpower, and that the reason why previous attempts to build a socialist society have not delivered it is that previous socialist leaders have lacked that willpower.

Nor is there a word on the failures of the Soviet economy. Again, Sunkara seems to believe that democratisation would also, somehow, have sorted out the Soviet Union's economic problems.

Another example is the article 'How to be a socialist without being an apologist for the atrocities of communist regimes' by Nathan Robinson, the editor of *Current Affairs* magazine. Robinson sees political and economic systems like a buffet, where we can pick and choose the elements that we like:

Because I am capable of holding two ideas in my head at the same time, and do not think in caveman-like grunts of 'This good' and 'This bad,' I can draw distinctions between the positive and negative aspects of a political program. I like the bit about allowing workers to reap greater benefits from their labor. I don't like the bit about putting dissidents in front of firing squads. And it seems to me as if an intelligent person ought to be capable of disaggregating those things.[28]

So, again, in this view, there is no specific reason why all socialist experiments have sooner or later turned towards authoritarianism. It was simply a political choice:

> Gulags only become possible if you have an ideology, like Leninism, that justifies Gulags. [...] [C]ommunist atrocities are a warning against committing atrocities in pursuit of fairness, not against fairness.[29]

Thus, socialists have nothing to learn from historical experience, because the various manifestations of authoritarianism under socialism are all completely unconnected to each other. The only lesson from the Gulags is that we should not build Gulags, the only lesson from the show trials is that we should not have show trials, the only lesson from the Berlin Wall is that we should not build walls through Berlin, and so on. Anything else would be caveman-like grunting.

What would real socialism look like, and what was unreal about previous attempts? According to Robinson:

---

28 How to be a socialist without being an apologist for the atrocities of communist regimes, *Current Affairs*, 25 October 2017 (https://www.current affairs.org/2017/10/how-to-be-a-socialist-without-being-an-apologist-for -the-atrocities-of-communist-regimes).

29 Ibid.

> [S]ocialism was about giving workers ownership over the means of production, which they don't have if they're being told what to produce at gunpoint. [...] The history of the Soviet Union doesn't really tell us much about 'communism', [...] it was a society dominated by the state, in which power was distributed according to a strict hierarchy.

Once again, 'giving workers ownership over the means of production' is just an abstract aspiration, not a tangible description of an economic system. What does this mean? In a society with a population of over 60 million people (such as the UK), how would 'the workers' manage 'their' means of production collectively? How would I be able to meaningfully exercise control over 'my' 60 millionth part of a steel mill or a car factory? Robinson does not address such questions.

Nor is there a word on the *economic* failures of socialism. Robinson claims that it is easy to separate the good bits (raising workers' living standards) from the bad bits (repression) – but fails to mention that socialism did *not* raise workers' living standards, at least not relative to any plausible counterfactual. Robinson takes it as a given that a socialism without Gulags and a secret police would not just be more humane, but also economically more successful. Why should it be?

A final example is *Washington Post* columnist Elizabeth Bruenig's case for socialism. Bruenig also distances herself from the forms of socialism that have so far been tried:

> Not to be confused for a totalitarian nostalgist, I would support a kind of socialism that would be democratic and

aimed primarily at decommodifying labor, reducing the vast inequality brought about by capitalism, and breaking capital's stranglehold over politics and culture.[30]

And elsewhere:

Socialism has a range of expressions, and though it's mostly argued against [...] in its twentieth-century historical forms, the effect of any strands I would advocate would be [...] 1) to de-commodify labor, and as many other domains of life as possible; 2) to reduce or eliminate workers' alienation from their labor, society, and themselves; 3) to reduce [...] the vast social and political inequality brought about by capitalism; and 4) to diminish or destroy capital's control over politics, society and the economy.[31]

Once again, 'real' socialism is defined in terms of abstract outcomes rather than tangible institutional characteristics. How would Bruenig's version of socialism work? This is a question she brushes aside as mere detail:

These four fronts are only a rough sketch of the sort of socialism I envision; my purpose here was to debate for

---

30 It's time to give socialism a try, *Washington Post*, 6 March 2018 (https://www.washingtonpost.com/opinions/its-time-to-give-socialism-a-try/2018/03/06/c603a1b6-2164-11e8-86f6-54bfff693d2b_story.html).

31 Case in favor of Socialism, debated at LibertyCon, *Medium*, 3 March 2018 (https://medium.com/@ebruenig/case-in-favor-of-socialism-debated-at-libertycon-5887336f4f88).

its merits rather than to supply particular policy parameters, which can be left to more talented policy-makers.[32]

An opinion piece is not a draft constitution, so nobody would
expect anything more than a 'rough sketch'. The problem is
that Bruenig does *not* provide a rough sketch. She merely
talks about a set of aspirations – and even then, only at a
very high level of abstraction – and effectively defines her
version of socialism as 'a system that would fulfil those aspirations'. There is not a word on why earlier forms of socialism
fell short of those ideals, or even on why they failed on more
tangible metrics, such as productivity and economic output.

Not for a lack of trying

Democracy and economic performance

Both of these leaps of faith are entirely unwarranted. Firstly, there is no reason to believe that the economic failure of
socialism had anything to do with the lack of democracy.
Democratisation improves many things, and is desirable
for many reasons, but it does not, in itself, tend to make
countries richer. Przeworski (2002) studies the relationship between political systems and economic performance,
looking at 135 countries during the period from 1950 to
1990. He finds that (ibid.: 21):

> Political regimes have no impact on the growth of total in-
> come [...] The few countries that developed spectacularly

---

32 Ibid.

during the past fifty years were as likely to achieve this feat under democracy as under dictatorship. On the average, total incomes grew at almost identical rates under the two regimes.

Democracy and economic progress are strongly related, but the causation runs in the opposite direction: rich democracies are much more stable than poor democracies (Przeworski and Limongi 1997).

Przeworski's findings are in line with an earlier, similar study by Barro (1994: 26), who uses an index of democratisation rather than a binary democracy/dictatorship distinction. Looking at a sample of about 100 countries over a 30-year period, he finds that

> [D]emocracy is not the key to economic growth, although it may have a weak positive effect for countries that start with few political rights. [...] [T]he advanced western countries would contribute more to the welfare of poor nations by exporting their economic systems, notably property rights and free markets, rather than their political systems, which typically developed after reasonable standards of living had been attained.

Again, democracy and prosperity are related, but the causation runs in the opposite direction (ibid.: 25):

> [I]mprovements in the standard of living—measured by a Country's real per capita GDP, life expectancy, and education—substantially raise the probability that political

> institutions will become more democratic over time. [...]
> Rich places consume more democracy *because this [...] is*
> *desirable for its own sake* [emphasis added].

One implication is that socialist dictatorships are (or were) not poor *because* they are (or were) dictatorships. They are poor because they are socialist.

It is therefore entirely fair to hold the *economic* failure of socialist countries against democratic socialists. It is not a straw man. Democratic socialists may not want to replicate the *political* systems of these countries, but they do want to pursue similar *economic* policies, and it is the *economic* policies – not the absence of democracy – that caused their economic failure.

Since Ludwig von Mises's (1922) seminal *Die Gemein-wirtschaft: Untersuchungen über den Sozialismus*, a lot has been written about the reasons why socialist economies must ultimately stagnate and fail. A discussion of those reasons would go far beyond the scope of this book. Suffice it to briefly allude to two major issues which no socialist economy has so far been able to solve.

It is a common misunderstanding that socialism failed because a socialist economy expects people to work primarily for the common good rather than their own good, and that most people were not altruistic enough to do that. This is not true. In practice, socialist economies never relied on altruism. There were statutory work norms, there were production quotas, there were differences in pay, and there were performance-related material incentives. Socialist economies were not leisurely places. East German workers, for example, tended to work longer hours than West German workers.[33] A lack of the right incentives *was* a huge issue under socialism (see Caplan 2009), but not simply in the sense that people did not work hard enough. Socialism's relative failure, and capitalism's relative success, had much more to do with capitalism's capacity to generate economically relevant knowledge.

Firstly, market prices have proven to be an indispensable way of collating and disseminating information about conditions of supply and demand. Market prices are determined by the buying and selling decisions of thousands, if not millions or billions of people, who are acting upon their knowledge of their own preferences, and of any information they possess that is relevant to the transaction. In this way, markets can tap into a vast body of knowledge that is dispersed across the minds of millions of people, and not accessible in its totality to anyone (see Hayek 1945). Much of this knowledge is 'tacit': it is specific to time and place, and it cannot be easily put into words or numbers. The people who possess it might struggle to articulate it. But in a market economy, they do not need to articulate it. They just need to act upon it.

Market prices are a distilled form of a vast amount of information, and they disseminate that information quickly and widely. Changed circumstances lead to price changes, which lead to market participants adjusting the behaviour accordingly. In Hayek's words (ibid.: 526):

---

33 DDR/Fünf-Tage-Woche: Samstags nie, *Der Spiegel*, 28 August 1967 (http://www.spiegel.de/spiegel/print/d-46265001.html).

Assume that somewhere in the world a new opportunity for the use of [...] tin, has arisen, or that one of the sources of supply of tin has been eliminated. It does not matter [...] – and it is very significant that it does not matter – which of these two causes has made tin more scarce. All that the users of tin need to know is that some of the tin they used to consume is now more profitably employed elsewhere and that, in consequence, they must economize tin. There is no need for the great majority of them even to know where the more urgent need has arisen, or in favor of what other needs they ought to husband the supply. If only some of them know directly of the new demand, and switch resources over to it, and if the people who are aware of the new gap thus created in turn fill it from still other sources, the effect will rapidly spread throughout the whole economic system and influence not only all the uses of tin but also those of its substitutes and the substitutes of these substitutes, the supply of all the things made of tin, and their substitutes, and so on; and all this without the great majority of those instrumental in bringing about these substitutions knowing anything at all about the original cause of these changes.

Planned economies have no way of replicating this knowledge-collecting and knowledge-disseminating function of market prices. They therefore deprive themselves of vast amounts of information, which must lead to worse economic decisions. This is not just a problem for fully planned economies, where prices are set by a planning board. It is also true in an economy where the private sector accounts for the bulk of economic activity, but where the government tampers with market prices.

Another indispensable feature of market economies, which no socialist economy has yet been able to replace, is the fact that market competition is an ongoing trial-and-error process, coupled with extensive feedback mechanisms (see Hayek 2002 [1968]). We do not know, from the outset, how to organise a successful enterprise or industry (let alone an entire economy). We find out by trying lots of different things, with most of them failing, but some succeeding, and the latter ones getting more widely adopted.

A market economy is a testing ground, in which different business ideas, different management styles, different organisational models and different industry structures can be tried and tested in competition with one another. For example, integrated models, where companies perform a lot of functions in-house, can compete freely with specialised models, where companies outsource many functions to external contractors. In this way, we find out where specialisation is more appropriate, and where integration is more appropriate.

It is a common misunderstanding that the main role of competition is to act as a spur: we work harder when we are under competitive pressure than we do when we can take our current position for granted. But this was never the main issue: socialist economies had other (less benign) ways of spurring people on. What they lacked, however, was the knowledge-creating capacity of competition. *This* is the main role of competition in economic life. Socialist economies deprive themselves of the vast amount of knowledge created by competition. To a lesser extent, so do market economies that hinder the competitive process, for example, by erecting barriers to market entry.

Socialism, technocracy and authoritarianism

The question whether socialism is inherently authoritarian, or whether it was a coincidence that socialist countries were also autocracies, is not new. In the 1970s, Jean-François Revel (1978: 41–42) wrote:

> [T]hey tell us it is unfair to judge 'socialism' on the basis of experience. [...] How, from a Marxist point of view, can one explain so many accidents and deviations over so many decades without finding their causes [...] in the economic system [...]? [...]
>
> [I]t is ironic that the spokesmen of 'scientific' socialism should be the first to offer us this odd application of Marx's historical materialism – one constant, [...] long-lived and showing no signs of decay, [...] is said to be the result of mere chance, [...] bearing no relation to the system.

And elsewhere (ibid.: 61):

> A Marxist-Leninist, that is to say a 'scientific' socialist, surely should seek out the cause of this recurring failure. In science a law is that hypothesis which is verified by all

experimental observation. Perhaps present-day Marxists are going to stage still another of their many epistemological revolutions by offering this innovative definition: the law shall be that hypothesis which is verified by none of the experiments.

Four decades later, we have still not seen a socialist experiment which has not, sooner or later, descended into authoritarianism, but socialists remain convinced that there is no deeper reason for that. In their account, socialism has just not been properly tried – but it could be tried any time. It is merely a matter of willpower.

When contemporary socialists talk about 'extending democracy to the economy' and 'democratising every aspect of society', they are not being dishonest. That is their aspiration. But the point they miss is that this has *always* been the aspiration, and the promise, of socialism. There was never a time when socialists aspired to create stratified societies, in which power would be concentrated in the hands of a technocratic elite. Much less did they aspire to create police states that relied on terror, torture, forced labour and mass murder for their very survival. Socialist experiments *ended up* that way, but they were not *intended* to be that way.

Take the following quote from a famous socialist, critiquing authoritarian tendencies in the nascent Soviet Union:

There are two methods: the method of coercion (the military method), and the method of persuasion (the trade-union method). [...] The mistake Trotsky makes is that he underrates the difference between the army and the working class, he [...] tries [...] to transfer military methods from the army into [...] the working class. [...]

[T]he Soviet power [...] can be directed only through the medium of the working class and with the forces of the working class. [...] Obviously, it is impossible to do this by coercive methods [...] Obviously, only [...] proletarian democracy [...], only methods of persuasion, can make it possible to unite the working class, to stimulate its independent activity.

That was Stalin (1921).

Or take the original meaning of the term 'Soviet Republic'. A 'soviet' was originally simply a democratically elected workers' council based at a factory, and a Soviet Republic was originally meant to be a semi-direct grassroots democracy, in which these workers' councils would form the main building blocks. The idea was that all political power would ultimately be derived from local workers' assemblies. This idea was never formally abandoned: on paper, that was how the Soviet Union worked.

When contemporary socialists talk about a non-autocratic, non-authoritarian, participatory and humanitarian version of socialism, they are not as original as they think they are. That was *always* the idea. This is what socialists have *always* said. It is not for a lack of trying that it has never turned out that way.

Democratic collective ownership can work perfectly well – but only in small, homogeneous, voluntary communities with simple economies. The classic example of this is the Israeli *kibbutz*. In a kibbutz, one can meaningfully say that the community, as a whole, organises its economic affairs collectively and democratically.

But even then, a kibbutz cannot be considered an alternative to the market economy. A kibbutz is not an 'economy' in its own right. It is an actor within an economy, namely the predominantly market-based economy of Israel (and beyond). This is what allows each kibbutz to specialise in a narrow, manageable range of economic activities. The kibbutz can be a perfectly viable model. But a quick glance at the history of the kibbutzim is enough to make clear that that model is neither scalable nor transferrable. Kibbutzim have never grown beyond a certain size; a kibbutz with more than 1,000 members would be counted as one of the largest. While the traditional, collectivist kibbutz model still works for many of them, some have moved away from it, introducing more conventional management methods, and becoming more like conventional private enterprises over time.[34] There has also been a tendency for kibbutzim to outsource functions they would once have provided internally.

Democratic collectivism requires small, homogeneous communities, characterised by a high degree of internal agreement on aims and means. And even then, such communities can only coordinate a very limited range of activities. It is all right for the members of a small agrarian

---

34 See, for example: The kibbutz movement adapts to a capitalist Israel, *Wall Street Journal*, 13 October 2017 (https://www.wsj.com/articles/the -kibbutz-movement-adapts-to-a-capitalist-israel-1507908175).

commune to organise a meeting, and debate whether they should cultivate more of this grain or that grain; whether they should buy new farming tools, or mend the old ones and spend the money on something else. But it would be impossible to run a whole economy in that way.

Economic planning is not amenable to democratic participation. It is, in fact, not even amenable to representative democracy. As Hayek (1993 [1944]: 48) pointed out in *The Road to Serfdom*:

> To draw up an economic plan in this fashion is even less possible than, for example, successfully to plan a military campaign by democratic procedure. [...] [I]t would become inevitable to delegate the task to the experts.
>
> Yet the difference is that, while the general who is put in charge of a campaign is given a single end [...] there can be no such single goal given to the economic planner [...] The general has not got to balance different independent aims against each other; there is for him only one supreme goal. But the ends of an economic plan [...] cannot be defined apart from the particular plan. It is the essence of the economic problem that [...] an economic plan involves the choice between conflicting and competing ends. But [...] the alternatives between which we must choose, can only be known to those who know all the facts; and only they, the experts, are in a position to decide.

Socialism does not always have to lead to industrial-scale murder and terror. The horrors of Stalinism, Maoism and the Khmer Rouge were extreme even by socialist standards.

The second half of the Soviet Union's history was nothing like as bad as the first half. Other Warsaw Pact countries were repressive, but not genocidal.

But socialism could never be anything other than a technocratic, hierarchical command-and-control system. The claim that the Warsaw Pact countries were not 'really' socialist, because they were not parliamentary democracies with free and fair elections, misses the point. Even if they *had* been parliamentary democracies, this would not have changed their ultra-technocratic character, because their parliaments, such as they were, did not play much of a role in the economic planning process anyway. (And as Hayek explained, they *could* not have). Five-Year Plans were drafted by expert commissions, under instructions from the upper tiers of the executive branch of government, and then rubberstamped by parliament. Steiner (2010: 4) explains this process, using the example of the German Democratic Republic:

> [T]he State Planning Commission (SPK) [...] had to work out the plans and be responsible for them, it had to establish the interdependencies of the various controlled economic fields, and in so doing reject the interests of individual partial spheres that might run counter to the macroeconomic [...] priorities. [...] Disregarding the *purely formal* approval of the plans by the People's Chamber [the GDR's parliament], the final decision [...] was up to the Council of Ministers [emphasis added].

We could, in theory, imagine a democratic GDR (or a different example of a socialist country), with free and fair elections. This would have given people a chance to oust the government and replace it with a new one. But it would not have brought the GDR any closer to the kind of participatory socialism described by authors such as Chomsky, Sunkara, Robinson or Jones, in which 'the people' run the economy together. In the GDR, as in all socialist countries, the process of economic planning was performed by a bureaucratic elite. A democratic GDR would still have been an extremely stratified, hierarchical society.

It is easy to see why the GDR's ruling party (or its counterparts in other socialist countries) never allowed a free and fair democratic election: they would have lost, and they knew it. This explains the GDR's dictatorial character. But it does not explain its *technocratic* character. It would not have threatened the party's position of power to allow public participation in the planning and running of the economy. On the contrary: this would, if anything, have strengthened its power, because it would have given the system a veneer of democratic legitimacy. The party could have neutralised parts of the pro-democratic resistance movement, and steered the public appetite for democracy into safe channels. ('Safe' as in 'safe from the party's perspective'.)

They did not do it, because it cannot be done. A country with 17 million inhabitants is not a kibbutz.

What was briefly tried was workers' participation in the running of state-owned enterprises, via democratically elected workers' councils. But a centrally planned economy cannot allow meaningful autonomy at the local level, for the simple reason that this would disrupt the plan.

The different parts of the plan intertwine and depend on each other. So the government cannot allow some actors of the economy to deviate from it. As Steiner (2010: 30–31) explains:

> The work councils [...] oriented themselves by the interests of their enterprises and their workforce rather than by the requirements of the economy as a whole. This was one of the reasons why they were abolished in 1948. [...] Thus there was no institution that would have enabled the workers to share in decision making.

In the GDR, the greatest source of disruption to the plan was emigration. This is why the Berlin Wall was not an aberration from the 'noble' ideal of socialism, but a logical correlate of a planned economy.

Planned economies typically restrict people's freedom of movement, including domestically (see, for example, Dowty 1988). They have to: large-scale movements of people would jumble the Five-Year Plans. One cannot plan an economy when the factors of production have a will of their own and move around all the time. Planners need to be able to allocate factors of production, including labour, and those factors then have to stay where they have been allocated to. It is therefore not a coincidence that the Soviet Union introduced its internal passport system at the same time as it implemented its first Five-Year Plan.

In a market economy, a law to restrict freedom of movement between, say, London and Cambridge would seem absurd. Citizens would feel that a decision like where they want to live is nobody else's business but their own. In a planned economy, it is not absurd at all, because a planned economy turns such decisions into everyone else's business. Moving residence and changing jobs has repercussions for complementary factors of production and other parts of the Five-Year Plan, and, unlike in a market economy, there is no price mechanism that leads to automatic adjustments. Therefore, people's movements must be controlled.

If the case for restricting freedom of movement within a country follows logically from the rationale of a planned economy, the case for restricting emigration follows even more strongly. One of the fundamental differences between a socialist economy and a market economy is that the former is a collective endeavour. We all know from our personal lives that, when we take part in collective endeavours, we give up some degree of personal autonomy. This is not a problem as long as we do so voluntarily. If we live on our own, we can do whatever we like at home (for example, decorate the home as we see fit, play loud music at night, etc.); if we share a home with other people, we can no longer do that. If we work on a project as part of a team, we have to act as a team player; we do not have the same flexibility that we have when we work on our own. And so on. In a liberal society, communities are voluntary and self-selecting. We choose to what extent we want to take part in collective endeavours, in which areas of life, and with whom. In a socialist society, most economic life is a collective endeavour. Limitations of personal liberty are therefore inevitable, and, within the logic of the system, justifiable. Emigration restrictions are an example of this. Dowty (1988: 86–88) explains:

> Emigration [...] becomes an act of disloyalty, desertion from a common cause, perhaps even a treacherous act [...]
>
> In 1922, both Russia and the Ukraine [...] practically closed off all departures. In 1923 a special corps of the GPU was organized to control the border, and by 1928 had become effective enough to cut off nearly all illegal departures. [...]
>
> Regarding exit policy generally, the Soviet model [...] was by the early 1950s followed by most states of Eastern Europe, China, Mongolia, and North Korea. [...]
>
> Eastern European spokesmen [...] stress the debt an individual owes society because of benefits received. In socialist states, it is argued, [...] [s]ociety makes a large investment in each person, [...] and one should therefore repay society by remaining a working member of it. [...] Accordingly, they show relative liberality on exit visas toward those who have done their part (retirees in East Germany, those over fifty-five in Hungary).

This is why the Berlin Wall and the Iron Curtain were not a 'betrayal' of socialism, but its consistent application.

Finally, socialism has always led, and must always lead, to an extreme concentration of power. As explained above, by abolishing market signals and competition, socialist economies deprive themselves of vast amounts of knowledge. But they also deprive themselves of something else: an extremely effective way of dispersing and limiting power. As Hayek (1993 [1944]) writes, 'the competitive system is the only system designed to minimize the power exercised by man over man'.

In a socialist economy, the state becomes the main employer, the main landlord, the main supplier of goods and services, the main financial intermediary, etc. There are not many things that F. A. Hayek and Leon Trotsky would have agreed on, but the fact that a socialist state requires a greater concentration of power than any other kind of state is one of them. Trotsky (1936: Chapter 2)[35] wrote about the Soviet government:

> There is no other government in the world in whose hands the fate of the whole country is concentrated to such a degree. [...] [T]he Soviet government occupies in relation to the whole economic system the position which a capitalist occupies in relation to a single enterprise. The centralized character of the national economy converts the state power into a factor of enormous significance.

And Hayek wrote, 'In order to achieve their ends the planners must create power – power over men wielded by other men – of a magnitude never before known'.

From a socialist perspective, this does not constitute a problem. It merely substitutes state power for corporate power, and state power is accountable to 'the people'

---

35 This book has been accessed via an online archive. Page numbers are therefore not available.

– state power is 'people power'. But this is a fundamental misunderstanding. As Hayek explains:

> [B]y concentrating power so that it can be used in the service of a single plan, it is not merely transformed, but infinitely heightened. By uniting in the hands of some single body power formerly exercised independently by many, an amount of power is created infinitely greater than any that existed before, so much more far-reaching as almost to be different in kind.
>
> It is entirely fallacious to argue that the great power exercised by a central planning board would be 'no greater than the power collectively exercised by private boards of directors'. There is, in a competitive society, no-body who can exercise even a fraction of the power which a socialist planning board would possess. *To decentralize power is to reduce the absolute amount of power* [emphasis added].

The idea that business owners are all in cahoots with one another, and act as one, is a socialist fantasy. Business owners *compete* with each other – often fiercely so. This greatly limits whatever 'power' any of them may wield.

Unlike Hayek, Trotsky did not object to the concentration of power under socialism. His only complaint was that in the Soviet Union power was no longer wielded by 'the working class' but by the Soviet bureaucracy, which had acquired features of a social class of its own. The solution, then, was for 'the working class' to reclaim the power it once held. However, Trotsky's supposed 'golden age', before 'the working class' was 'betrayed', happens to coincide with the period in which *he*, Trotsky, was one of the country's most powerful figures. The 'corruption' of the workers' state happens to coincide with *his own* fall from grace. Had Trotsky prevailed and expelled Stalin, then presumably the exiled Stalin would have written a book about how 'the working class' had been betrayed, and how the Soviet Union had ceased to be a 'true' workers' state.

The concentration of power under socialism does not *have* to lead to a tyranny as murderous as Stalinism or Maoism. Khrushchev's de-Stalinisation policy shows that the Soviet system had *some* capacity for self-reform, and most other socialist countries never produced an equivalent of Stalinism or Maoism. But even Stalinism and Maoism were not aberrations. They were periods during which tendencies that are always present in socialist societies were taken to extremes.

One of the persistent features of socialist regimes is that they often respond to economic failures by searching for scapegoats – imaginary 'saboteurs', 'wreckers', 'hoarders', 'speculators', 'counterrevolutionaries', etc. – and engaging in witch-hunts. They have to: since economic problems under socialism can never possibly be the fault of socialism itself, there must be *somebody* who is deliberately working to undermine the economy.

Stalin's killing sprees were not always random; they were often linked to economic events. For example, during and after the famines, Stalin targeted all sectors that had some connection with agriculture, however loose. As Udy (2017: 436–37) explains:

The kulaks had already been named as the instigators of wrecking in the fields and farms, but the dekulakisation campaign of 1929–31 had been fought to 'smash the kulaks as a class'; they could not now [in 1932–33] be held up as the sole cause of the trouble [...] More scapegoats were needed. So vets were shot for secretly engineering livestock mortality; meteorologists were arrested for falsifying weather forecasts in order to damage crops; [...] there was a mass purge of governmental and academic institutions, as well as newspapers; the Ukrainian Chamber of Weights and Measures was held responsible for deliberately sabotaging the measurement of the harvest. [...]

Casting around for more people to blame, agricultural specialists were an obvious target. [...] They were convicted of 'agricultural sabotage' – a charge which included [...] 'the deliberate propagation of weeds with a view to lowering crop yields'.

If in far less extreme forms, the same basic pattern recurred in many other socialist countries. The most recent example is Venezuela, where paranoia about 'saboteurs' and 'hoarders' has become a fixed feature of the government's rhetoric.[36] Venezuela's government once promised

---

36 See, for example: Venezuela's power cut was 'sabotage' – President Maduro, *BBC News*, 4 December 2013 (http://www.bbc.co.uk/news/world -latin-america-25210984); Venezuelan President Maduro 'to expand price controls', *BBC News*, 11 November 2013 (http://www.bbc.co.uk/news/world -latin-america-24897407); Venezuela announces new plan to tackle food crisis, *BBC News*, 9 June 2016 (http://www.bbc.co.uk/news/world-latin -america-36486246); Venezuela seizes millions of toys, accuses importer

to build a completely different form of socialism, defined explicitly in opposition to the Soviet model (more on this later). Yet today, a press release from the Venezuelan government sounds suspiciously like a 1930s copy of *Pravda*.

When contemporary democratic socialists protest at the mention of a real-world example of socialism, and insist that they are not condoning the abuses committed by any of those regimes, they are missing the point: nobody is accusing them of that. Critics of socialism are perfectly aware that contemporary socialists have no intention of bringing back forced labour camps, mass executions, show trials, forced confessions, the Stasi or the Berlin Wall. But no socialist project ever started with that intention. When critics of socialism bring up the oppressive nature of past socialist regimes, the intention is not to score rhetorical points against their opponents. The intention is to draw attention to the fact that these systems were not just randomly oppressive. They were all oppressive *in similar ways*. There are recognisable, recurring patterns of oppression under socialist regimes, and they are intimately linked with socialist economics.

The straw men that were once alive

If socialism has made a comeback, it is not because people have 'forgotten' about how bad things were in the Warsaw Pact countries, Maoist China or other socialist countries.

---

of hoarding, *Bloomberg*, 9 December 2016 (https://www.bloomberg.com/news/articles/2016-12-09/venezuela-seizes-millions-of-toys-accuses-importer-of-hoarding).

It is because socialists have successfully managed to distance themselves from those examples.

Democratic socialists have been so successful at convincing themselves (and others) that historical examples of socialism had nothing to do with socialism, they tend to react with genuine irritation when a political opponent brings up any such example.[37] They tend to see the mention of these examples as either disinguous, or simple-minded (or both). It is either a straw man – a rhetorical stick which anti-socialists use to beat socialists with – or a sign that an opponent is intellectually incapable of understanding the difference between a good idea and a distorted application.

Given that more than two dozen attempts to build a socialist society have ended in varying degrees of failure, insisting that none of them were ever 'really' socialist is the only way in which modern-day socialists can protect their worldview from refutation. However, this book will show that there is a major flaw in the not-*real*-socialism narrative: the fact that it is usually only deployed *after the event*, that is, *after* a socialist experiment has already been widely discredited.

---

37 A good illustration is an article exchange between the writer James Bartholomew and his nephew Sebastian Vella in *The Spectator* magazine. Bartholomew talks about his memories of travelling through the Soviet Union, pre-liberalisation China, and Ceausescu's Romania. His nephew, who sympathises with socialism, does *not* reply with a defence of any of these examples, or with a romanticised description of them. Rather, he reacts with surprise that his uncle brings them up at all. See: Letter to a young Corbynista, *The Spectator*, 24 June 2017 (https://www.spectator.co.uk/2017/06/letter-to-a-young-corbynista/); A letter from a Corbynista, *The Spectator*, 1 July 2017 (https://www.spectator.co.uk/2017/07/a-letter-from-a-corbynista/); for an example, see: *The Daily Politics* show, BBC, 1 November 2013 (https://www.facebook.com/BBCPolitics/videos/758283277521866/).

This book will show that as long as a socialist experiment is in its prime, its socialist credentials are rarely in doubt. As long as socialism seems to work, it is always 'real' socialism. It is only when it fails, and when it becomes an embarrassment for the socialist cause, that it is retroactively recategorised as unreal.

This book will show that virtually *all* socialist experiments in history – including and in fact *especially* the Soviet Union and Maoist China – were, at some point or other, widely endorsed by prominent Western intellectuals. They were all held up as 'real' socialism. Until they ceased to be 'real' socialism, and retroactively became unreal socialism.

More precisely, this book will show that in terms of their reception in Western countries, socialist experiments usually go through three distinct phases.

1. The honeymoon period
The first stage is a honeymoon period, during which the experiment has, or at least *seems* to have, some initial success in some areas. During this period, its international standing is relatively high. Even anti-socialists concede, grudgingly, that the country in question has something to show for it.

During the honeymoon period, very few dispute the experiment's socialist character; almost nobody claims that the country is not 'really' socialist. On the contrary: during the honeymoon period, large numbers of Western intellectuals enthusiastically embrace the experiment. Self-declared socialists claim ownership of it, and parade it as an example of their ideas in action.

2. The excuses-and-whataboutery period

But the honeymoon period never lasts forever. The country's luck either comes to an end, or its already existing failures become more widely known in the West. As a result, its international standing deteriorates. It ceases to be an example that socialists hold against their opponents, and becomes an example that their opponents hold against them.

During this period, Western intellectuals still support the experiment, but their tone becomes angry and defensive. The focus changes from the experiment's supposed achievements to the supposed ulterior motives of its critics. There is a frantic search for excuses, with the blame usually placed on imaginary 'saboteurs' and unspecified attempts to 'undermine' it. There is plenty of whataboutery.[38]

3. The not-real-socialism stage

Eventually, there always comes a point when the experiment has been widely discredited, and is seen as a failure

---

38 'Whataboutery' or 'Whataboutism' is defined by the Oxford Dictionary as 'The technique or practice of responding to an accusation or difficult question by making a counter-accusation or raising a different issue'. In practice, it is usually both, because it normally comes with implied accusations of hypocrisy. The most common form of socialist whataboutery is to shift the attention to Western colonialism, US foreign policy interventions, Western countries' ties with non-socialist dictators, etc. This comes with the implied accusation that critics of socialism are blasé about or even supportive of these. It is a strange accusation, because it is not even true on its own terms. Historically, some of the most committed proponents of free trade, such as the British Anti-Corn Law League, were also strongly opposed to militarism and colonialism. More recently, some of the most effective critiques of US foreign policy have come from US libertarians (for example, Bandow 2006).

by most of the general public. The experiment becomes a liability for the socialist cause, and an embarrassment for Western socialists.

This is the stage when intellectuals begin to dispute the experiment's socialist credentials, and, crucially, they do so with retroactive effect. They argue that the country was never socialist in the first place, and that its leaders never even tried to implement socialism. This is the deeper meaning behind the old adage that 'real' socialism has never been tried: socialism gets retroactively redefined as 'unreal' whenever it fails. So it has never been tried, in the same way in which, in Orwell's *Nineteen Eighty-four*, the government of Oceania has always been at war with East Asia.

This is not a conscious process, let alone a purposefully orchestrated one. There is no equivalent of an industrial standards body, which awards a '*real* socialism' certificate of authenticity, and then withdraws it again with retroactive effect. Socialists do not hold clandestine conferences in secret hideouts; they do not deliberately cover up their former support for the regime in question. They simply fall silent on the issue, and move on to the next cause.

At some point, the claim that the country in question was never 'really' socialist becomes the conventional wisdom. Since it is only the opponents of socialism who still refer to that example, while socialists themselves no longer do, it is easy to gain the impression that it must be a straw man argument.

This book will show that these alleged 'straw men' were all once very much alive. They are not straw men at all. They are the failed utopias of yesteryear.

2   THE SOVIET UNION UNDER STALIN: 'A WHOLE NATION MARCHED BEHIND A VISION'

Soviet socialism

According to Marxist theory, the socialist revolution was supposed to start where capitalism was most advanced. In 1917, the Russian Empire, a semi-feudal, predominantly agrarian economy, was one of the least likely candidates. Trotsky (1936: Chapter 3) writes:

> Marx expected that the Frenchman would begin the social revolution, the German continue it, the Englishman finish it; and as to the Russian, Marx left him far in the rear. [...] Russia was not the strongest, but the weakest link in the chain of capitalism.

Tsarist Russia did not have much of a working class, partly because Tsarist economic policy restricted movements from agriculture to industry, thus artificially slowing down the pace of industrialisation and urbanisation (Cheremukhin 2013: 3–7). The dominant position of government-backed cartels, and high levels of protectionism, further arrested industrial development. Politically, before

World War I, the Bolsheviks were a fringe group with no serious hope of coming to power.

The chaos and misery of World War I then prepared the ground for the 'bourgeois' February Revolution of 1917. The February revolutionaries managed to overthrow the Tsarist system, but they did not manage to replace it with a stable government of their own. Eight months later, the Bolsheviks exploited this weakness to stage their own follow-up revolution.

Initial attempts to build a socialist economy under conditions of civil war proved disastrous, leading to a collapse in industrial output and to the famine of 1921–22. So the Bolsheviks put the socialist transformation on hold, and, under the guise of the 'New Economic Policy' (NEP), allowed a limited range of market activity again. Once the economy had recovered to pre-war levels, the NEP was abandoned, and with the commencement of the first Five-Year-Plan in 1928, the socialist transformation project was resumed (ibid.: 8).

The government takeover of the economy's commanding heights enabled a forced reallocation of the factors of production, from agriculture to industry, from rural to urban areas, and from consumer goods to capital goods. Living standards fell. The Soviet famine of 1932–33 was initially caused by the forced collectivisation of agriculture, which caused a massive disruption of agricultural production patterns. But it was exacerbated further by the government's decision to export large amounts of grain, even at the height of the famine, in order to import industrial equipment (see Udy 2017: 435–36).

The Soviet experiment quickly descended into a murderous tyranny. According to one estimate based mainly on Soviet archives, it claimed about 20 million lives (Courtois 1999: 4), mainly through avoidable famines, mass executions and terrible conditions in forced labour camps. This descent into tyranny started at a very early stage. As Udy (2017: 5) explains:

> Although the Gulag [...] gets its name from the administrative body which was set up by Stalin in 1930, its foundations were laid in the early days of the Revolution [...] [B]y September 1918, the process of setting up labour camps to intern counter-revolutionaries was well advanced [...] [B]y October 1923, there were over 350 camps [...] holding around 70,000 prisoners.

Through eyewitness accounts from Russian refugees, this was also well-known – or at least *knowable* – in the West. Ramsay MacDonald, Britain's future prime minister, was an early sympathiser with the Russian revolution, which, in his 1919 book *Parliament in Revolution*, he described as 'one of the greatest events in the history of the world' (quoted in Udy 2017: 76). Even in those early days, MacDonald felt obliged to mention some of the atrocities committed by the regime, if only to dismiss them quickly (quoted in ibid.: 77):

> I leave out of account the Terror and similar incidents, not only because most of them are mere fabrications [...] Besides, Lenin abhors them [...] We know that some

expedients have been purely temporary [...] For them a comprehensive excuse, which is a justification under the circumstances, can be made that they belong to the stress of the revolution.

Although he blames them on external factors, MacDonald does mention 'chaotic "dictatorship" stages of the revolution [...] Red Terror, [...] revolutionary tribunals, [...] the execution of politicals' (ibid.).

This suggests that, already in 1919, a reasonably well-informed observer would have known what was going on, and that denying it took some effort.

This was *a fortiori* true a decade later. Udy explains (ibid.: 529):

The excesses were widely known; they were simply not accepted by many on the left. Over a million people had joined in prayers for the persecuted in 1930. Fifty thousand had attended a special service in St Peter's square. [...]

[Foreign Office] Reports of Soviet oppression and brutality were frequent throughout the years from 1917 to 1929.

However, the 1930s and 1940s were also a period of rapid industrialisation and modernisation, which contrasted favourably with the Great Depression in the West. It was during this period that the Soviet Union rose to the status of a global superpower. Even its fiercest critics acknowledged that it had become a force to be reckoned with. In terms of its international standing, this was the Soviet Union's honeymoon period.

During this honeymoon period, the Soviet Union was widely admired by Western intellectuals. As Paul Hollander (1990) documents in his book *Political Pilgrims: Travels of Western Intellectuals to the Soviet Union, China, and Cuba 1928–1979*, Western cheerleaders flocked to the Soviet Union in their thousands, and returned full of praise. At that time, the claim that Stalinism did not constitute 'real' socialism would have seemed outlandish.

Stalin's pilgrims

As co-founders of the London School of Economics, of the Fabian Society and of the *New Statesman* magazine, Sidney and Beatrice Webb were undoubtedly two of the leading figures of the British left at the time. They were also devout Stalinists. Today, the *New Statesman* is upfront about this legacy:

> Stalin's regime had been eulogised by the Webbs [...] after visits to the USSR from which they returned gushing with enthusiasm. In this they were not unusual. Throughout the 1930s [...] streams of Western fellow-travellers went to the Soviet Union and came back convinced that it embodied humankind's best hopes for the future. [...]
>
> The gaggles of *bien pensant* writers and journalists, liberal teachers and academics, radical aristocrats and businessmen who flocked to the Soviet Union and later

Mao's China [...] believed that only a thinking minority – themselves – could see the outlines of a better future.[1]

What attracted the Webbs to the Soviet Union? In 'Is Soviet Russia a democracy?' Sidney Webb described the Soviet Union as a genuine grassroots democracy, run by the workers, for the workers (Webb 1933: 533–36):

> All the elected representatives in the U.S.S.R. [...] habit-ually appear before their electors in open meeting every few weeks [...] to give an explanatory account of the business in which they have been occupied, to answer all questions addressed to them and to hear the complaints on all sorts of subjects that their electors freely express. Thus, in literally hundreds of thousands of small public meetings, there goes on [...] an almost ceaseless discus-sion of public affairs, to which there is in other countries no parallel [...]
>
> We may perhaps sum up the Constitution of the U.S.S.R. by emphasizing its reliance on the widest possible partici-pation of the whole adult population in the public business, which includes the planned control of the whole social environment [...] Power does actually emanate from the people, as Lenin insisted – 'All power to the soviets.'

Webb emphatically rejected the idea that the USSR is a one-party dictatorship. The Communist Party, he claims,

---

1   Fellow-travellers and useful idiots, *New Statesman*, 8 May 2017 (http://www.newstatesman.com/politics/uk/2017/05/fellow-travellers-and-use ful-idiots).

does not exercise any power; it only provides moral guidance. It is (ibid.: 535–36):

> the spiritual power in the State, pointing out always what ought to be done, in big things and small, but not itself exercising any but the authority of persuasion [...] a spiritual power, apart from but influential with the legislative and executive authorities.

He also rejected the idea that Stalin is a dictator. Stalin is merely a party functionary, who holds neither legislative nor executive powers (ibid.: 535):

> [Comrade Stalin] is merely the General Secretary of the Communist party [...] His orders are not law [...] They are not enforced by the police or the law courts. The Commissars [...] must seek to carry them out, but they can do so only by persuading those actually concerned to put them in execution. Nor are the decisions of 'Comrade Stalin' his own autocratic commands. He is not that sort of man.

Insofar as Stalin's influence goes beyond what the letter of the Soviet constitution would suggest, this is, according to Webb, explained by the fact that he is simply a very persuasive man: 'He is [...] extraordinarily skillful in influencing, by deft questions and persuasive interjections, the conclusions at which the committees arrive' (ibid.).

A few years later, in 'Is Soviet communism a new civilisation?', the Webbs described the Soviet economy as an economy characterised by almost perfect social harmony, in which people strive jointly for the common good (Webb and Webb 1936: 8–10):

> [T]here is no longer any conflict of interests in produc-tion. [...] [N]o person's gain is rooted in another person's loss. [...] There is a universal and continuous incentive to every producer [...] to improve his qualifications, and to render the utmost service [...]
>
> Hence the eager zeal and devotion of the 'shock bri-gades' [...] to do more work than is customary [...] Hence the unpaid service of the 'Saturdayers' [...] who give up their free time to clearing off arrears in any enterprise that lags behind its programme. Hence the 'socialist competitions' [...] it is from the same unity of interest that springs the custom of the winning team in these competitions making it a matter of honour immediately to proceed to the assistance of the losing team, in order to teach those who have failed in the competition how they can improve their production [...]
>
> Each [enterprise] becomes eager to help every other enterprise [...] to attain the greatest possible product, be-cause it is the aggregate net product of all the enterprises in the USSR that provides [...] all the social services.

According to the Webbs, this harmony in economic life ra-diates outwards, permeating all aspects of social life (ibid.: 11):

> [T]he principle of social equality goes much further [...] It extends, in a manner and to a degree unknown elsewhere,

to the relations between the sexes [...] Husbands and wives, parents and children, teachers and scholars, [...] administrators and typists, and even army officers and the rank and file, live in an atmosphere of social equality and of freedom from servility [...] that is unknown elsewhere.

The Gulags are not mentioned, although the paranoia about 'saboteurs' is vaguely alluded to. In the Webbs' account, however, 'sabotage' is dealt with through benign peer pressure (ibid.: 22):

Any person who neglects or refuses to pay this debt by contributing, according to his ability, to satisfying the needs of the present or future generations, is held to be a thief, and will be dealt with as such. He will, to begin with, be faced everywhere and at all times with the manifest disapproval of his mates. If his idleness or slackness continues [...] he may have to be isolated for appropriate remedial treatment. But [...] prevention is better than cure. The encouragement of good habits is deemed even more effective in producing virtuous conduct than the discouragement of bad ones.

The famines are not mentioned either, unless one counts the following vague allusion (ibid.: 29):

About the complete success of collectivised and mechanised agriculture there may be, in certain quarters, still some doubt. But [...] the initial difficulties of this gigantic transformation have been overcome.

The Soviet system of governance is presented as a more authentic and more comprehensive form of democracy (ibid.: 13–14):

> It is impossible to enumerate all the channels, and it would be difficult to exaggerate the extent, of the participation in the public affairs of the Soviet electorate [...] [T]he universal electorate in the USSR does a great deal more than elect. At its incessant meetings it debates and passes resolutions by the hundred thousand, in which it expresses its desires on great matters and on small [...] In every village, as in every city, a large part of the detailed work of public administration is actually performed, not [...] by paid officials [...] but by a far larger number of the adult inhabitants themselves.

All of these features are contrasted favourably with the capitalist West (ibid.: 24):

> The characteristics of Soviet Communism [...] exhibit [...] a distinct unity, itself in striking contrast with the disunity of western civilisation. The code of conduct based on service to the community in social equality, and on the maximum development of health and capacity in every individual, is in harmony with the exclusion of exploitation and the profit-making motive, and with the deliberate planning of production for community consumption; whilst both are in full accord with that universal participation in a multiform administration which characterises the soviet system.

The pilgrims were, of course, not a homogeneous group. Different people admired different aspects of the Soviet system. But there are a few common threads, repeated by many of the system's admirers. The Webbs' characterisation of the Soviet economy as a thoroughly democratised economy, run collectively by all workers together, is one of them. Joseph Freeman, an American writer and magazine editor, reported (quoted in Hollander 1990: 115):

[E]veryone acted as though the general good was his personal good, as though his personal difficulties could be solved by conquering the common difficulties. [...] [I]n America, [...] the worker [...] had no real voice in the management of the national economy [...] Here the 'average man' felt himself master of everything.

Waldo Frank, an American historian, novelist and literary critic, described his visit to a Soviet factory in the following terms (ibid.: 109):

Here are happy workers, because they are whole men and women. [...] Dream, thought, love collaborate in the tedious business of making electric parts, since these toilers are not working for a boss – not even for a living.

Alexander Wicksteed, an English writer and author of the book *Ten Years in Soviet Moscow*, also argued (ibid.: 115):

[F]or the first time in history the common man feels that the country belongs to him and not the privileged class that are his masters. [...] [O]n the economic plane the Marxian ideal of a classless society may still be a thing of the future, but on the social side it has been realized to an extent that is wonderfully refreshing to any Englishman of democratic aspirations.

Corliss Lamont, an American philosopher and director of the American Civil Liberties Union (ACLU), described his impression of Soviet housing construction works (ibid.: 139):

Those workers up there, carelessly dressed, coatless and collarless – lacking most of the superficial qualities found in capitalist society – those workers, and men like them are running the new Russia.

Herbert Dyson Carter, a Canadian writer and scientist, and future president of the Canadian–Soviet Friendship Society, describes Soviet agriculture in similar terms (ibid.: 139):

[T]he Soviet farmer is constantly striving to increase the crop yield [...] and the milk output [...] without the slightest regard for market prices [...] His concern is to step up farm production so that there will be ever more food available.

Louis Fischer, an American journalist and writer, summarised his impression of the Soviet economy thus: 'The entire Soviet Union felt inspired in the presence of this spectacle of creation and self-sacrifice [...] A whole nation marched behind a vision' (ibid.: 137).

Similarly, Joseph Freeman wrote (ibid.: 132):

[F]or the first time I saw the greatest of human dreams assuming the shape of reality. Men, women and children were uniting their efforts into a gigantic stream of energy directed toward destroying the evils of life, toward creating what was healthy and good for all.

What also appealed to many pilgrims was the apparent equality of material conditions. Equality made poverty seem palatable, even romantic. Theodore Dreiser, an American journalist and novelist, wrote (ibid.: 111):

[Y]ou will see thousands who are comparatively poorly dressed to ten – at most a hundred – who are well dressed. And yet generally speaking, a sense of well-being – none of that haunting sense of poverty [...] that so distressed one in western Europe and America. It is not to be found. Yet in Moscow there is poverty. There are beggars in the streets. [...] But Lord, how picturesque! The multi-colored and voluminous rags of them!

This sentiment was echoed by Eugene Lyons, an American journalist and Moscow correspondent for United Press: 'Elsewhere dinginess might be depressing. Here it seemed to us romantically proletarian' (ibid.: 108).

These contributors at least acknowledged the existence of poverty. Others denied it outright; famine-denial, in particular, became a way of signalling one's socialist credentials. The Irish–British playwright George Bernard Shaw visited the Soviet Union during the famines, travelling by train via Poland. To make a point, Shaw threw his food provisions out of the window just before his train crossed the Polish–Soviet border (Hollander 1990: 118).

During a lunch at a luxury restaurant, Shaw was challenged about this by another Western visitor. He replied by pointing to the other tables, and asking, 'Where do you see any food shortage?' (ibid.).

Julian Huxley, the first President of the British Humanist Association, a founding member of the World Wildlife Fund, and later the first Director of UNESCO, also claimed that he 'got the impression of a population not at all undernourished, and at a level of physique and general health rather above that to be seen in England' (ibid.: 118).

Even the prisons and the Gulags were marvelled at by many of the pilgrims (ibid.: 140–60). They were presented as places of rehabilitation, not punishment, where inmates were given a chance to engage in useful activities, while reflecting upon their mistakes. The pilgrims saw Soviet prisons and Gulags as a transitory phenomenon. Crime, in their view, was not committed out of base motives, but as a response to social injustice. Since social injustice no longer existed under socialism, crime was merely a hangover from the pre-socialist period, which would eventually die out.

Anna Louise Strong, an American author and journalist, wrote that 'The labor camps have won high reputation throughout the Soviet Union as places where tens of thousands of men have been reclaimed' (ibid.: 145).

On the same subject, Mary Stevenson Callcott, author of the book *Russian Justice*, argued that "The authorities seek to use labor that is constructive as to character and useful economically, and not the kind that brings indignity and resentment when resorted to as punishment' (ibid.: 146).

Describing her impression of one of the labour camps she visited, Callcott said, 'I could never see what kept men in this camp unless they wanted to stay there. No convicts I have known would have any difficulty if they wanted to break away' (ibid.: 146).

And in a prison she visited, the inmates were (ibid.: 148):

> talking and laughing as they worked, evidently enjoying themselves. This was the first glimpse of the informal atmosphere that prevailed throughout, and which caused us to look in some amazement [...] It was difficult to believe that this was indeed a prison.

According to George Bernard Shaw's description, being incarcerated in the Soviet Union was such an enjoyable experience that it was hard to convince the inmates to leave again:

> In England a delinquent enters as an ordinary man and comes out a 'criminal type', whereas in Russia he enters [...] as a criminal type and would come out an ordinary man but for the difficulty of inducing them to come out at all. As far as I could make out they could stay as long as they liked.

A persistent feature of the Soviet system was the obsession with 'wreckers' and 'saboteurs'. Since the fault for economic failures could never possibly lie within the socialist system itself, scapegoats had to be found whenever failures became apparent. This led to permanent witch hunts, mass arrests and mass executions on fabricated charges. For the Soviet Union's defenders, however, it was inconceivable that the Soviet justice system randomly executed people, so charges of wrecking and sabotage had to be genuine.

A good illustration is the Western response to the Metropolitan-Vickers trial in 1933. Metropolitan-Vickers was a British engineering company, which had been commissioned by the Soviet government to carry out an engineering project in Moscow. Some of its engineers were arrested on charges of 'wreckage' and 'sabotage', and were made to sign pre-prepared 'confessions' under torture. Since they were British nationals, the British parliament had to debate the issue.

The MP for Tavistock, Colin Patrick, had previously worked at the British embassy in Moscow, and described his observations of the Soviet practices (quoted in Udy 2017: 445–46):

Having obtained the necessary number of prisoners, and determined on the plan of action, the next step is to get the evidence [...] In most cases the accused have been selected from among the remnants of the pre-War bourgeoisie. [...] [T]he supply of the bourgeoisie seems to be running short and [...] the Proletariat is becoming increasingly involved. The charge is almost always one of wrecking and sabotage. One has to be on the spot to realise how utterly unreal that charge may be. In all these numerous trials I am convinced that there has very seldom been a single conviction that has really been based on reality.

Several other MPs, however, took the side of the Soviet government. The MP for Glasgow Bridgeton, James Maxton, replied to Patrick (ibid.: 446):

The hon. Member for Tavistock has given a very clear indication of how his prejudices guide him to look at Soviet Russia [...] [H]e was not completely conscious of the amount of prejudice that was displaying itself in his utterances. I stand here as one who has been very anxious, and is anxious now, that the great experiment of the Russian people should work out to a complete success, but [...] in the House there is a large number of people who are very anxious that the Russian experiment should fail.

Aneurin Bevan, the future Minister of Health and Minister of Labour, said (ibid.: 447–48):

Such an individual has no right to complain of the operation of the laws of a foreign State [...] [A]n Englishman going into a foreign country accepts the authority of its legislation [...] and subjects himself to all the consequent inconveniences.

I do not believe the Foreign Secretary, when he tells the House that the purpose [...] is to seek justice for these

Englishmen. I believe its purpose is wider and more sin-ister [...]

[T]he Foreign Secretary and his chauvinistic and jin-goistic followers [...] for years have sought an opportunity of declaring war against the one nation, which, despite all the difficulties, is still showing that it is possible to have a world order in which people can live with more security than we have here.

Sir Stafford Cripps, the future Chancellor of the Exchequer and Minister for Economic Affairs, said (ibid.: 443):

If the Russian system is a system of justice, as I accept, and if they have a crime the penalty of which is death, then the person who is guilty of that crime must be put to death, just as a Russian in this country, if he has done a murder, will be hanged.

Some supporters of Stalinism were less starry-eyed than others. Some used a language of tough trade-offs rather than a language of unicorns and rainbows; they acknowledged Stalinist atrocities, but justified them as necessary for the greater good. Harold Laski, a British po-litical theorist and economist, as well as chairman of the Labour Party in the immediate post-war period, did call the Soviet system a one-party dictatorship (Laski 1946: 58–59). But he saw Soviet authoritarianism as explicable – and excusable – by the country's special circumstances. And he believed that a socialist economy, even in the ab-sence of 'formal' freedoms, gives ordinary people greater freedom and control over their lives than other systems (ibid.: 49–51):

> The expropriation of landlord and capitalist [...] has made possible the ending of social dependence upon the profit-making motive as the stimulus to productive effort. The outcome of this freedom has been, unquestionably, immense social advantage. It has meant that, in the planning of the productive effort, attention can be concentrated not upon effective demand but upon social need. [...] [I]n the narrow economic sphere, there is a more genuine basis for economic freedom for the masses than they have elsewhere previously enjoyed. [...]
>
> [T]here is this widespread sense [...] that millions, in every field and factory, help to make the conditions under which they live, [...] there are the effective beginnings of constitutional government in industry. The rules of an enterprise are not made at the discretion of an employer who owns it [...] The rules are genuinely the outcome of a real discussion in which men and management participate. And the absence of the profit-making motive [...] gives men the sense of freedom because they find their own wills represented.

Laski also believed that social advances more than outweigh the lack of 'bourgeois' freedoms (ibid.: 46–47):

> [T]he sense of wide horizons opening to a population hitherto confined to narrow perspectives of opportunity is bound to evoke what is best in the spirit of a people. [...]

> [T]his has taken place on an immense scale in the Soviet Union [...] The scale, for example, upon which education has been organized has given to millions [...] a power to make themselves articulate, an ability to explain the wants they have, which is of the essence of freedom. [...] That educational achievement has gone hand in hand with important achievements in other social spheres.

G. D. H. Cole, the chairman and later president of the Fabian Society, and a Professor of Social and Political Theory at Oxford University, took a similar line (quoted in Udy 2017: 508):

> Critics of Russian institutions [...] dwell very greatly on the alleged suppression of liberty in Russia [...] But though the Soviet system in its present working does undoubtedly restrict individual liberty very seriously in certain directions [...] it has resulted in other directions in an enormous extension of the liberties of the great mass of the Russian people. Observers who come back from Russia, unless they are too prejudiced to notice what they see, practically all report that there exists among the Russian people [...] a sense of freedom of self-expression quite unknown among the mass of the people in any capitalist country.

By the early 1940s, the Soviet occupation of eastern Poland and the Baltic states, as well as the attempted invasion of Finland, had cooled Stalin-mania somewhat. Cole, however, saw Soviet expansionism as a force for good. In 1942, he wrote (quoted in Udy 2017: 513–14):

I have never allowed my dislike of much that Stalin has done to blind me to the fact that the USSR remains fundamentally Socialist, or that the Soviet form of revolution and of government may be the only one that is capable of sweeping clean the stables of Eastern and Southern Europe [...] I would much sooner see the Soviet Union, even with its policy unchanged, dominant over *all* Europe, including Great Britain, than [...] restore [...] capitalist domination. Much better be ruled by Stalin than by [...] Western capitalism. [...] I am fully convinced that what matters most is to eradicate the class system, even if [...] liberties [...] suffer severe damage in the process.

The American writer and journalist Upton Sinclair used a similar language of tough trade-offs when he talked about the forced collectivisation of agriculture (ibid.: 162):

They drove rich peasants off the land and sent them wholesale to work in lumber camps and on railroads. Maybe it cost a million lives – maybe it cost five million – but you cannot think intelligently about it unless you ask yourself how many millions it might have cost if the changes had not been made [...] There has never been in human history a great social change without killing.

Perhaps the most famous representative of this harsh-but-necessary line of argument is Walter Duranty, the *New York Times*'s Moscow Bureau Chief from 1922 to 1936. On the famines, Duranty wrote:

It is all too true that the novelty and mismanagement of collective farming, plus the quite efficient conspiracy of Feodor M. Konar and his associates in agricultural commissariats [alleged 'saboteurs' who had just been executed], have made a mess of Soviet food production.

But – to put it brutally – you can't make an omelette without breaking eggs and the Bolshevist leaders are just as indifferent to the casualties that may be involved in their drive toward socialization as any General during the World War who ordered a costly attack.[2]

On the issue of individual liberties, Duranty said:

Stalin is giving the Russian people – the Russian masses, [...] Russia's 150,000,000 peasants and workers – what they really want, namely, joint efforts, communal effort. And communal life is as acceptable to them as it is repugnant to a Westerner. [...] Russian Bolshevism [...] suits the Russians, and is [...] familiar, natural and right to the Russian mind.[3]

Duranty saw Lenin and Stalin as men of action, who knew that the creation of a classless society was not a walk in the park:

---

2   Russians hungry, but not starving, *New York Times*, 31 March 1933 (http://www.nytimes.com/2003/10/26/weekinreview/word-for-word-soft-touch-our-man-moscow-praise-stalinist-future.html).

3   Stalinism dominates Russia of today, *New York Times*, 14 June 1931.

Marx theorized about 'the elimination of class distinctions' in his proletarian Utopia, but Leninism and Stalinism showed what the words meant in practice. [...] The old ruling class – royalty, nobles, generals and officials [...] have disappeared already. [...] [W]hat is happening now to the Kulaks is leading to the same result [...]

'The liquidation of the kulak as a class' runs the present slogan whose meaning in terms of reality is that 5,000,000 human beings [...] are to be dispossessed, dispersed, demolished, to be literally melted or 'liquidated' into the rising flood of classless proletarians.

Here, when you get right down to it, is the supreme justification from the Bolshevik angle of the cruel and often bloody pressure upon [...] class enemies from Czar to kulak. Where Marxism theorized Stalin acts. Marxism says, 'Eliminate class distinctions' and Stalinism does so by the simple and effective process of destructions [...]

But truth it is – ant-heap system, ant-heap morality – each for all and all for each, not each for self and the devil take the hindmost.[4]

That was also the line of the British historian Eric Hobsbawm. In an interview in 1995, Hobsbawm was asked about his commitment to socialism and the Soviet Union in his youth (during the Stalinist period):

---

4   Stalinism smashes foes in Marx's name, *New York Times*, 24 June 1931 (http://www.garethjones.org/soviet_articles/duranty_1931_8.htm).

SOCIALISM: THE FAILED IDEA THAT NEVER DIES

> [Interviewer:] 'So you're saying that such was your com-
> mitment and your dedication that if there was a chance
> of bringing about this communist utopia, which was
> your dream, it was worth any kind of sacrifice?'
> [Hobsbawm:] 'Yes, I think so.'
> [Interviewer:] 'Even the sacrifice of millions of lives?'
> [Hobsbawm:] 'Well, that's what we felt when we fought
> World War II, didn't we?'[5]

Hollander's book contains an extensive discussion of the psychological self-manipulation techniques the pilgrims used in order to see what they wanted to see, and overlook or unsee what they did not want to see. Discussing these techniques is beyond the scope of this book, but suffice it to say this: the possibility that pilgrims were naive people, who were simply tricked by Soviet propaganda, can be safely ruled out. The basic facts were known in the West, if not in their exact extent. Denying them took some mental effort.

The 1930s were the heyday of Western intellectuals' enthusiasm for the Soviet Union. It was not ended by a single event, but decreased in stages, as subsequent Soviet actions made it harder and harder to rationalise the regime's behaviour. The Soviet invasion of eastern Poland, the Baltic states and the attempted invasion of Finland marked the end of the most enthusiastic period. But support for

---

5 Professor Eric Hobsbawm, *BBC Radio 4*, 10 March 1995 (http://www.bbc
.co.uk/programmes/p0093pss). Hobsbawn is reminiscing about what he
thought *at the time*, the period when Stalin was alive. It does not necessarily reflect what he thought in 1995.

Stalinism had not completely disappeared yet. In the mid-1940s, George Orwell still had difficulties finding a publisher for *Animal Farm*, since the book's anti-Stalinist message was still deemed controversial at the time. Just after Stalin's death in 1953, William Gallacher, who had been the MP for West Fife until three years before, still wrote (Gallacher 1953):

> The people of the Soviet Union, the progressive forces and the Peace Movement throughout the world have suffered an irreparable loss through the death of our great and well-beloved Comrade Joseph Stalin. [...]
>
> [H]e worked out the strategy that destroyed forever the hopes of the counter-revolutionaries and their imperialist backers. [...] From this the legend was started that he was 'rude' and 'ruthless'. [...] If he had been a petty-bourgeois 'intellectual' he would have lost the revolution and earned the praise of the workers' enemies. But to save the revolution – that was 'rude', 'ruthless'. [...]
>
> [T]hrough the years his wise guidance has led the Soviet people along the Lenin road to a happy, joyful life [...] only communism can give. [...]
>
> [W]ith his work completed, [...] the Soviet people still under his wise guidance will go forward, resolute as he was resolute—to the new truly free society of Marx and Engels, of Lenin and of Stalin.

Bertolt Brecht, a German poet, playwright and theatre director, added:

> The oppressed of five continents, those who have already liberated themselves, and all those who are fighting for world peace – their heartbeat must have paused when they learned about Stalin's death. He was the embodiment of their hope. But the intellectual and physical weapons that he built are still there, and so is the creed to produce new ones.[6]

Paul Robeson, an American musician and political activist, went even further (quoted in Udy 2017: 526):

> Here was one who was wise and good – the world and especially the socialist world was fortunate indeed to have his daily guidance. [...] [T]ens of millions [...] have sung – sing now and will sing his praise – in song and story. [...] Glory to Stalin. Forever will his name be honored and beloved in all lands. [...] He leaves tens of millions all over the earth bowed in heart-aching grief. Inspired by his noble example, let us lift our heads slowly but proudly high and march forward.

And in 1956, Peter Shore, the future MP for Bethnal Green and Stepney, Secretary of State for the Environment and Secretary of State for Trade, wrote in the *New Statesman* (quoted in Udy 2017: 515):

> [O]ur attitude to Communism [...] must begin with the recognition that Communism has proved to be the most

---

6   Quoted in Deutscher Bundestag 2006: 4 (translation mine).

speedy, effective, and in some ways attractive instrument yet devised for transforming primitive into modern societies [...] [W]hen its repulsive features are weighed Communism remains an infinitely superior system of social organization to the feudalism which, with minor exceptions, it has so far replaced.

Ironically, Stalin-mania only fully came to an end in the West when it came to an end in the Soviet Union itself, with Khrushchev's 'secret speech' in 1956 and his subsequent policy of 'de-Stalinisation'. Vivian Gornick, an American journalist and a socialist at the time, remembers:

I was 20 years old in February 1956 when Nikita Khrushchev addressed the 20th Congress of the Soviet Communist Party and revealed to the world the incalculable horror of Stalin's rule. [...] I was beside myself with youthful rage. 'Lies!' I screamed [...]

The 20th Congress report brought with it political devastation for the organized left around the world. Within weeks of its publication, 30,000 people in this country quit the [Communist] party[7]

But once it was over, it was well and truly over, and disappeared without a trace. As Hollander (1990: 433) explains:

---

7 When communism inspired Americans, *New York Times*, 29 April 2017 (https://www.nytimes.com/2017/04/29/opinion/sunday/when-communism-inspired-americans.html).

> [T]he sympathies which prevailed earlier in many circles of intellectual and public opinion were wiped out [...] With few exceptions, the intellectuals [...] who had earlier favored the Soviet Union repudiated their pro-Soviet fervor or fell silent on the issue [...]
>
> Several of these earlier pro-Soviet or old-left intellectuals emerged into public life in the 1960s lending their support to the student protest [...] Most of them, however, did not rekindle their pro-Soviet sentiments.

From then on, Soviet socialism was increasingly presented as a rigid, stifling and bureaucratic form of socialism, a perversion of the original socialist idea. A rhetoric of equidistance, presenting Soviet socialism and Western capitalism as roughly equally flawed, became the norm (Revel 1978).

Remnants of Soviet apologetics today

Soviet apologetics has long ceased to be a mainstream pursuit, but it never disappeared completely. During the final stages of the dissolution of the Soviet Union in 1991, Jeremy Corbyn MP, the current leader of the opposition, said:

> People marched and organised in this area of London in support of the Soviet Revolution of 1917. I certainly haven't come here to bury those ideas. [...] [W]e should not go around saying, or allowing others to say, that democracy equals liberal economics and market forces. It doesn't. Nor should we say that Socialism or the ideas of Socialism are dead. They are not. [...] [O]nly Socialism

and socialist ideas can bring about peace, democracy and a reasonable life expectancy.[8]

Corbyn's account contains only two mildly critical remarks about the Soviet Union:

> I am not defending everything that has happened in the Soviet Union in the last seventy years. [...]
>
> If there are two areas where I think grave mistakes were made by the Soviet Union, it was the inability of the system to recognise the importance of the national question and the way in which the Communist Party of the Soviet Union became an extremely elitist body.

The Soviet Union is otherwise presented as a force for good, especially on the global stage:

> Had the Soviet Union at the time of the Gulf war played a somewhat stronger role at the United Nations, then perhaps that piece of carnage would not have been able to take place in the name of the United Nations. [...]
>
> [T]he only country in the world that was prepared to help [Cuba] break the blockade of the US was the Soviet Union. [...] We should also recognise the changes that have happened in other parts of the world since it came into being. The Soviet Union supported the revolution in Nicaragua and it supported large numbers of anti-colonial struggles in Africa and other places.

---

8   Where do we go from here? *Morning Star*, 24 September 1991.

Consequently, Corbyn believed that nothing good could come out of the Soviet Union's demise:

> We are dealing with a whole new scenario in which the IMF and the World Bank are in effect running the world economy. [...]
>
> I am alarmed at the consequences of what has happened in the past two years in the Soviet Union and Eastern Europe [...] The changes taking place in the Soviet Union are going to bring with them the old class struggles. That of course is where the Bolsheviks came in in the first place.

For socialists in Britain, the relevant lesson from the USSR's collapse was not to move away from socialism, but, on the contrary, to double down on it:

> What we should be asking ourselves is what are we doing about Socialism here in this country? Why are so many people now becoming so defensive about Socialism? I am fed up with the leadership of the labour movement continually denying the birthright of this movement [...]
>
> We have to look at what we mean by Socialism. Is it the anarchy of the free market with a few ameliorating features [...], or is Socialism really production for need rather than profit?

Seumas Milne, the Labour Party's Executive Director of Strategy and Communications, still regularly defends the Soviet Union and the former Eastern bloc. Milne concedes that there were 'excesses' during the Stalinist period, but believes that these have been greatly exaggerated for political purposes. What Milne rejects with particular vehemence is the idea that Stalinism is in any way comparable to Nazism.

In 2002, Milne wrote in *The Guardian*:

[T]he number of victims of Stalin's terror has been progressively inflated [...] Despite the cruelties of the Stalin terror, there was no Soviet Treblinka, no extermination camps built to murder people in their millions. [...] [T]hose who demonise past attempts to build an alternative to capitalist society are determined to prove that there is none.[9]

He goes on to relativise the death toll of Stalinism through whataboutery:

Perhaps most grotesque in this postmodern calculus of political repression is the moral blindness displayed towards the record of colonialism. [...] Throughout the 20th-century British empire, the authorities gassed, bombed and massacred indigenous populations [...] If Lenin and Stalin are regarded as having killed those who died of hunger in the famines of the 1920s and 1930s, then Churchill is certainly responsible for the 4 million deaths in the avoidable Bengal famine of 1943.

---

9 The battle for history, *The Guardian*, 12 September 2002 (https://www .theguardian.com/education/2002/sep/12/highereducation.historyand historyofart).

In 2006, Milne argued:

> The [...] attempt to equate communism and Nazism is in reality a moral and historical nonsense. [...] For all its brutalities and failures, communism in the Soviet Union, eastern Europe and elsewhere delivered rapid industrialisation, mass education, job security and huge advances in social and gender equality. It encompassed genuine idealism and commitment [...] Its existence helped to drive up welfare standards in the west [...]
>
> [T]he current enthusiasm in official western circles for dancing on the grave of communism [...] reflects a determination to prove there is no alternative to the new global capitalist order.[10]

And in 2007:

> [Communism's] crimes and failures are now so well rehearsed that they are in danger of obliterating any understanding of its achievements – both of which have lessons for the future of progressive politics and the search for a social alternative to globalised capitalism. It was a communist state, after all, that played the decisive role in the defeat of Nazi Germany [...]
>
> [A]long with its brutalities and authoritarianism, communism delivered rapid industrialisation, mass education, full employment and unprecedented advances in

---

10 Communism may be dead, but clearly not dead enough, *The Guardian*, 16 February 2006 (https://www.theguardian.com/Columnists/Column/0,,17 10891,00.html).

social and gender equality. Its collapse, by contrast, has brought an explosion of poverty and inequality [...] There certainly was mass support for these regimes.[11]

Similarly, Kostas Papadakis, a Member of the European Parliament, talks about:

an orchestrated campaign that aims to slander socialism, rewrite history, and to unacceptably and provocatively equate communism with the monster of fascism. [...] A basic goal is to conceal the fact that fascism is a form of capital's power in specific conditions. In Germany, Nazism constituted the ideal form to support capital in the conditions of [...] the increase of the prestige of the KPD [the Communist Party of Germany] and the USSR. [...]

Nazism-fascism met its deadliest and most determined opponent in the socialist society of the USSR [...] A self-evident consequence of the anti-communist campaign is the justification, prettification and exoneration of Nazism-fascism and its atrocities.[12]

In 1999, Andrew Murray, a Labour Party campaign manager in the 2017 General Election, and formerly chair of the

---

11 Movement of the people, *The Guardian*. 12 May 2007 (https://www.the guardian.com/books/2007/may/12/featuresreviews.guardianreview8).

12 The equation of Communism with Nazism is unacceptable and provocative, *In Defense of Communism* blog, 30 August 2017 (https://communism gr.blogspot.co.uk/2017/08/kostas-papadakis-equation-of-communism .html).

Stop the War coalition and chief of staff at Unite the Union, wrote in a column for the *Morning Star* newspaper:

> Next Tuesday is the 120th anniversary of the birth of Josef Stalin. [...] A socialist system embracing a third of the world and the defeat of Nazi Germany on the one hand. On the other, all accompanied by harsh measures [...] Nevertheless, if you believe that the worst crimes visited on humanity this century [...] have been caused by imperialism, then [Stalin's birthday] might at least be a moment to ponder why the authors of those crimes and their hack propagandists abominate the name of Stalin beyond all others. It was, after all, Stalin's best-known critic, Nikita Khrushchev, who remarked in 1956 that 'against imperialists, we are all Stalinists'.[13]

Milne, Papadakis and Murray stand for a view of the world in which a condemnation of Leninism/Stalinism, which is not coupled with an explicit condemnation of Nazism, colonialism, the Vietnam War, etc., constitutes a tacit endorsement of the latter. They do not explain where they get this idea from. If somebody does not couple a condemnation of Stalinism with an explicit condemnation of, say, Attila the Hun, Vlad the Impaler and Genghis Khan – should we also interpret this as a tacit endorsement of the latter?

It may well be true that most critics of socialism pay much less attention to atrocities committed under different systems. But this does not indicate tacit approval of the

---

13 Eye's Left, *Morning Star*, 17 December 1999. Quoted in Mosbacher (2004).

latter. There is a perfectly good reason for it, which is that Nazism, colonialism, the slave trade, the Vietnam War, etc., are, to put it mildly, not fashionable causes today. There is no political force of any relevance today which wants to resurrect any of these. Nobody argues that Nazism or slavery were 'noble' causes that had just been 'badly implemented'. Nobody argues that Hitler's version of Nazism was not 'real' Nazism, or that slavery as it was practised during the slave trade was not 'real' slavery.

Such arguments are only made with reference to socialism. It is socialism which remains extremely fashionable to this day. It makes perfect sense to focus one's energies on refuting bad ideas that remain in vogue, rather than bad ideas that have already been defeated.

Ironically, the apologists' own careers are the performative contradiction of the claim that we pay too much attention to the crimes of Stalinism relative to those of other systems. If somebody in a comparable position attempted to relativise the horrors of Nazism in the same way in which modern-day Soviet apologists attempted to relativise the horrors of Stalinism, their career would be finished.

A positive view of the Soviet Union, as expressed by Milne, Papadakis and Murray, is clearly a minority view on the left today. But it is a view which is tolerated on the left, and it is certainly not a career obstacle. Indeed, the ease with which those who insist that any mention of the Soviet Union is a straw man share platforms with those who openly defend the Soviet Union gives an impression of just how illusory the difference between 'real' and 'unreal' socialism is.

Conclusion

The short summary of this chapter is *not* that the socialist left, as a whole, was in thrall to Stalinism in its heyday. The above quotations are a selection, not a representative cross sample. Even Hollander's book, which contains hundreds of pages filled with similar quotes, is still a selection.[14] If we define the term 'intellectual' broadly enough, if we look at a large enough number of countries, and over a long enough period of time, then even several hundred sympathisers need not be a huge proportion of the total.

One can also find critical left-wing voices; indeed, some of the Soviet Union's fiercest critics were disappointed socialists. The two most famous critiques of the Soviet regime (among other themes), George Orwell's *Animal Farm* and *Nineteen Eighty-Four*, were written by one of them. And some of those left-wing critics saw the Soviet regime for what it was from a very early stage. Bertrand Russell, the British philosopher and logician, was initially supportive of the October Revolution, but already disavowed the regime in 1920 (although he remained committed to the communist 'ideal') (Russell 1920: 170):

---

14 It is not even clear what would constitute a 'representative cross sample' in this case. Professional associations, such as the American Economic Association, sometimes conduct surveys of their members to find out where they stand on various issues. It is possible to extrapolate from such surveys, and make statements such as 'most economists oppose rent controls'. We cannot quantify support for Stalinism among socialist intellectuals in a comparable way. Who counts as an 'intellectual'? Who counts as a 'socialist'? Obvious cases aside, what counts as 'support'? Are we just interested in a headcount, or would we give a higher weight to a more prominent intellectual, such as Sidney Webb?

> Owing to unpopularity, the Bolsheviks have had to rely upon the army and the Extraordinary Commission, and have been compelled to reduce the Soviet system to an empty form. More and more the pretence of representing the proletariat has grown threadbare.

According to Russell, Soviet socialism represented (ibid.:):

> a slavery far more complete than that of capitalism. A sweated wage, long hours, industrial conscription, prohibition of strikes, prison for slackers, diminution of the already insufficient rations in factories where the production falls below what the authorities expect, an army of spies ready to report any tendency to political disaffection and to procure imprisonment for its promoters – this is the reality of a system which still professes to govern in the name of the proletariat.

Russell was not alone. In the early 1920s, when the Bolsheviks crushed a series of strikes, protests and uprisings (such as the 1921 Kronstadt Rebellion), a number of initial sympathisers turned their backs on the regime (Hollander 1990: 349; Berkman 1925).

Nor is the short summary of this chapter that *only* the socialist left had a soft spot for murderous tyrants at the time. Richard Griffiths's (2011) book *Fellow Travellers of the Right: British Enthusiasts for Nazi Germany* shows that during the 1930s, admiration for the Third Reich was much more widespread in Britain than is commonly acknowledged today.

But at the same time, the people quoted here were not obscure fringe figures. They were prominent, respectable mainstream intellectuals in their day. Some of them were among the left's leading figures. They include a British prime minister, various cabinet ministers, various MPs, a chairman of the British Labour Party, co-founders of the LSE, the Fabian Society and the *New Statesman*, a Nobel Peace Prize laureate, a Nobel Literature Prize laureate, and so on.

And while the pilgrim's uncritical enthusiasm may not have been representative of left-wing opinion overall, it represented an end of a spectrum. On the same spectrum, we can find plenty of people who were not as enthusiastic and not as starry-eyed about socialist regimes as the pilgrims were, but still clearly supportive overall – the people who are often described as 'fellow-travellers' (see Caute 1988). Unlike pilgrims, fellow-travellers typically maintained some critical distance to the socialist regime *du jour*.[15] They were, for example, more aware of the systems' repressive aspects. Nonetheless, they ultimately supported the same regimes, and for similar reasons.

It should also be noted that, for obvious reasons, we can only quote people who have left a written testimony of their impressions of the Soviet Union. This is why the above selection is heavily biased towards journalists and writers from English-speaking countries. But the guided tours also included large numbers of doctors, teachers and

---

15 There is, of course, no hard-and-fast dividing line between 'pilgrims' and 'fellow-travellers', and such categories are somewhat made-up. Unsurprisingly, a lot of the names that appear in *Political Pilgrims* also appear in Caute's book about the fellow-travellers.

members of other professions, most of whom may not have put their views into writing, but who may still have been opinion multipliers in other ways.

And while it is absolutely true that there have always been socialist critics of the Soviet Union, these critics tended to be socialists of the anarchist, utopian variety. They rejected the Leninist system simply because they rejected *all* real-world systems. They were 'right' about the Soviet Union in the same way in which a stopped clock is right twice a day.

For example, the Socialist Party of Great Britain (SPGB) had already distanced itself from Soviet Russia in 1920, if not earlier (SPGB n.d.). But this was not because they had come up with an especially lucid critique of where Russian socialism had gone wrong. It was because they judged it against their definition of 'true' socialism, which is:

> a wageless, moneyless, worldwide society of common (not state) ownership and democratic control of the means of wealth production and distribution. [...] [S]ocialism will be a sharp break with capitalism with no 'transition period' or gradual implementation of socialism [...] [T]here can be no state in a socialist society. [...] [T]here can be no classes in a socialist society.[16]

Of course, socialists who judge real-world experiments against such utopian standards would not have found

---

16 How the SPGB is different, Socialist Party of Great Britain (http://www .worldsocialism.org/spgb/how-spgb-different).

much to like in Lenin's system. If one's idea of socialism demands the immediate abolition of the police, the army, the court system, the prison system, etc., if it requires people to voluntarily give up money, private property, exchange, etc., and if one does not accept any compromises, halfway measures or phase-in periods, then yes, such a person would not have been seduced by Leninism. But this is simply because they would have set the bar impossibly high.

A lot of the early socialist critics of the Soviet Union fall into this category. Emma Goldman, an initial supporter of the revolution, published a book with the self-explanatory title *My Disillusionment in Russia* in 1923.[17] In a similar vein, Alexander Berkman, another initial supporter, published *The Bolshevik Myth (Diary 1920–1922)* in 1925. Both Goldman and Berkman had spent some time in Russia, arriving with high hopes, and left disenchanted. But both were anarcho-socialists of a Bakuninite variety, who were bound to end up disappointed.

Ultimately, it is impossible to tell how widespread support for Stalinism was among Western intellectuals. But one thing is safe to say: the idea that Soviet socialism was only ever supported by a few extremists, and that Stalinism is merely a stick which anti-socialists use to beat socialists, is demonstrably false. The relevant answer to the question 'How many reasonably high-profile Western socialists supported Stalinism in its heyday?' is not 'four out of five' or 'one in two' or 'one in four'. The relevant answer

---

17 https://www.marxists.org/reference/archive/goldman/works/1920s/disil
lusionment/index.htm

is 'far more than commonly assumed, and far more than contemporary socialists would have you believe'.

The short summary of this chapter is that the claim that Soviet socialism was not 'real' socialism is a post-hoc rationalisation. During the Stalinist period, it *was* real socialism to plenty of prominent, self-described socialists.

3 CHINA UNDER MAO TSE-TUNG: 'A REVOLUTIONARY REGIME MUST GET RID OF A CERTAIN NUMBER OF INDIVIDUALS THAT THREATEN IT'

Maoist socialism

By the 1950s, Western intellectuals had fallen out of love with the Soviet Union. But it did not take long for new utopias to fill that void: North Vietnam, Cuba (see Chapter 4), and above all, Maoist China.

The People's Republic of China was established in 1949, but during its first decade or so, it attracted little attention from Western intellectuals. Then, in the late 1950s, two things happened.

Firstly, the socialist transformation of the country began in earnest, first with the Great Leap Forward, and later with the Great Proletarian Cultural Revolution. The Great Leap Forward was the government takeover of the commanding heights of the economy – including the forced collectivisation of agriculture – and an attempted industrialisation campaign, comparable to Soviet economic policies in the 1930s. The Cultural Revolution was a programme of purging society of 'counterrevolutionaries', 'saboteurs', and remnants of 'bourgeois' traditions, vaguely comparable to Stalin's Great Terror.

Secondly, while China was initially closely aligned with the Soviet Union, the relationship between the two socialist regimes increasingly soured, leading to their eventual fallout, the so-called Sino-Soviet split. Relations became so hostile that for a while, a war between the two former sister states seemed likely.

The Sino-Soviet split radically changed perceptions of China in the West. It meant that Chinese socialism was no longer tainted by association with the – now discredited – Soviet model of socialism. It represented the promise of a fresh start, a genuinely novel, independent form of socialism. Maoism came to be seen as an alternative to Western capitalism on the one hand, and the unreal socialism of the Soviet Union on the other hand.

The period from, roughly, the beginning of the 1960s to the mid-1970s became the honeymoon period of Maoism. Echoing the pilgrimages to the Soviet Union in the 1930s, Western admirers flocked to China in large numbers, and returned full of praise.

This was, of course, a period during which millions of alleged 'saboteurs' and 'counterrevolutionaries' were executed, or worked to death in the Chinese version of the Gulags, the Laogai. The Great Leap Forward led to what may well have been the worst famine in human history. Taken together, Chinese socialism was responsible for about 65 million deaths, according to one estimate (Courtois et al. 1997: 4).

Unlike in the Soviet case, China's honeymoon period was not even a period of initial economic success. The closest thing to a counterfactual has to be Taiwan, the former Chinese province which declared independence from mainland China during the socialist revolution. Taiwan did not just avoid the famine and the economic dislocation that the mainland went through. In the 1960s, Taiwan became one of the four 'Asian Tigers' (together with Hong Kong, Singapore and, later, South Korea), while mainland China remained a poorhouse. By 1980, Taiwan had become more than ten times as rich as mainland China (IMF 2017). Today, Taiwan's GDP per capita (PPP) is higher than the UK's, and virtually identical to Germany's and Austria's.

The difference between the two is that Taiwan became a magnet for Western investors, while mainland China became a magnet for Western intellectuals.

Mao's pilgrims

By the time China entered its honeymoon period, many Western intellectuals had given up on economic progress. It had become fashionable to dismiss material prosperity as soulless, morally corrupting and alienating, and to praise ascetic living standards as more 'authentic'. Thus, Maoism's lack of economic success did not constitute a problem for its admirers. It was, if anything, an advantage, because it was seen as a deliberate avoidance of the perils of 'consumerism'. Peter Worsley, a British sociologist and social anthropologist, and one of the founders of the 'New Left', wrote (cited in Hollander 1990: 319):

> The Chinese [...] do not wish to create a consumer society. They have not *tried* to produce cars, television [*sic*] or phones on a mass scale, since they do not wish to. Hopefully the boulevards of Peking will never be choked with thousands of private cars.

The American philosopher Corliss Lamont wrote that 'The Communists [...] will not permit the bad by-products of modern technology that had brought pollution and other evils to the United States and other capitalist nations' (ibid.: 319).

In the pilgrims' eyes, Mao's China stood for social progress rather than economic progress. Carol Tavris, an American social psychologist, wrote (ibid.):

> It is the certainty of success that dominates the Chinese mood today. Their accomplishments assume dreamlike proportions in the cold light of an American day. They virtually have eliminated many of the social problems that nations are heir to: prostitution, drugs, theft, rape, murder and litter. They have eradicated many [...] diseases [...] No one starves, no one begs.

Joshua Horn, a British surgeon and member of the Socialist Medical Association, also found 'a complete absence of beggars, vagrants [...] and prostitutes. In the shops, fixed prices, no persuasion, scrupulous honesty and no bartering' (ibid.: 318).

According to John Fairbank, an American historian (ibid.: 278):

> The people seem healthy, well fed and articulate about their role as citizens of Chairman Mao's new China [...] The Maoist revolution is on the whole the best thing that happened to the Chinese people in centuries.

A group of authors from the Committee of Concerned Asian Scholars wrote that 'After Hong Kong – noisy, pushy and crowded – the busy streets of Canton seemed gentle by comparison. [...] Everyone looked healthy, no one wore rags, or begged' (ibid.: 309).

Differences in attitudes to economic progress aside, the testimonies of Mao's pilgrims sound remarkably similar to those of Stalin's pilgrims. In a 'blind test' (i.e. if we blacked out time- and place-specific references), it would be difficult to tell them apart. The main theme is the characterisation of the Chinese economy as an economy run collectively by 'the people', and the idea that this economic model produces all-round social harmony. Maria-Antonietta Macciocchi, an Italian journalist, writer and later an MP and an MEP, wrote (ibid.: 315):

> There is no trace of alienation in China, nor of those neuroses or that inner disintegration of the individual found in the parts of the world dominated by consumerism. The Chinese world is compact, integrated, an absolute whole.

And elsewhere (ibid.: 278):

> [A] people is marching with a light step and with fervour
> toward the future. This people may be the incarnation of
> the new civilization of the world. China has made an un-
> precedented leap into history.

Alberto Jacoviello, another Italian writer and foreign affairs editor of the newspaper l'Unità, agreed (ibid.: 315):

> [T]he most striking observation is the absolute absence
> of [...] alienation [...] There is no alienation in China. And
> [...] there is mass political passion such as I have not
> found in any other part of the world.

Joshua Horn believed that 'the ending of exploitation has
greatly reduced social tensions and insecurity' (ibid.: 313).

Basil Davidson, a British historian, described his impression of Chinese soldiers and railway workers thus
(ibid.: 310):

> [T]hey were exceedingly different from any other peas-
> ant army I have seen [...] they looked like men who had
> elected to serve. [...] The railwaymen [...] produced the
> same kind of effect in me, they looked so sure that they
> owned their own railways, so determined to make their
> railways run well.

Norma Lundholm Djerassi, an American poet, saw 'none
of the role-playing and power-pushing I find so unpleasant

in my own society. [...] To feel none of that here is most refreshing. People are who they are and are happy in their usefulness to society' (ibid.: 309).

While some pilgrims insisted that China was a grass-roots democracy run by 'the workers' and 'the peasants', others ascribed a more active role to Mao Tse-Tung and his entourage. Urie Bronfenbrenner, an American developmental psychologist, explained that 'To me China seemed a kind of benign monarchy ruled by an emperor priest who has won the complete devotion of his subjects. In short, a religious and highly moralistic society' (ibid.: 278).

Simone de Beauvoir, the French philosopher and social theorist, saw Maoist China as a kind of Platonic republic, run by 'philosopher kings' (ibid.: 278):

> [L]ife in China today is exceptionally pleasant. [...] Plenty of fond dreams are authorized by the idea of a country [...] where generals and statesmen are scholars and poets.

Hewlett Johnson, an English priest, Dean of Manchester and later Dean of Canterbury, reported (ibid.: 328):

> It was not hard [...] to understand the deep affection men feel for this man [...] All men – intellectuals, peasants, merchants – regard Mao as the symbol of their deliverance, the man who [...] raised their burdens. The peasant looks at the land he tills: Mao's gift. The factory worker thinks of a wage of 100 lb. rice instead of 10: Mao's gift.

Some of the pilgrims acknowledged the existence of restrictions on individual liberty, but nonetheless maintained that 'the workers' and 'the peasants' were in control. Arthur Galston, an American scientist and bioethicist, wrote that 'they are not free to change residence or job, but in spite of that [...] the Chinese masses seem to enjoy a greater measure of control over those agencies that directly affect their daily lives than do most Western city workers' (ibid.: 336).

The British historian Basil Davidson described the regime as 'authoritarian only towards a minority – a minority who are not workers or peasants. [...] [T]he truth is that China's successes are being achieved [...] by the voluntary and even enthusiastic effort of most of the people in China' (ibid.: 337).

Simone de Beauvoir argued that police state methods were only a problem in capitalist countries, where the state apparatus acted against the interests of 'the people'. Since in Maoist China, 'the people' were in charge, those methods became a force for good, a legitimate self-defence against saboteurs and counterrevolutionaries (ibid.: 337):

Urging people to vigilance the government does indeed exhort them to report the counterrevolutionary activities [...] but we must not forget that these activities consist in arson, the sabotage of bridges and dikes, in assassinations [...]

This cooperation with the police seems more shocking to me in our country where law is determined by the interests of a class than where justice is made to correspond to the welfare of the people.

Peter Townsend, the UK's leading poverty researcher (who invented the concept of 'relative poverty'), and Lord Boyd Orr, a Scottish scientist and Nobel Peace Prize laureate, acknowledge that the collectivisation of agriculture was not entirely voluntary. But in their version of events, it was driven by peer pressure rather than the liquidation of dissenters (ibid.: 338):

> Inevitably, of course, there was a good deal of public pressure. [...] [W]hen a majority of villagers decided to form a cooperative, the minority probably found it difficult to remain outside.

Others were more hard-nosed. In the can't-make-an-omelette-without-breaking-a-few-eggs tradition, Jean-Paul Sartre said that:

> A revolutionary regime must get rid of a certain number of individuals that threaten it and I see no other means for this than death; it is always possible to get out of a prison; the revolutionaries of 1793 probably didn't kill enough people.[1]

As with the Soviet Gulags, Chinese Laogai were described as places of rehabilitation, not punishment, where inmates were given the opportunity to perform socially useful work, while being encouraged to think about their mistakes.

---

1   Quoted in: The Absolute Intellectual, *Policy Review*, Hoover Institution, 1 February 2004 (http://www.hoover.org/research/absolute-intellectual).

John Gittings, a British author and *The Guardian*'s future assistant foreign editor and chief foreign leader-writer, wrote (ibid.: 338):

> [R]eform through labour, which to a Western visitor has something of the flavor of the kibbutz combined with the Marxist weekend school (except that it may last for a couple of years), seemed to be working for the great majority.

Felix Greene, a British–American journalist and documentary maker, found 'the Chinese doing what we had been trying to get the English authorities to do for years without success. Mainly, of course, to get the stigma, the moral stigma, out of imprisonment' (ibid.: 342).

Bernard Frolic, a professor at the Department of Politics at York University, compared China's labour camps to an 'adult Boy Scout Camp, or maybe what the Civilian Conservation Corps was like during the Depression' (ibid.: 343).

Harrison Evans Salisbury, an American writer and a *New York Times* correspondent, likened them to 'a combination of a YMCA camp and a Catholic retreat' (ibid.: 344).

Unlike Stalin-mania, Mao-mania was not the preserve of established mainstream intellectuals. Maoist iconography, such as Mao's 'Little Red Book', became a fixed feature of the student protests that gripped most Western countries in the 1960s and 1970s. Ironically, one of the world's most authoritarian and hierarchical societies became the chosen utopia for a protest movement that saw itself as socially liberal, anti-authoritarian and libertine (see Wolin (2010) on Mao-mania in France and Aly (2012) on the similar situation in West Germany).

Just as ironically, the enthusiasm of Western intellectuals for China began to fade when the most murderous period was over (Hollander 1990: 344–46). After Mao's death, mainstream intellectuals moved on to other causes, and Maoism quickly became the preserve of sectarian fringe groups. By the late 1970s, Maoism had become something of a joke, and the factionalism of Maoist groups was occasionally mocked in popular culture (most famously in Monty Python's film *Life of Brian*, which plotted the 'People's Front of Judea' against the 'Judean People's Front').

China, meanwhile, gradually moved away from socialist economics. The country's Economic Freedom score rose from 3.6 (on a scale from 0 to 10) in 1980 to over 4 in the mid-1980s, over 5 in the mid-1990s, and over 6 in the mid-2000s. This is still far behind the score of Taiwan, not to mention Hong Kong: China's economy is still very far away from free-market capitalism. But it is a million miles away from Maoism.

The result was a genuine 'great leap forward'. Since 1980, China's GDP per capita has increased 50-fold in constant prices. In the early 1980s, Taiwan, the closest thing to a counterfactual, was more than ten times as rich as China. Today, it is 'only' three times as rich (see Figure 6).

In the early 1980s, virtually the whole population of China lived in extreme poverty. Since then, this share has fallen to about one in ten (see Figure 7).

Figure 6 GDP per capita (PPP), People's Republic of China vs. Republic of China (Taiwan), 1980–2017

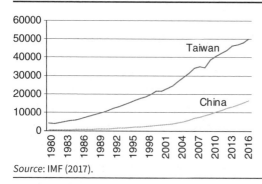

Source: IMF (2017).

Figure 7 Poverty in China, 1981–2013 (poverty line = $3.10 PPP per day)

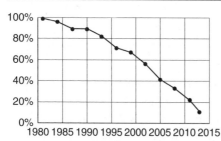

Source: Based on Our World in Data (2013/17).

Western intellectuals had lavishly heaped praise on China when millions of Chinese people were starving or worked to death in forced labour camps. But when a programme of relative liberalisation lifted millions of people out of poverty, those intellectuals were conspicuous by their silence. Market-based reform programmes, no matter how successful, will never inspire pilgrimages. They may, in a narrow sense, 'work'. But they will never capture the imagination of Western intellectuals.

Remnants of Maoist apologetics today

Support for Maoism has never completely disappeared. In 1986, some members of the British House of Commons praised Deng Xiaoping's policy of relative liberalisation, and the subsequent acceleration in the growth of the Chinese economy. Jeremy Corbyn MP countered these claims, insisting that China's recent improvements, far from being the result of liberalisation, were really a belated vindication of socialism (Hansard 1986):

> The conditions enjoyed by people in China now, compared to 1948, are immeasurably better. The country has pulled itself up [...] by collectivising its economy, its efforts and its energy.
>
> Starvation and poverty are not common in China as they were in 1948. Before the hon. Gentleman lectures the world on the way in which capitalism can improve living standards he should look at some of the countries which had to develop their own economies without the assistance of anybody else. [...] [T]he present prosperity in China is based upon a collective economy and not on an individual and market oriented economy.

A lukewarm version of Maoist apologetics survives to this day. In 2010, Benton and Chun (2010) published the book *Was Mao Really a Monster?*, in which seventeen authors try to 'set the record straight' on Maoism. The book does not present itself as a defence of Mao Tse-Tung and his policies, but as merely an exercise in 'fact checking'. It is, of course, entirely possible that some estimates of the death toll of Maoism are inflated. Most genocidal regimes do not meticulously keep records. But one wonders whether any academic would have gone to such great lengths to show that the death toll of, say, Genghis Khan or Attila the Hun may not have been as high as commonly assumed.

The book was referenced favourably by Seumas Milne, who believes that:

> a determined rewriting of history [...] has sought to portray 20th-century communist leaders as monsters equal to or surpassing Hitler in their depravity [...] The latest contribution was last year's bestselling biography of Mao by Jung Chang and Jon Halliday, [...] dismissed by China specialists as 'bad history' and 'misleading'.[2]

On a BBC *This Week* programme in 2008, the MP for Stoke Newington, Diane Abbott, argued:

> I suppose some people would judge that on balance, Mao did more good than harm. [...] He led his country from feudalism, he helped to defeat the Japanese, and he left

---

2 Communism may be dead, but clearly not dead enough, *The Guardian*, 16 February 2006 (https://www.theguardian.com/comment/story/0,,1710 890,00.html).

his country on the verge [...] of the [...] great economic
success they're having now.[3]

These are minority views on the left today, but the ease
with which such views are tolerated in socialist circles
suggests, again, how illusory the distinction between 'real'
and 'unreal' socialism is.

Conclusion

As before, the short summary of this chapter is *not* that
the Western left, as a whole, was in thrall to Maoism in the
1960s and early 1970s. The above quotes are a selection, not
a representative sample.

Nor was the tendency to make excuses for dictatorships
confined to the left. It is well-known that under the eu-
phemistic label of *realpolitik*, governments of the political
right were often willing to forge alliances with dictatorial
regimes, provided they shared a common interest.

But it is entirely fair to say that Maoism had its fair
share of prominent admirers in the West. Some of the left's
leading thinkers were sympathetic to Maoism. Since the
late 1970s, Maoism has been widely associated with eccen-
tric, politically irrelevant fringe groups – but that is only
because around that time, mainstream intellectuals had
already moved on to other causes, leaving only the eccen-
trics behind. Before then, Maoism *was* a mainstream cause.

---

3   *This Week*, BBC, 21 February 2008 (https://www.youtube.com/watch?v
    =uB4o5n2EGyA).

The claim that Maoist socialism was not 'real' socialism is a post-hoc fabrication. It *was* 'real' socialism. Until it was not.

4 CUBA UNDER FIDEL CASTRO: 'THE BEGINNING OF BUILDING THE NEW MAN'

¡Hasta Siempre, Comandante!

In 1997, the French pop singer Nathalie Cardone recorded a cover version of the old Cuban revolutionary song *Hasta Siempre, Comandante*. The music video shows the singer, armed with a machine gun, leading a band of peasants, apparently to a rebellion. More and more people join in, and the band grows into a peasant army. The song became an overnight hit in France, Belgium and the Netherlands.

The iconography of the Cuban revolution has long been absorbed into mainstream fashion and pop culture. In this process, it has lost most of its connection with Cuba as an actual country, or with the Cuban system as an actual political and economic model. It has simply become a way of projecting a generic 'rebel' image of oneself. A quick search on Amazon UK has come up with a 'Che Guevara Cuban Mens Revolutionist Hat', a pack of 'Che Organic Green Mate', a 'Metal Tin Sign Plaque Cafe Bar Wall Decor Art Poster Sheet – CHE GUEVARA 726', an 'Ernesto "Che" Guevara Revolution Mens/Womens Wallet', Che Guevara lighters, Che Guevara birthday cards, a Che Guevara

'Unisex Long wood or acrylic beaded fashion bling, hip-hop, gangster necklace' (although this is a customisable product, where Che can also be swapped for Superman), a 'Che Guevara Decal Vinyl Wall Sticker', Che keyrings, a 'Celebrity Star Hard Back iPhone Case – Che Guevara Pop Art', a 'Che Guevara Shoulder Bag made from recycled material', a 'Che Guevara Toiletry and Make Up Bag', Che Guevara mousepads, Che Guevara cufflinks, Che Guevara mugs, and so on. This comes on top of a wide range of Che Guevara shirts, flags, posters and stickers.

Maybe it is because of this absorption into 'rebel chic' culture that Cuba has never become toxic in the West. In this respect, Cuba deviates from the three-stage pattern described in this book (honeymoon period, period of excuse-making and whataboutery, period of retroactive dismissal). Cuba is the only example of a socialist experiment for which many Western commentators have retained a soft spot to this day, although its honeymoon period ended ages ago.[1]

Support for Cuba takes a peculiar form. Cuba-admirers usually focus on aspects of the system that are not specifically socialist. It has become a cliché to say that while Cubans are neither prosperous nor, in a Western sense, free, at least

---

1   For example, after Fidel Castro's death, the prime minister of Canada, Justin Trudeau, called Castro a 'larger than life' figure and a 'legendary revolutionary'. 'While a controversial figure, both Mr Castro's supporters and detractors recognized his tremendous dedication and love for the Cuban people who had a deep and lasting affection for "el Comandante"'. See Fidel Castro: Justin Trudeau ridiculed over praise of 'remarkable leader', *The Guardian*, 27 November 2016 (https://www.theguardian.com/world/2016/nov/27/justin-trudeau-ridiculed-over-praise-of-remarkable-fidel-castro).

they have access to healthcare and education. But those are, of course, hardly hallmarks of socialism. The vast majority of countries in the top quartile of the Economic Freedom list also offer universal access to healthcare and education.

Cuba still routinely receives praise from Western commentators, but more as an example of a comprehensive welfare state than as an example of socialism per se. Even the most uncritical supporters rarely defend Cuban socialism *qua* socialism. A good example is London's former mayor Ken Livingstone, who, after Fidel Castro's death, referred to Castro as 'an absolute giant of the 20th century' and to Cuba as 'a beacon of light'.[2] Livingstone recited all of the well-rehearsed pro-Cuba clichés, but even he made no reference to those features of the Cuban economy that make it specifically socialist. Even Livingstone did not, for example, praise Cuba's state-run sugar plantations, or its system of food rationing.

Cuba-romanticism is not shared by all left-wing commentators. Some specifically dispute the country's socialist credentials. Zoe Williams writes in *The Guardian*:

> Castro was an authoritarian. [...] Pluralism, democracy and universal rights are the foundations of progressive politics. One man [...] does not get to govern by force

---

2 Ken Livingstone: Castro was a giant, *BBC News*, 26 November 2016 (http://www.bbc.co.uk/news/av/world-latin-america-38115935/ken-livingstone -castro-was-a-giant); Fidel Castro: Ken Livingstone mentions Hitler while defending Cuban leader as 'absolute giant of 20th century', *Independent*, 26 November 2016 (http://www.independent.co.uk/news/people/fidel-castro -dies-dead-ken-livingstone-hitler-cuba-human-rights-abuses-giant-of -20th-century-a7440536.html).

and decree. One oppressed group [...] is an oppression of everybody. One nation, even if it's tiny [...] is as great an insult to the principles of the left as one dictatorial superpower.[3]

Owen Jones, after a long detour of whataboutery and Cuba-clichés, writes that 'Cuba [...] is a dictatorship. Socialism without democracy [...] isn't socialism'.[4]

So, in short, left-wing critics of Cuba dispute that Cuba is (or was ever) socialist at all, while left-wing supporters of Cuba avoid talking about those features that make it socialist. This means that in terms of our three-stage pattern, Cuba is permanently stuck somewhere between stage two and stage three.

But it was not always thus. In the 1960s, Cuba was a popular destination for political pilgrimages, just as the Soviet Union had been three decades earlier, and as China still was at around the same time. With some differences in emphasis, the accounts of Castro's pilgrims are remarkably similar to those of Mao's and Stalin's pilgrims. The pilgrims saw Cuba as far more than a country that tried to expand access to healthcare and education. They saw it as a new model of socialism, an alternative to both Western capitalism and to the now discredited variants of socialism that were practised in the Warsaw Pact countries.

---

3   Forget Fidel Castro's policies. What matters is that he was a dictator, *The Guardian*, 27 November 2016 (https://www.theguardian.com/commentis free/2016/nov/27/fidel-castro-policies-dictator).

4   My thoughts on Cuba, *Medium*, 29 November 2016 (https://medium.com/@ OwenJones84/my-thoughts-on-cuba-32280774222f).

Cuba's revolution was homegrown. There was no involvement of either the Soviet Union, or of any other Warsaw Pact country. Cuba's version of socialism was therefore untainted by associations with 'unreal' socialism. It contained the promise of a fresh start. This time would be different.

Castro's pilgrims

Different visitors admired different aspects of the Cuban system, but, again, a few common themes emerge. Various pilgrims were fascinated by the political rallies organised by the regime, which they interpreted as spontaneous outbreaks of genuine mass euphoria. In the pilgrims' accounts, it was this euphoria from which the regime derived its legitimacy. This form of 'street democracy' was, in their view, far more authentic and lively than the stale, formalistic Western variants.

A member of the Venceremos Brigade, a US-based Cuba-support organisation, reported (quoted in Hollander 1990: 246):

Here people are high on their lives all the time. [...] [T]hat much unadulterated emotional give is almost unbearable. I begin to really conceive of being part of a current, that in the process of a revolution you are both very important and very small; we're talking about something bigger than all of us, and that is the transformation of an entire people, [...] the beginning of building the new man.

Waldo Frank, an American historian and novelist, saw an 'absolute frenzy of brotherhood and excitement' everywhere and 'young men and women sparkling with animal spirits' (ibid.: 246). This led him to conclude that 'a revolution such as Castro's is nourished by the direct, almost physical embrace of leaders and people' (ibid.: 248).

LeRoi Jones, an American writer, reported: 'At each town, the chanting crowds. The unbelievable joy and excitement. The same idea, and people made beautiful because of it' (ibid.: 247).

Huey Newton, an American political activist and co-founder of the Black Panther party, believed that the revolution had made people more caring and compassionate: '[T]ruly everybody is an extended family and [has] concern for everybody else's welfare [...] They are interested in each other's life in a brotherly way' (ibid.: 244–45).

Susan Sontag, an American writer and film-maker, wrote (ibid.: 245):

> The Cubans know a lot about spontaneity, gaiety, sensuality, and freaking out. [...] The increase in energy comes because they have found a new focus for it: the community. [...] Perhaps the first thing a visitor to Cuba notices is the enormous energy level. It is still common, as it has been throughout the ten years of the revolution, for people to go without sleep – talking and working for several nights a week.

David Caute, a British novelist, playwright and journalist, described a political rally he attended as 'a gigantic demonstration of solidarity': 'the demonstrators are [...] euphorically happy and proud as any festival's children could be' (ibid.: 246).

Abbot Hoffman, an American writer and activist, describes a New Year's Day parade (ibid.: 238):

> Fidel sits on the side of a tank rumbling into Havana [...] Girls throw flowers at the tank and rush to tug playfully at his black beard. He laughs joyously [...] Fidel lets the gun drop to the ground, slaps his thigh and stands erect [...] [T]he crowd immediately is transformed.

Similarly, state-organised 'volunteering' activities were also seen as spontaneous and self-organised expressions of popular enthusiasm. Angela Davis, the director of the University of California's Feminist Studies department, saw 'young and old, proudly dressed in work clothes, singing as they made their way to the country [...] On these faces reigned the serenity of meaningful work – the passion of commitment' (ibid.: 250).

Joseph A. Kahl, a professor of sociology at Cornell University, thought that (ibid.: 249–50):

> the young militants are convinced that they are building a superior society [...] To talk with them was profoundly moving, especially in contrast to the disillusionment and cynicism of many of the best of young Americans. Cuban youth are not alienated, bitter, or 'turned off'.

Many pilgrims did not really see the Cuban economy as 'state planned', but as run collectively by Cuba's workers and peasants, and fuelled by the enthusiasm of the masses. Cuba, in this view, was not run by Fidel Castro and his entourage, but by 'the people', with Castro merely serving as their medium.

Julius Lester, an American writer and a professor at the University of Massachusetts Amherst, wrote (ibid.: 239):

> To become a public personality in a revolutionary society is to become so at one with the people that quite unconsciously they see you in them and you see yourself in them. The West says a 'cult of personality' exists in the figures of Mao and Fidel. That is not true. Revolutionary consciousness and revolutionary commitment have destroyed the ego in Mao and Fidel [...] Mao is China. Fidel is Cuba. China is Mao. Cuba is Fidel.

Other pilgrims saw Castro as an almost superhuman leader figure. Norman Mailer, an American novelist, journalist, playwright, filmmaker and actor, wrote an open letter to him, which stated (ibid.: 236):

> You were the first and greatest hero to appear in the world since the Second World War. [...] [Y]ou give a bit of life to the best and most passionate men and women all over the earth, you are the answer to the argument [...] that revolutions cannot last, that they turn corrupt or total.

Angela Davis wrote (ibid.: 239):

> Talking to almost any Cuban about Fidel, it soon became clear that they did not see him as anything more than extraordinarily intelligent, exceptionally committed and an extremely warm human being [...] Fidel was their leader, but most important he was also their brother in the largest sense of the word.

In a joint publication, Leo Huberman, the chair of the Department of Social Science at Columbia University and co-editor of the *Monthly Review*, and Paul Sweezy, a Harvard economist, wrote (ibid.):

> First and foremost, Fidel is a passionate humanitarian [...] he feels compassion for human suffering, hates injustice [...] and is totally committed to building in Cuba a society in which the poor and the underprivileged shall be able to hold up their heads.

René Dumont, a French agronomist, sociologist and a politician, went on a guided tour with Castro himself, and reported (ibid.: 241):

> He finds a bridge in bad shape and gives orders for it to be repaired immediately. Fifty miles further along, [...] 'See to it that a good asphalt road is built here.' On another occasion [...] 'See to it that the area gets a little dam.' At another place the crops appear neglected. 'I want an agricultural school here'.

Frank Mankiewicz, a political adviser to Robert F. Kennedy and George McGovern, as well as president of National Public Radio, wrote that Castro knew (ibid.: 242):

> the annual construction rate of schools, housing, factories and hospitals. He knows the number built and being built, their scheduled dates for conclusion, and the building plans projected for the next five to ten years. He knows the number of students at each level of the educational process, is familiar with the curriculum [...] He knows the monthly water temperatures at the fishing ports.

Elizabeth Sutherland, a journalist, critic and arts editor of *The Nation*, wrote that Castro 'seems, first of all, utterly devoted to the welfare of his people – and his people are the poor, not the rich. When he speaks, it is as if his own dedication and energy were being directly transfused into his listeners with an almost physical force' (ibid.: 238).

Not all sympathisers were quite so starry-eyed. Some did recognise the authoritarian character of the system, but thought that the entitlement to free services more than outweighed any lack of 'negative' liberties. Joe Nicholson, author of the book *Inside Cuba*, argued that most of Latin America's poor people would be vastly better off if they lived in Cuba. There, they (ibid.: 257):

> wouldn't be assured all of the civil liberties of a Jeffersonian democracy, but [...] [f]or the poor of Latin America, Cuba offers dignity that is even beyond the grasp

> of large segments of American citizens [...] This dignity
> is composed of rights Cubans have gained under their
> Communist revolution: the right to a decent job [...] to an
> equal – and adequate although not yet generous – share
> of rationed food and clothing, the right to inexpensive
> housing.

Castro-mania had one lasting PR problem that would not go away: the ongoing exodus of people from the People's State. The first wave of emigration, which saw about a quarter of a million Cubans relocate to the US (Duany 2017), did not constitute a problem for Western Cuba-enthusiasts. Those were predominantly upper- and middle-class emigrants, so from a socialist perspective, they were not really part of The People. But in the second half of the 1960s, the social composition of the Cuban expat community in the US began to change radically, as blue-collar workers and agricultural workers began to arrive in large numbers. It was now no longer possible to claim that they were all just Batista-cronies or expropriated large-scale landowners.

At the same time, Cuba developed closer ties with the Soviet Union, East Germany and other Warsaw Pact countries. When Soviet troops invaded Czechoslovakia in 1968 to crush the Prague Spring, Castro stood firmly on Moscow's side, describing the Czech protestors as 'pro-Yankee agents and spies, the enemies of socialism, the agents of West Germany, [...] fascist and reactionary rabble.'[5]

---

5   Castro speech database (https://web.archive.org/web/20120402043602/
    http://lanic.utexas.edu/project/castro/db/1968/19680824.html).

Cuba was supposed to be different. But the distinction between the 'good' and the 'bad' kind of socialism became blurrier. The golden age of (presumed) innocence was coming to an end.

Cuba entered stage two, the period of whataboutery, relativisation, faux counterfactuals, and a focus on the presumed motives of the regime's critics. For example, Castro apologists have always benchmarked the Castro regime against the seven-year dictatorship that immediately preceded it, ignoring the much longer period of Cuban republicanism. As an extension of this, they have always implicitly linked Castro's critics to the Batista regime, even decades after Batista's death.

For example, in 1991, Jeremy Corbyn, the current leader of the opposition, said:

> [U]ntil 1959 [...] [Cuba] was a place whose culture and identity was denied by the worst form of market economy. [...] The revolution of 1959 was an entirely popular affair. Castro didn't do it on his own [...] He did it with [...] hundreds of thousands of people who were prepared to take part [...]
>
> [T]he choice that now faces Cuba is to capitulate to the gangsters in Miami who want to take over and destroy the gains of the revolution, or to soldier on to build the best form of socialism that can be achieved in Cuba. Sections of the left attacking Cuba at the present time with all the problems it has got are, frankly, not very helpful at all.[6]

---

6   Where do we go from here? *Morning Star*, 24 September 1991.

It is not quite clear who 'the gangsters in Miami' are, but by that time there must have been a million-strong Cuban exile community in Florida. They cannot all have been henchmen of the former dictator who had been dead for nearly two decades by then. But this, as we have seen in earlier chapters, is the rhetoric which characterises stage two.

Why is Cuba different?

The enthusiasm for Cuba was greatest in the years immediately after the revolution, when Cuban socialism was seen as a novel and different model of socialism. That initial euphoria did not last long. But as mentioned, Cuba is the only example of a socialist country that never fully entered the not-*real*-socialism stage, the stage of retroactive disowning. Support for Cuba turned from euphoric to lukewarm, and it became more narrowly about healthcare and schooling rather than socialism per se. But the country remained permanently stuck somewhere in between stage two and stage three. We do not know exactly what explains the difference, but there are a number of (mutually reinforcing) plausible explanations.

Firstly, and most obviously, the Cuban regime was never nearly as atrocious as the Stalinist and the Maoist regimes. The Cuban regime is dictatorial and oppressive, but it is not genocidal. The relevant section in *The Black Book of Communism* reads like a watered-down version of Stalinism or Maoism. There were summary executions, purges, extrajudicial arrests, an extensive secret police network and all the rest of it, but the scale was much smaller, and the details less grim. As far as socialism goes, the Cuban regime is far from being the worst.

Secondly, and perhaps most importantly, Cuba has (at least implicitly) always been benchmarked against less ambitious counterfactuals than other socialist systems. East Germany was far more economically and technologically advanced than Cuba, but East Germany was benchmarked against West Germany, and it paled in that comparison. Cuba, in contrast, is part of a world region where, for much of the twentieth century, poverty, underdevelopment, dictatorial rule and woeful human rights records were the norm, not the exception. This has changed in the meantime: most Latin American and Caribbean countries are now democratic middle-income countries, and many have made serious inroads in reducing poverty (see Our World in Data 2017). But Cuba is usually compared to the region's poorest countries, not to its relative success stories such as Chile or Costa Rica.[7]

Thirdly, the Cuban revolutionaries were able to pick a number of low-hanging fruits. By regional standards, Cuba was already relatively highly developed around the time of the revolution, and well ahead in terms of social indicators. Life expectancy at birth was eight years above the Latin American and Caribbean average, while infant mortality was only one third of the regional average (Tupy 2016). Cuba already had an adult literacy rate of about 80 per cent,

---

7   See, for example: Caribbean communism v capitalism, *The Guardian*, 22 January 2010 (https://www.theguardian.com/commentisfree/cifamer ica/2010/jan/22/cuba-communism-human-rights).

one of the highest in the region (Roser and Ortiz-Ospina 2017). Such indicators were already improving before the revolution, and kept improving afterwards – but Western sympathisers were able to ascribe all post-revolution improvements to Castro's government.

Fourthly, the persistence of the US trade embargo against Cuba provided not just the Cuban government, but also its Western sympathisers, with a convenient excuse for the country's economic underdevelopment. It contains a grain of truth. If tariffs and import quotas reduce prosperity – as virtually every economist would confirm they do – then logically, a wholesale embargo must do so.

However, Cuba's isolation is mainly self-imposed. In far-left circles, it remains fashionable to refer to the US embargo as the 'Cuba blockade', as if the US somehow prevented Cuba from trading with third countries. It is, of course, not a blockade. Cuba has always had the option of developing more extensive trade links with, for example, Canada, the EU, Mexico or Brazil, which is what other countries in the region have done. But the Cuban regime has chosen not to do so. Cuba does not trade very much with *anyone* (European Commission 2017). Nor is the US embargo an absolute embargo. In terms of imports of goods, the US is still Cuba's seventh most important trading partner (ibid.).

And yet: the excuses for the failures of socialism that are usually put forward during stage two do not have to be plausible. They just need to be widely believed.

Taken together, these factors might explain why Cuba never quite completed the move from the second stage (excuse-making and whataboutery) to the third stage (retroactive disowning). But today's Cuba romantics have little in common with the Cuba pilgrims of the 1960s. The latter saw Cuba not just as a place that sought to expand access to healthcare and schooling. They saw it as a model of a new socialist society.

5   NORTH KOREA UNDER KIM IL SUNG: 'A MESSIAH RATHER THAN A DICTATOR'

North Korean socialism

The division of Korea into a broadly capitalist South (the Republic of Korea) and a socialist North (the Democratic People's Republic of Korea) represents a natural economic experiment. Reliable figures for the DPRK are hard to obtain, but what we know is enough to consider the matter settled. In per capita terms, South Korea is more than twenty times richer than North Korea (CIA World Factbook 2017). The DPRK still suffered from severe famines as recently as in the 1990s, and without humanitarian aid from the ROK and Western countries, they probably still would. On average, South Koreans live about twelve years longer than North Koreans (Our World In Data 2017). The ROK is a relatively liberal democracy, while the DPRK is a Stalinist garrison state, complete with forced labour camps and an extensive secret police. Every year, thousands of North Koreans risk their lives trying to escape.

It is therefore no surprise that almost no mainstream Western leftist wants to be associated with that system today. But the situation was not always so clear-cut. Before the division in the 1940s, the North of Korea was more industrialised than the South, and the South only overtook the North in the mid-1970s (Young 1995: 6). Even then, the ROK's increased prosperity did not immediately lead to democratisation, or an improvement in its record on civil liberties and human rights. South Korea remained a military dictatorship until the late 1980s.

The DPRK never enjoyed *widespread* support among the Western left. But it used to have some reasonably prominent Western admirers, and attracted some small-scale pilgrimages. It was once hailed by some as an earthly paradise in the making. Qualitatively, Kim-Il-Sung-mania was indistinguishable from Stalin-mania, Mao-mania and Castro-mania. The difference is purely one of scale.

Kim Il Sung's pilgrims

In 1964, the Cambridge economist Joan Robinson, a leading figure in the Cambridge School of Economics, went on a pilgrimage to North Korea, and subsequently summed up her research and observations in the paper 'Korean Miracle'. Robinson (1965) described North Korea's version of socialism as an unmitigated social and economic success story, powered by the enthusiasm of the people. After reciting various official figures on industrial and agricultural output, her verdict was that 'All the economic miracles of the postwar world are put in the shade by these achievements' (ibid.: 542).

The country's social achievements were, in her account, even more impressive. Pyongyang is 'a city without slums' (ibid.: 541) and North Korea 'a nation without poverty' (ibid.: 542). There is a cradle-to-grave welfare state far more encompassing than any Western equivalent (ibid.: 542–45):

> There is already universal education [...] There are numerous nursery schools and creches, all without charge. There is a complete system of social security [...] The medical service is free. [...]
>
> In all enterprises there is an eight-hour day, with an hour's break for lunch [...] The general manager of an enterprise is responsible for the housing estate in which the workers live, the nurseries and nursery school, and supplies to the shops, so that no one need worry about his home affairs.

What are the sources of this economic and social miracle? According to Robinson, it is a collaborative, participatory process of economic planning (ibid.: 544):

> Workers are consulted by management when the Plan is being framed and encouraged to make suggestions about methods of work. Through this means, startling increases in productivity are achieved. A steel works with furnaces of a nominal capacity of 60 thousand tons was actually producing 40 thousand. The Prime Minister came for 'on-the-spot guidance' and told the workers that the nation needed 90 thousand tons from them. The workers and technicians decided that it was possible and pledged themselves publicly to carry out the assignment. Actually they produced 120 thousand tons.

Robinson conceded that, to a Western observer, North Korea will look very much like a dictatorship, but argued that in truth Kim Il Sung is more like a benevolent father figure, who provides spiritual guidance (ibid.: 548–49):

> The outward signs of a 'cult' are very marked – photographs, street names, toddlers in the nursery singing hymns to the beloved leader. But Prime Minister Kim Il Sung seems to function as a messiah rather than a dictator [...]
>
> He visits every plant and every rural district for 'on-the-spot consultation' to clear up their problems. He comes to a hospital to say that the life of doctors and nurses must be devoted to the welfare of their patients, and this thought inspires their work every day. He explains to the workers in the heavy machine plant that their products are the basis of industrialization, and pride renews their zeal.

The author also credited North Korea's economic isolationism (ibid.: 548):

> [T]heir policy of self-reliance has some economic advantages also. [...] Imported equipment, with imported know-how, inspires awe and does not help to throw off colonial mentality.

In her version of events, South Korea must go to great lengths to prevent people from emigrating to the North (ibid.: 549):

[G]reat pains are taken to keep the Southerners in the dark. The demarcation line is manned exclusively by American troops, down to the cleaners, with an empty stretch of territory behind. No Southern eye can be allowed a peep into the North.

Robinson concluded with a prediction that did not age well: 'As the North continues to develop and the South to degenerate, sooner or later the curtain of lies must surely begin to tear' (ibid.).

In the US, the Black Panther Party (BPP), the socialist extension of the Civil Rights Movement, became the most enthusiastic supporters of the DPRK. As the Wilson Center (2013: 1) explains:

Though other American leftist groups were drawn to North Korea during the 'long 1960s,' the BPP established perhaps the most firm connection with the North Koreans. The DPRK's links to the American radical left have long been known [...] [T]he American radical left regarded Pyongyang as an important alternative from [*sic*] Moscow and Beijing.

Eldridge Cleaver, a BPP spokesman and a former presidential candidate of the Peace and Freedom Party, visited the DPRK several times. After a pilgrimage in 1970, he wrote (ibid.: 11–12):

Here in Korea we have found a people who have laid the foundations of communism and who are now rushing

[...] to transform their society into an earthly paradise (Cleaver 1970: 2B). [...]

[W]e will tell the American people of the glorious victories of [...] socialist revolution, of the miraculous economic construction that has built a paradise [...] No other people in the history of the world have been able to achieve such fantastic results in all areas of the economy at one time [...]

The workers [...] of the world have much to envy in the lives of the working people in the Democratic People's Republic of Korea.

A year later, Cleaver sent an open letter to Kim Il Sung, celebrating the 23rd anniversary of the founding of the DPRK (Cleaver 1971: 1–2):

The miraculous strides that the Korean revolution has made in building a powerful nation with its economy, culture, politics and social system firmly in the hands of the Korean people and dedicated to serving their needs provides a brilliant inspiration to those peoples still fighting for [...] democratic freedoms. The long dark yesterdays [...] have born fruit [*sic*] today in the wonderful life available to the people in the Democratic People's Republic of Korea. [...] Today, the [DPRK] is [...] expressing for the world to see the superiority of the socialist system.

Fred J. Carrier, a Professor of History at Villanova University, Pennsylvania, also went on a number of pilgrimages to the DPRK in the 1970s, and summarised his research in the book *North Korean Journey: The Revolution Against Colonialism.*

Like Robinson, Carrier saw North Korea as a huge economic success story: 'socialist Korea is capable of producing its own heavy industry in whatever special fields it chooses [...] the success of Korea in this regard is amazing' (Carrier 1975: 31). He spoke of an 'industrial capacity and technical skill that only a few dozen countries of the world could display' (ibid.: 34).

Carrier saw equally impressive progress in areas such as public housing (ibid.: 78, 83):

> [T]he bright new high-rise apartments that abound in Pyongyang, Hamhung, and everywhere else [...] provide comfortable living with central heating, running water, electricity — all at a cost approximating three percent of a family income.
>
> [I]n socialist Korea the mass of people are housed as well as any people in Asia, and far better than most. If one adds the social conditions which provide the total environment— the absence of anything resembling ghetto culture marked by cultural deprivation, crime, drug addiction, sexual abuse — then the apartments of Pyongyang offer better living standards than large sections of American cities like New York or Philadelphia.

The same applies to the area of nutrition: 'hunger has been erased throughout the land. [...] hunger stalks the Third World. Not socialist Korea, however!' (ibid.: 82–83).

North Koreans may not be rich by Western standards, but this is not a problem in a society which has not been contaminated by Western consumerism (ibid.: 83–84):

Everywhere in the People's Republic [...] one has the sense of a decent society in which equality of goods, services and opportunities prevails. [...] [E]veryone enjoys a certain richness of life. The stores are not lavish with luxuries but good foods are plentiful and everyone in the country is decently clothed. Koreans have not been conditioned to conceive themselves as consumers whose lives are measured by the quantity, novelty and expense of their acquisitions. One can hope that their collective values will spare them such a fate.

What was the source of the DPRK's success? According to Carrier (ibid.: 33–34):

At the heart of the process is a hard-working people, willing to work long hours not because of coercion but because of dedication to the socialist revolution. [...]

The morale of the workers [...] emanates from a cultural revolution that is central to socialism. Workers must [...] be concerned with the economic plans of their country, support these goals, and contribute to both the physical and political efforts toward fulfillment of these plans. Maintaining such morale [...] can be accomplished through a close relationship between the people and the state. The state cannot act apart from the people, nor could plans be more than hollow figures if workers do not support them in practice.

For Carrier, the DPRK was the very opposite of a dictatorship. It was a 'peasant democracy' (ibid.: 107) and a 'workers' society' (ibid.: 73): 'the masters of the revolution are the masses of the people' (ibid.: 96). The DPRK was well on its way to becoming 'a society which is democratic in the ultimate meaning of the word – economic and social democracy which can only emanate from the end of class rule' (ibid.: 84–85).

The basic building blocks of this grassroots democracy are worker cooperatives. Carrier visited one of those cooperatives, and explained (ibid.: 70):

> [I]mportant decisions are made by general meetings of all the men and women 18 years or older. For the first time in their lives peasants are making choices affecting more than a chongbo [a plot] of land! What shall the cooperative plant? What proportion of its earnings shall be placed in social funds or invested in new machinery? Who shall serve on the Management Committee? What treatment shall be accorded a shirker?

Carrier contrasted North Korea's achievements to the 'hardships suffered by the mass of south Koreans' (ibid.: 100). But he was optimistic that North Korea would lead by example (ibid.: 118):

> The people of the south part of Korea are bound to be stirred by such a vision, their revolutionary sentiments awakened again and strengthened. The victory of the revolutionary forces in Vietnam and Cambodia has

encouraged a resurgence of the liberation struggle in south Korea.

North Korea's version of socialism, in Carrier's view, was a model not just for South Korea, but far beyond (ibid.: 47):

[T]he People's Republic of Korea stands in stark contrast to much of the Third World for it has begun a democratic cultural revolution which benefits all of the people. The door has been opened to a future socialist world.

In the 1980s, Luise Rinser, a West German novelist and the Green Party's presidential candidate in 1984, travelled to North Korea several times, and described her impressions in the book *Nordkoreanisches Reisetagebuch* (North Korean Travel Diary). If we replace 'Kim Il Sung' with 'Stalin' or 'Mao', and 'North Korea' with 'the USSR' or 'China', the *Reisetagebuch* reads like a classic pilgrimage account from one of the earlier waves. North Korea is described as a country in which everything is owned by 'the people', and in which 'the people' run the economy jointly, as a collaborative effort. These economic arrangements, in Rinser's account, gave rise to a society characterised by all-round harmony, in which social conflicts, crime and disaffection all but disappeared.

Rinser was impressed by the country's social achievements in various areas, such as public housing (Rinser 1986; translation mine):

Where there used to be a cluster of hastily constructed post-war buildings two years ago, there is now a whole new borough of high-rise buildings with modern apartments [...] I saw some of those apartments, they are such that you would wish all of the world's workers could live like this. And it really is mainly workers living here [...] And the rents for the new homes, are they high? Rents? Here in North Korea, nobody pays rent, the houses belong to the people [...]

There is no land or real estate speculation, and nobody needs to be afraid of being evicted from their flat: this creates a sense of calm security and comfort, just as everything here aims to create that comfort.

She was no less impressed by the country's health system and public health measures (ibid.):

There are lots of medical colleges. [...] Who pays the doctors? The state, obviously. [...]

I did notice how flourishingly healthy people look. [...] The younger ones, and especially the children, are bursting with health and a lust for life. Of course: Exercise and dance from an early age, no drugs, no alcohol, healthy, uncontaminated food, no medicines during pregnancy, constant medical supervision and a friendly communal life, that creates inner harmony, which expresses itself in good physical and mental health.

North Korea's children, in Rinser's version, are 'the little kings of the country' (ibid.):

The children have it good here. They could not have it any better. They have their doctors, their examinations, their carers, their trained nursery school teachers. A huge number of personnel. [...]

Ah, being a child in North Korea!

Her account of the North Korean justice system, which she describes as humane and rehabilitation-oriented, echoes those of Stalin's and Mao's pilgrims, romanticising the Gulags and the Laogai. After visiting a prison, she wrote (ibid.):

It does not match my Western concept of a 'prison'. No walls, no watchtowers, no barbed wire, no bars in front of the windows. [...] The legal maximum prison sentence is one year, but it is up to each inmate when they are released. [...]

I think about my own time in prison, under Hitler, but also about all the inmates in West German prisons, and I think about Stammheim.[1] And the Western press calls North Korea a sinister dictatorship? [...]

I notice that the guards and the director are unarmed. Why would we need a firearm? In case a prisoner tries to escape? But nobody tries to escape. Everybody understandingly atones for their guilt. [...]

---

1   Stammheim is the prison where the leaders of the Red Army Faction (RAF) terrorist group were held in the 1970s. Since their rhetoric was left-wing and anti-capitalist, RAF terrorists enjoyed considerable sympathy among West German intellectuals, including Rinser herself, at the time (see Fleischhauer 2009: 236-247). They carefully cultivated the image of being 'mistreated' in Stammheim, and when they eventually committed suicide, they set it up in such a way that it looked like murder. All of this was debunked, but the RAF terrorists held martyr status among the West German intelligentsia for a while (ibid.).

> So this is what a North Korean prison looks like. Why can a German prison [...] or a prison elsewhere in the world not also look like this? Why: because [...] no other country lives in this spirit of community.

One can find the odd critical thought in the book, but it is immediately dismissed, or relativised by a tirade against the evils of the Western world. For example (ibid.):

> Is there not a form of steady, subtle brainwashing going on here?
> But where does that not happen? Only the contents differ. We, in the West, are being indoctrinated with the dogma of progress, of attaching a high value to material possessions, [...] of the dangers of [...] socialism [...]
> It is here [in North Korea] that I realise how programmed we are.

What explains North Korea's success? Like Robinson, Rinser believed that North Korea's economy was not *centrally* planned, but *collaboratively* planned (ibid.):

> It really is true, I experience it, that the president does not govern from his desk, he goes out to the people, giving and receiving advice at the grassroots. What is then worked out as an official plan in Pyongyang is the result of Kim Il Sung's consultations with experts and workers.

In North Korea, people do not work for themselves, but for the community (ibid.):

The realisation that everything belongs to everyone is truly overwhelming; and the experience that money really plays no role puts the Westerner – who does everything just for money, because he doesn't know what else to strive for – to shame.

Rinser cannot help feeling somewhat disturbed by the leadership cult around Kim Il Sung, but manages to reconcile it with her preconception of a country run by 'the people' (ibid.):

I have finally understood what this is really about. [...] [T]o the people, this man is a lot more than an individual figure, he is the Higher Self [Über-Ich in the original] of the people as a whole. In him, the people recognise and honour themselves. He is the personification of the soul of Korea. The cult is seemingly about him as a person, but it is much more about the people as a whole, it is about the idea whose representative he is.

In this way, the leadership cult becomes a 'people's cult', in which the people really celebrate themselves.

Rinser repeatedly contrasted North Korea's 'real' socialism to the 'unreal' socialism of East Germany and the Soviet Union. She believed that North Korean socialism was becoming more popular around the world (ibid.):

Delegations from various countries, capitalist as well as socialist ones, come [to North Korea] to study economic problems and the Juche ideology. In some countries, such

145

as Austria, universities already have institutes for the study of Juche ideology.

This growing popularity was, in Rinser's book, the real reason why Western governments were indifferent or hostile towards North Korea. They feared that it might become a threat by example: 'That the USA [...] declares North Korea off limits [...] proves what role it ascribes to this small country at the end of the world: It could awaken a taste for a new form of socialism' (ibid.).

Remnants of North Korea apologetics today

The naive pro-DPRK enthusiasm expressed by Robinson, Cleaver, Carrier and Rinser has not completely disappeared. Today, the Korean Friendship Association (KFA), a pro-DPRK outlet, has around 17,000 members worldwide,[2] with branches in the US, Canada and most of Western Europe.[3] Admirers of North Korea have their own internal lingo: for example, they always spell 'south Korea' with a lowercase 's', and they refer to North Korea as 'People's Korea' or by its official name. North Korea aficionados can, however, safely be dismissed as irrelevant fringe groups, with no detectable impact on the mainstream left.

---

2   Personal e-mail correspondence between the author and a KFA delegate. *The Diplomat* magazine put the number at 15,000 in 2014. See: The Westerners who love North Korea, *The Diplomat*, 25 February 2014 (http://thediplomat.com/2014/02/the-westerners-who-love-north-korea/).

3   Organization, Korean Friendship Association (http://www.korea-dpr.com/organization.html).

The closest thing to a DPRK apologist in mainstream academia today has to be Bruce Cumings, the former chair of the University of Chicago's history department and a Fellow at the American Academy of Arts and Sciences, who has been described as 'the left's leading scholar of Korean history'.[4]

Cumings's book *North Korea: Another Country* is not in the same league as the above accounts. He does not see North Korea as an earthly paradise. He states: 'I have no sympathy for the North, which is the author of most of its own troubles', and 'Does North Korea have political prisoners? Of course it does – at least 100,000' (Cumings 2004).[5] His stated aim is not to glorify North Korea, but to offer a more 'balanced' and 'nuanced' account. This may seem uncontroversial. But the book is, in fact, a good illustration of the so-called 'Golden Mean Fallacy' or 'Equidistance Fallacy', the logical fallacy that a clear position on a subject can never be right, and that the truth must always be somewhere in between two or more opposing positions.

The Golden Mean Fallacy usually works on the insinuation that having a clear position on a subject is low-brow and unsophisticated, and that having a somewhere-in-between position is a sign of intellectual sophistication. This book is no exception. Cumings often starts by citing

---

4   The historian who defends North Korea, *History News Network*, Columbian College of Arts and Sciences, George Washington University (http://historynewsnetwork.org/article/2742).

5   This book has been accessed via Amazon kindle. Page numbers are therefore not available.

negative accounts of North Korea in the American media, which, unsurprisingly, are often somewhat sensationalist, and not particularly well-researched. Cumings thereby provides himself with plenty of easy targets to shoot down, creating the impression that strong criticism of North Korea can only be based on ignorance.

This is then contrasted with positive statements about the DPRK, although Cumings usually does not make these points himself. He hides behind other people, quoting or summarising their positive statements, which he then neither explicitly endorses nor challenges.

For example, Cumings summarises the work of Erik Cornell, a Swedish diplomat who visited North Korea in the 1970s and 1980s (ibid.):

> Ambassador Cornell [...] ably represents the achievements of the regime in rapid industrialization, [...] providing free healthcare and education to everyone [...] and certainly lacking in the widespread poverty and homelessness visible in the ROK.

He also refers to a book by Andrew Holloway, an English translator who lived in North Korea in the 1980s (ibid.):

> Until things fell apart in the 1990s, honesty was the rule [...] Crime was nonexistent [...] There was no squalor, no begging [...] The average North Korean lived 'an incredibly simple and hardworking life but also has a secure and happy existence, and the comradeship between these highly collectivized people is moving to behold.'

And he quotes Bernard Krishner, an American journalist, who 'was also amazed by how successful the leadership had been in cultivating a spirit of communal effort, he likened the North to "one big kibbutz"' (ibid.).

According to Cumings, it is not just Western visitors who find a lot to like in the DPRK (ibid.):

> [A] large (and growing) number of younger South Koreans [...] find appealing the doctrine of self-reliance and the North's strong anti-imperialism. The Korean Youth Federation [...], the leading organization in student demonstrations [...] subscribes to many central tenets of the North's ideology [...] Meanwhile prominent novelists [...] depict the North as unspoilt, unpolluted, plain, and bucolic [...]

Where he uses his own words, Cumings still talks about the 'various achievements of this regime: compassionate care for children [...], "radical change" in the position of women, genuinely free housing, free healthcare, and preventive medicine' (ibid.).

Cumings tries to cast doubt on stories told by defectors:

> One famous defector, Kim Sinjo [...] was an all-purpose source for exaggerated and inflamed propaganda about the North, as well as a well-known alcoholic. He later tried to re-defect back to the North.

He acknowledges the existence of Gulag-like prison camps, but engages in the usual whataboutery and false equivalence (ibid.):

> [W]e [in the US] have a long-standing, never-ending gulag full of black men in our prisons, incarcerating up to 25 percent of all black youths. This doesn't excuse North Korea's police state, but perhaps it suggests that Americans should do something about the pathologies of our inner cities [...] before pointing the finger.

In the same vein, he accuses people in 'human rights circles' of

> look[ing] one way and condemn[ing] the communists, while ignoring the reprehensible behaviour of our allies, that is, US support for dictators who make Kim Jong Il look enlightened (the Saudis, for example) [...]

And he engages in the usual faux-relativism (ibid.):

> Does this system promote human freedom? Not from any liberal's standpoint. But from a Korean standpoint, where freedom is also defined as [...] freedom for the Korean nation [...] the vitriolic judgements do not flow so easily. [...] [T]here is one undeniable freedom in North Korea, and that is the freedom to be Korean [...]

In 2013, Gareth Morgan, a New Zealand economist, businessman and politician, travelled to North Korea. He opined that 'the West's "beat-up" view of North Korea is completely wrong'. Morgan found a people who were poor, yes, but wonderfully engaged, well-dressed, fully employed and well informed. [...] [W]hat North Korea has achieved economically despite its lack of access to international money has been magnificent.[6]

In 2017, the Center for Research on Globalization's Geopolitical Analyst and correspondent at the United Nations headquarters, Carla Stea, went on a pilgrimage to North Korea. She described it as 'a successful example of a socialist system' and 'a paradise for children, providing excellent, up-to-date health care and education, free of charge'.[7]

[I]t is difficult, if not impossible to convey in words, or even in photographs, the absolutely awe-inspiring achievements of the people and government of North Korea [...]

North Koreans heroically persevere in their socialist development, [...] this noble example of an economically and socially equitable and democratic society. The DPRK remains an example of the courageous pursuit of social and economic justice [...]

---

6 The West needs to rethink its ideas about Korea, 2 September 2013 (https:// web.archive.org/web/20130905014559/http://worldbybike.com/2013/ 09/02/gareth-combats-global-media-frenzy/).

7 The Social and Economic Achievements of North Korea, Center for Research on Globalization, 11 June 2017 (https://www.globalresearch.ca/the -social-and-economic-achievements-of-north-korea/5594234).

Stea is particularly impressed by the country's progress on gender equality, although her reasoning is a bit unconventional:

> To my amazement, a woman [...] was wearing gold stiletto high heels [...] I then noticed, with fascination, that other women, too, wore glamourous high heels [...] I emphasize this detail, because a woman's shoes, especially high heels, are very often an expression of her self-esteem. And these women, throughout Pyongyang, evidently enjoy high self-esteem. And as my visit progressed, I recognized that the DPRK has achieved notable progress on gender-equity [...]

She is convinced that human rights abuses are

> a propaganda fabrication based upon reports by defectors who were highly paid for their gruesome fabrications [...]
> [C]ontriving disinformation slandering the DPRK is becoming a very profitable industry, a lucrative profession comparable to the oldest one.

She does not get an audience with Kim Jong Un, but hears many positive things about him:

> [M]any people told me that their President Kim Jung-un loves children, and there is strong evidence of this in the many facilities available to encourage and assist children in health, education, and recreational activities [...]

> The DPRK President [...] is evidently very dedicated to his people, attending to the needs of orphans, and the disabled, providing the highest level of education for his people, building factories to supply women with excellent leather shoes [...]

What explains the West's hostility to the country? According to Stea:

> North Korea's development [...] remains today so successful a model of socialist economic and social development and its achievement is so threatening to the deteriorating capitalist economies of the US and Western Europe that those capitalist countries are pathologically obsessed with destroying what their own systems cannot achieve.

And in the UK, Andrew Murray, who would become a Labour Party election campaign manager in the 2017 General Election, wrote in 2003:

> The drive to seize command of the world economy in the interests of its own monopoly groups now propels the US government to seek to seize command of every corner of the world itself. [...] [W]e should [...] be alert to the very real dangers [...] around Peoples Korea. The clear desire of the USA [is] to effect regime change [...] Our Party [the Communist Party of Great Britain] has

already made its basic position of solidarity with Peoples Korea clear.[8]

These are isolated examples. Today, views like these are tolerated on the left, but not actively taken up more widely. But it has not always been this way. Albeit never comparable in scale to the pilgrimages to the USSR, China and Cuba, the DPRK was once a pilgrimage destination for a few relatively prominent Western intellectuals. Juche socialism was certainly 'real' socialism to them.

---

8 Political report – March 2003 Executive Committee meeting, 10 March 2003 (https://web.archive.org/web/20031210230502/http://www.communist -party.org.uk/articles/2003/march/10-03-03.shtml).

6 CAMBODIA UNDER THE KHMER ROUGE: 'THE KINGDOM OF JUSTICE'

Debates about whether one genocidal regime was a bit worse, or a bit less bad, than another genocidal regime, tend to be rather tedious. But if we *had* to rank dictatorial regimes on such terms, it is hard to see how the Khmer Rouge would not come out on top. For this regime, the death toll is usually not stated as an absolute number, but as a proportion of the population, like for the Black Death or the Thirty Years' War. Between 1975 and 1979, the regime led by Pol Pot – or 'Brother Number One', as he was officially known – managed to kill between a fifth and a quarter of the Cambodian population, through mass executions, famine, forced labour and a general increase in abject poverty.

The Khmer Rouge were an exceptionally murderous regime. But there was method in what they did. Comparable to Mao's Cultural Revolution, Khmer Rouge socialism was an attempt to not just restructure the economy, but to completely remake society from scratch. They forcibly evacuated the cities, which they thought of as cesspits of capitalist corruption, and forced people to live and work in rural communes. They banned money, exchange, books, religion, and all cultural norms and practices they associated with class differences. They confiscated not just the means of production, but personal property as well, as part of an attempt to create equality. They isolated the country from the outside world, and strove for autarky. Since such extreme measures, unsurprisingly, provoked resistance, the Khmer Rouge had to resort to extreme brutality to push them through.

Socialist Cambodia did not receive a great deal of attention from Western intellectuals. In absolute numbers, the circle of Western Khmer Rouge supporters was never large. But they were a large proportion of scholars in the relevant academic fields. Sophal Ear, a Cambodian-born (now American) political scientist, has reviewed the scholarly literature on Cambodia that was written while the Khmer Rouge were in power. His verdict (Ear 1995: 4):

> [T]his community [of sympathisers] was not some extreme 'fringe' faction of Cambodian scholars, but virtually all of them. [...] [T]heir view of the Khmer revolution [...] became the Standard Total Academic View on Cambodia [...] These scholars [...] became the Khmer Rouge's most effective apologists in the West. [...] [T]hey expressed unreserved support for the Khmer revolution.

For example, Laura Summers, a politics lecturer at the University of Lancaster, wrote two papers about the Khmer Rouge, 'Cambodia: Consolidating the Revolution' and 'Defining the Revolutionary State in Cambodia'. She described how, after what she calls 'the day of liberation', 'the awesome task was to transform accumulated bitterness and suffering into impetus for socio-economic reconstruction of the country' (quoted in ibid.: 19).

There was, she believed, 'little evidence of famine'. She conceded that 'food allowances in the solidarity groups are small', but claimed that there was 'greater security for fishing and livestock industries' (ibid.: 20). She did not see life under the Khmer as paradisal, but as a relative improvement, and believed that the revolution enjoyed popular support (ibid.):

> Life is without doubt confusing and arduous in many regions of the country, but current hardships are probably less than those endured during the war. It is mistaken to interpret postwar social disorganization or confusion as nascent opposition to the revolution.

For her, the fact that few people had emigrated represented further evidence of the popularity of the Khmer Rouge government (ibid.):

> Thus far, few Khmers have left the country and many of these are former officers from Lon Nol's [the former president] army or former civil servants who fear prosecution for wartime activities.

Emigration was punishable by death under the Khmer Rouge. But according to Summers, it was easy to emigrate (ibid.: 25):

> Most Cambodians leaving the country in 1975 managed to do so without much difficulty as if the regime were acknowledging that they were among the few whose values could not be accommodated in a people's state.

The forced clearing out of the cities, and forced agricultural labour, were reinterpreted as necessities, and as a success: 'universal conscription for work prevented a postwar famine' (ibid.: 23). She did, vaguely, concede that repression existed: 'It [...] appears that some work groups, in lieu of other forms of reeducation, are obliged to work harder and longer than others' (ibid.: 24). But she did not consider this a major issue (ibid.):

> What the urban dwellers consider 'hard' labor may not be punishment or community service beyond human endurance [...] Such associations take what is happening in Cambodia out of its historical and cultural context.

As in the cases of Stalinism and Maoism, the exact scale of the atrocities was not known at the time – but fragmentary evidence, such as accounts from refugees, was available from a very early stage. As in these earlier cases, those who wanted to maintain the illusion of a romantic, revolutionary country had to actively deny them. About negative coverage in the French media, based on such eyewitness accounts, Summers wrote (ibid.: 23):

> [P]ublic concern raised by sensational, but false, documents finally provoked the Paris Mission of Democratic

Kampuchea to protest that some journalists were degrading their profession and that the French held a major share of the responsibility for allowing these activities to continue.

The American press was no better (ibid.: 25):

The United States press, not to be outdone, produced dramatic news reports and editorials based on refugee and unnamed intelligence sources. In retrospect, these reports were partly inaccurate and are still largely unverified. The flap illustrates the powerful and potentially dangerous force that is generated when the political machinations of a few capture the attention of a concerned and uninformed public.

In 1976, the Southeast Asia scholars Gareth Porter and George Hildebrand published their book *Cambodia: Starvation and Revolution*. They saw the Khmer Rouge as victims of a relentless smear campaign in the Western media (ibid.: 26):

[T]he U.S. government and news media commentary have [...] gone to great lengths to paint a picture of a country ruled by irrational revolutionaries, without human feelings, determined to reduce their country to barbarism.

But this negative coverage of the Khmer Rouge, they believed, merely reflected the authors' prejudices (ibid.: 28):

> [C]ommentators and editorialists expected revolutionaries to be 'unbending' and to have no regard for human life, and [...] they were totally unprepared to examine the possibility that radical change might be required in that particular situation.

And (ibid.: 33):

> Cambodia is only the latest victim of the enforcement of an ideology that demands that social revolutions be portrayed as negatively as possible, rather than as responses to real human needs which the existing social and economic structure was incapable of meeting.

Apologists for Stalinism and Maoism made use of the fact that evidence of human rights abuses was often of low quality and thus easy to challenge. Pol Pot apologists did the same. The initial reports about the forced evacuation of Phnom Penh were mainly based on the accounts of a *New York Times* journalist, who had been on site, but who was not an 'eyewitness' in the conventional sense, because he had spent those days hiding in the French embassy. Porter and Hildebrand called this (ibid.: 27–28):

> a weak foundation for the massive historical judgment rendered by the news media. It contained no eyewitness reports on how the evacuation was carried out in terms of food, medical treatment, transportation, or the general treatment of evacuees [...] Nor was there any extensive

analysis of the reasons [...] attributed to the revolutionary leadership for the action.

In Porter and Hildebrand's account, the clearing out of the cities was a laudable measure to increase agricultural production (ibid.: 30):

> Above all else, the [...] leadership had to be concerned with food and health. The concentration of a large part of the population in the cities, where they were unproductive [...], posed grave dangers. [...]
>
> The 500,000 to 600,000 urban dwellers would by growing their own food, by freeing others from the task of getting food to them, substantially increase the total produced. By remaining unproductive during the crucial months, on the other hand, they would reduce the amount of food available to everyone.

Their assumption seemed to be that unless urbanites were forced to work in the countryside, they would just loiter unproductively in their cities, waiting for other people to bring them food.

The Khmer Rouge's forced evacuation even extended to the hospitals. But Porter and Hildebrand argued that since sanitary conditions in the hospitals were poor, 'the temporary clearing of most hospitals, far from being inhumane, was an act of mercy for the patients' (ibid.: 31).

In summary (ibid.):

A careful examination of the facts regarding the evacuation of Cambodia's cities thus shows that the description and interpretation of the move conveyed to the American public was an inexcusable distortion of reality. What was portrayed as a destructive, backward-looking policy motivated by doctrinaire hatred was actually a rationally conceived strategy for dealing with the urgent problems that faced postwar Cambodia.

The Khmer Rouge's agricultural policy was celebrated as another success story (ibid.: 32):

For the Cambodian people this bumper harvest represents 250 grams of rice per meal per adult, and 350 grams per meal [per] worker on the production force [...] In addition meat eating has increased.

Two other authors, Bob Hering and Ernst Utrecht, wrote (ibid.: 34):

The Western Press, apparently feeling insulted and being outraged, excelled in negative reporting on developments in Kampuchea under the Pol Pot-Ieng Sary regime [Ieng Sary was 'Brother Number Three']. Not only did strongly exaggerated reports on the mass killings in the regime appear in the Western mass media, but also reports of crop failures and hunger in Kampuchea. Contrary to this unfavorable reporting in the Western newspapers, Malcolm [Caldwell] was able to find more reliable data and compose a much more favorable account of economic development in Kampuchea in the last two years before the Vietnamese invasion of January 1979.

Malcolm Caldwell, who is referenced here, was a lecturer at the University of London's School of Oriental and African Studies (SOAS), and perhaps Pol Pot's greatest Western admirer. One of Caldwell's main themes was the denying, downplaying or excusing of accounts of mass executions in Cambodia. According to Caldwell, 'only the most serious criminals were executed' (ibid.: 34, footnote 70). So were 'arch-Quislings who well knew what their fate would be were they to linger in Kampuchea'.[1]

When Caldwell wrote those words, he could not have known that he was soon to join the ranks of these 'most serious criminals' and 'arch-Quislings' himself. In 1978, he became a victim of one of those executions he claimed were not happening.

Caldwell went on a pilgrimage to Cambodia, where he was granted an audience with Pol Pot. According to an American journalist he met immediately afterwards, Caldwell was deeply impressed by the dictator. But apparently, the feeling was not mutual. A few hours later, armed men turned up at the hotel, and shot Caldwell. The exact reason is unknown, but to some, it looked like a spontaneous politically motivated execution.[2]

---

1 Lost in Cambodia, *The Guardian*, 10 January 2010 (https://www.theguard ian.com/lifeandstyle/2010/jan/10/malcolm-caldwell-pol-pot-murder).

2 Ibid.

Caldwell's book, *Cambodia: Rationale for a Rural Policy*, appeared posthumously. The editor's preface read (quoted in ibid.: 35):

> Caldwell's paper nails the lie to another aspect of the propaganda, viz. that the Kampuchean revolutionaries were following a mad path of building a socialist society. He has not only shown this path is correct but that it is the best-suited, not only for Kampuchea, but also for most of the underdeveloped Third World countries in the age of imperialism.

Caldwell's own overall assessment was that (ibid.: 37):

> [T]he leaders of the Cambodian Revolution had evolved both short-term tactics and long-term socio-economic strategy, based upon a sound analysis of the realities of the country's society and economy [...] [I]n the face of great difficulties they have attempted with some successes to implement these in the last three years; and the chosen course is a sound one whether one judges it in terms of its domestic appositeness or in terms of its reading of the future international economy [...]

He praised the 'forethought, ingenuity [and] dedication [...] of the liberation forces in the face of extreme adversity [...] and even outright sabotage' (ibid.: 38).

Caldwell saw Cambodia as a romantic, egalitarian place, in which revolutionary leaders and peasants toil in the fields side by side (ibid.):

[R]adicals like Khieu Samphan ['Brother Number Four'] and the others were not 'theoretical leftists'. [...] [T]hey always not only stressed the importance of cadres throwing themselves into manual labour alongside peasants, but set a personal example. They scorned material rewards and comforts, fully sharing the lives of the poor. [...] [S]ince liberation they have continued to retain their working offices deep in the rural areas and to take turns at field work.

He acknowledged that his enthusiasm was not universally shared in Cambodia, and that especially the former urbanites needed a bit of nudging, but saw this as mere teething problems (ibid.):

Urban dwellers re-settled from Phnom Penh in 1975 could not possibly have at once shared that outlook and it need occasion us no surprise that to begin with they required close supervision when put to work shifting earth and collecting boulders; we should bear this in mind when evaluating refugee stories.

He believed that the success story of Cambodian socialism might inspire peasants elsewhere to rise up, and establish a similar system: 'the lesson will not long be lost upon the as yet unliberated peasants' (ibid.: 40).

His worry was that the general public in the West was deluded about the reality of Cambodia, a situation which more enlightened observers had to rectify: 'manipulators have a very good reason to distort and obscure the truth

[...] we have a clear obligation to establish and propagate it with every resource at our command' (ibid.: 39).

A year before, Caldwell had written (ibid.: 36):

> Faced with determined attempts on the part of both the Western and the Soviet media to portray it as a crazed pariah, Kampuchea has succeeded in convincing many of its Asian neighbours and other Third World countries that the calumny is unwarranted. [...] [M]uch of the [...] propaganda is drawn from the notorious Reader's Digest book [...] Murder of a Gentle Land, which has long since been refuted and discredited.

So much for the prevailing view among Southeast Asia scholars. Khmer Rouge support was not limited to them. Just a month after the revolution, the Swedish author Per Olov Enquist wrote for the newspaper *Expressen* (quoted in Fröberg Idling 2006):

> [T]he people rose, freed themselves, threw out the intruders, found that their fine towns needed restoration. So they emptied the houses and began to clear up the mess. [...] [P]eople were never meant to live in degradation here, but in peace and with dignity. Then crocodile tears poured forth in the West. The brothel has been emptied and the clean-up is in progress. Only pimps can regret what is happening.

During their first three years in power, the Khmer Rouge made it almost impossible for foreigners to enter the country. But in their final year, they started to open their borders for political pilgrims, and the pilgrims started to turn up. As Locard (2015: 216) explains:

> There were [...] visits from Maoist communist parties all over the world who wanted to see this collectivist paradise first-hand. [...] Members came from the United States [...] Italy and Denmark [...] and France, Norway and Canada [...] [R]epresentatives from friendship associations came from Belgium [...] Sweden [...] Japan and were received by Pol Pot himself. Journalists also came [...] [M]any were given an interview with Brother Number One at the end of their visit – this was the apex of the pilgrimage to the new Mecca of communism.

In 1978, a Swedish delegation of the Sweden–Kampuchea Friendship Association went on a pilgrimage to Cambodia, and wrote about 'the wonderful achievements and feats of the Kampuchean people in defending and building Democratic Kampuchea' (quoted in Locard 2015: 217).

One member of the delegation, Gunnar Bergström, was especially impressed by the regime's agricultural policy. He explained in a radio interview (ibid.: 218):

> Everywhere we saw vast rice fields and numerous waterworks. We had learned already about all these achievements [...] but it was even more illuminating to see [them] with our own eyes [...] The '6th January' dam, that thousands of people are busily and arduously striving to complete, is concrete evidence attesting to how a people

who rely on their own strength and means can score wonderful feats.

Bergström's logic was simple: the group did not witness any atrocities, ergo, there could not have been any. As he put it (Bergström 1978: 11):

[I]f it was the case that one third of the people died from hardships and executions and that the slightest deviation from the 'right behaviour' led to death – then it would be evident in the mood of the people.

And '[N]owhere did we see the bloodthirsty [...] army. During the entire trip we saw four soldiers' (ibid.: 4).

Another member of the same delegation, Jan Myrdal, produced a documentary in which he described Khmer Rouge socialism as a rustic, communitarian socialism, with great achievements for the poor (quoted in Fröberg Idling 2006):

In the centre of the villages are large common dining halls. [...] People eat together. The pattern of life is new and old at the same time. New collectives, and at the same time village traditions [...]

City dwellers who once lived in villas with servants do find the food a bit meager. But the co-operative guarantees food for all. [...]

[T]he simple guarantees of dwelling space, clothes, and food that the new society provides, turn the dreams of a poor peasant into reality [...]

According to Myrdal, Pol Pot was building 'the kingdom of justice'.[3] Myrdal (1978: 10–11) wrote:

> The old society is gone. Then, there was luxury and fine wines and the sweet life for the selected few. But the people had it hard. Now everyone can satisfy their hunger and all can cover their nakedness. There is rice and there are clothes [...] [T]wice a month, it is said, everybody is able to eat dessert. A few have it worse and most have it better. Justice prevails.

In 1978, a Norwegian delegation went on a pilgrimage to Cambodia. They met with Brother Number One and Brother Number Three, and later praised Cambodian socialism in similar terms to the Swedish delegation.[4] One of the Norwegian pilgrims, the writer and editor Pål Steigan, has since revoked his support for the Khmer Rouge – but only on the basis that their version of socialism was not 'real' socialism: 'the Pol Pot regime was never a Marxist one. It violates the fundamental points of the whole theoretical basis for Marxism. That I did not understand then'.[5]

---

3   Mannen utan skam, *Expressen*, 25 July 2007 (https://www.expressen.se/kul tur/mannen-utan-skam/); Myrdal: Efter festen, *Sundsvalls Tidning*, 26 July 2007 (http://www.st.nu/kultur/myrdal-efter-festen). Translated with Google Translate and cross-checked via the dict.cc online dictionary.

4   Norwegian delegation 1978. Cambodia to Kampuchea, Archive and Readings (https://cambodiatokampuchea.wordpress.com/2015/08/30/norweg ian-delegation-1978/).

5   Ibid.

Towards the end, the Khmer Rouge regime was planning to increase pilgrimage tourism further (Locard 2015: 216). If their plans had gone ahead, Cambodia might well have become a more popular pilgrimage destination for Western socialists. But their plans were nipped in the bud. About a year after the opening to Western visitors began, Cambodia was invaded by Vietnam and the Khmer Rouge were ousted.

The most famous apologist for the Khmer Rouge must have been Noam Chomsky. 'Apologist' – as opposed to 'supporter' – is the right word here: Chomsky's writings on the subject contain a few sentences on the alleged positive achievements of the Khmer Rouge, but this is not the focus of his writings. They are primarily a denial and downplaying of Khmer Rouge atrocities. They are not pro–Pol Pot papers, but anti-anti–Pol Pot papers.

In 1977, Chomsky and Edward Herman published the paper 'Distortions at Fourth Hand'. By then, there were numerous accounts of what was happening in Cambodia, alongside estimates of the scale of the horrors. But the quality of the evidence was low, eyewitness accounts were usually unverifiable, different sources often contradicted each other and estimates of the body count varied hugely. This made it easy for Chomsky and Herman to pick holes in those accounts and imply that it was all a big hoax.

Their main target is the book *Murder of a Gentle Land: The Untold Story of Communist Genocide in Cambodia* by John Barron and Anthony Paul, which they describe as 'a third-rate propaganda tract'. Chomsky and Herman (1977) spot the odd mistake in it, and imply, on this basis, that the whole book is untrustworthy:

Their scholarship collapses under the barest scrutiny. To cite a few cases, they state that among those evacuated from Phnom Penh, 'virtually everybody saw the consequences of [summary executions] in the form of the corpses of men, women and children rapidly bloating and rotting in the hot sun,' citing, among others, J. J. Cazaux, who wrote, in fact, that 'not a single corpse was seen along our evacuation route,' and that early reports of massacres proved fallacious.

They also highlight irregularities in the way the death toll is calculated, which they use as a way to effectively dismiss them (ibid.:):

Barron and Paul [...] base their calculations on a variety of interesting assumptions [...]; curiously, their 'calculations' lead them to the figure of 1.2 million deaths [...] by January 1, 1977 ('at a very minimum'); by a coincidence, the number reported much earlier by the American Embassy [...] [S]imilar numbers are bandied about, with equal credibility.

Another target is the 1977 book *Cambodge année zéro* (*Cambodia: Year Zero*) by François Ponchaud (ibid.):

Ponchaud plays fast and loose with quotes and with numbers. [...] [W]here an independent check is possible, Ponchaud's account seems at best careless, sometimes in rather significant ways. [...] Ponchaud's [...] work has an anti-Communist bias and message.

Ponchaud's book is mostly based on interviews with and reports from refugees, which Chomsky and Herman do not put much stock in (ibid.):

> Refugees [...] naturally tend to report what they believe their interlocuters wish to hear. [...] [R]efugees questioned by Westerners or Thais have a vested interest in reporting atrocities on the part of Cambodian revolutionaries.

Eyewitness accounts from people who have not, in fact, witnessed anything are presented as evidence that nothing much can have happened (ibid.):

> [T]he Swedish journalist, Olle Tolgraven [and] [...] Richard Boyle of Pacific News Service, the last newsman to leave Cambodia [...] denied the existence of wholesale executions [...] Father Jacques Engelmann [...] who was evacuated at the same time [...] reported that evacuated priests 'were not witness to any cruelties'.

They also dismiss various *New York Times* articles by Robert Moss, whom they describe as 'editor of a dubious offshoot of Britain's *Economist* called "Foreign Report" which specializes in sensational rumors', on the basis of an ambiguous quote in his article (ibid.):

> Moss [...] asserts that 'Cambodia's pursuit of total revolution has resulted, by the official admission of its Head of State, Khieu Samphan, in the slaughter of a million people.' [...] [N]owhere [...] does Khieu Samphan suggest

that the million postwar deaths were a result of official policies [...] as opposed to the lag effects of a war [...] The 'slaughter' by the Khmer Rouge is a Moss–*New York Times* creation.

If all these negative reports are false, what, then, is the true situation in Cambodia? On the one hand, Chomsky and Herman hedge their bets, stating 'We do not pretend to know where the truth lies amidst these sharply conflicting assessments' (ibid.). But then, they also claim (ibid.):

[A]nalyses by highly qualified specialists who have studied the full range of evidence available [...] concluded that executions have numbered at most in the thousands; that these were localized in areas of limited Khmer Rouge influence and unusual peasant discontent [...] These reports also emphasize [...] repeated discoveries that massacre reports were false.

They compare Cambodia to France after the ousting of the Nazi regime, where former collaborators had also been dealt with harshly (ibid.):

[I]f postwar Cambodia is [...] similar to France after liberation [...] then perhaps a rather different judgement is in order. That the latter conclusion may be more nearly correct is suggested by the analyses mentioned earlier. What filters through to the American public is a seriously distorted version of the evidence available, emphasizing alleged Khmer Rouge atrocities.

In their general assessment of Cambodia under the Khmer Rouge, they draw on the aforementioned Hildebrand and Porter, who 'present a carefully documented study of [...] the success of the Cambodian revolutionaries [...], giving a very favorable picture of their programs and policies, based on a wide range of sources' (ibid.).

Two years later, Chomsky and Herman took the issue up again in their book *After the Cataclysm*, repeating most claims from their earlier paper. In addition, they ask why, if the Khmer Rouge are as bad their critics allege, there is not more resistance to their rule (Chomsky and Herman 1979: 156–58):

> If 1/3 of the population has been killed by a murderous band that has taken over the government – which some-how manages to control every village – or have died as a result of their genocidal policies, then surely one would expect if not a rebellion then at least unwillingness to fight for the Paris-educated fanatics at the top [...] [O]ne conceivable hypothesis does not seem to have been con-sidered, even to be rejected: that there was a significant degree of peasant support for the Khmer Rouge and the measures they had instituted in the countryside.

They also cite the historian Ben Kiernan, who (ibid.: 227–29):

> believes that there is little evidence that the government planned and approved a systematic large-scale purge. '[A]part from the execution of high-ranking army officers

and officials, the killing [...] was instigated by untrained and vengeful local Khmer Rouge soldiers, despite orders to the contrary from Phnom Penh. [...] Most of the brutality shown by local Khmer Rouge soldiers is attributable to lack of training [...].' [...]

[Kiernan] quotes one Khmer refugee who said that in Battambang the rich were being 'persecuted' while the poor were better off than before, and adds that 'where the Khmer Rouge were better organised, "persecution" of the rich was much less violent'.

Overall, Chomsky and Herman's writings are not an endorsement of the Khmer Rouge. They are an attempt to debunk and discredit criticism of the regime, rather than actively praise it. But it is notable that they refer to the Khmer Rouge as 'the communists' throughout their paper – not 'the so-called communists' or 'the self-declared communists', but 'the communists'. It may be linguistic pedantry to point this out, but then, Chomsky *is* a linguist, who insists that one must not call countries such as the Soviet Union 'socialist'.[6]

Chomsky could have taken a much safer line of defence, namely that the atrocities may all be real, but that they tell us nothing about socialism, because the Khmer Rouge were not 'really' socialist. But that was apparently not his perception at the time.

---

6   The Soviet Union vs socialism (https://www.youtube.com/watch?v=06-X cAiswY4&feature=youtu.be). See also Chomsky (1986).

After the Vietnamese invasion, enthusiasm for Cambodia quickly faded. Cambodia remained socialist, but it became closely aligned with Vietnam and the Soviet Union, and thus with two variants of socialism which, by that stage, had already been widely discredited.

Some former Khmer Rouge supporters in the West admitted that they had been wrong. Others simply fell silent on the issue (Ear 1995). The Khmer Rouge were subtly reclassified: they were now no longer socialists, but fascists, or simply a group of sadistic psychopaths without any particular ideology. This is the prevailing view to this day.

On the whole, the case of Cambodia represents the most complete, and the most successful example of the retroactive disowning of a socialist experiment. It is virtually impossible to find a Western supporter of the Khmer Rouge today.[7] Holding the Soviet Union or Maoist China against a contemporary socialist is considered gauche today, but holding the Khmer Rouge against them is considered beyond the pale. And yet, Khmer Rouge socialism was once seen as a romantic, agrarian, back-to-the-roots socialism by some mainstream Western intellectuals. Their absolute numbers were never large, but they included some of the leading scholars in the relevant academic disciplines.

---

7   An exception is Israel Shamir, who writes for *Counterpunch* magazine. He still describes Pol Pot as a saint-like figure, denies the genocide and portrays Cambodia under the Khmer Rouge as a bucolic egalitarian paradise. See: Pol Pot revisited, *Counterpunch*, 18 September 2012 (https://www.counter punch.org/2012/09/18/pol-pot-revisited/).

7 ALBANIA UNDER ENVER HOXHA: 'THE WORKING CLASS IS IN POWER'

Mao-mania began with the Sino-Soviet split. For Western utopia-seekers, this split represented not just a foreign policy issue, but the hope of a fresh start. It created a clear dividing line between the old, discredited Soviet model on the one hand, and the great white hope of a genuine workers' and peasants' state on the other hand.

With the Sino-Albanian split in the mid-1970s, something similar happened again, albeit on a much smaller scale. This time, it was the Chinese model which represented the old and discredited form of socialism, while Albania represented the new hopeful.

It was a very unlikely candidate. By then, Enver Hoxha, the country's socialist dictator, had already been in power for three decades. But Albania's fallout with the Soviet Union, its withdrawal from the Warsaw Pact, and finally, its fallout with China and its re-foundation as the 'People's Socialist Republic of Albania' created the impression of a fresh start (at least for those who were desperately looking for a fresh start). Since the country was no longer aligned with anyone, its version of socialism was not tainted by off-putting examples of socialism elsewhere.

'Hoxhaism' was a particularly uncompromising, isolationist version of socialism, which, even relative to other socialist countries, severely retarded the country's economic development. When Enver Hoxha died in 1985, Albania was far behind even the poorest members of the Warsaw Pact, never mind the West. Today, despite some catch-up growth after a messy transition away from socialism, it remains one of the poorest countries in Europe (see Figure 8).

Figure 8   GDP per capita (PPP), Albania vs. Romania and Bulgaria, 1985–2017 (in current international $)

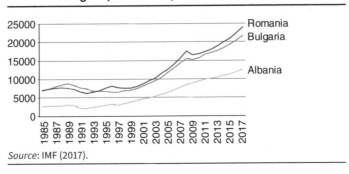

Source: IMF (2017).

But in the mid-1970s, in Marxist circles, 'Hoxhaism' became the new Maoism. Hoxhaist parties, such as the Revolutionary Communist Party of Britain (Marxist–Leninist), emerged all over the Western world, including in the US, Canada, France, West Germany, the Netherlands, Sweden, Norway, Spain and Italy. Even East Germany had a little Hoxhaist party, which criticised its own country for having deviated from 'true' socialism (although unsurprisingly, that party was quickly infiltrated and shut down by the Stasi (Wunschik 1997)).

Unlike Maoism, Hoxhaism was always a minority pursuit in the West. But it was 'a thing'. As Hollander (1990: 275) explains:

> [T]here was a loss of novelty and revolutionary freshness as the twentieth anniversary of the Cuban revolution approached [...] [S]ome Western intellectuals had reason to turn their attentions to other countries in the Third World. [...] [T]here were fleeting flirtations with Algeria, Albania, North Korea, Tanzania, Mozambique, and even Cambodia. Albania and Mozambique in particular enjoyed some measure of popularity

Western Hoxhaists did not leave extensive written statements, so it is hard to reconstruct what exactly they saw in Albania's variant of socialism. The exception is the book *Albania Defiant* by Jan Myrdal – the son of the Nobel Laureates Gunnar and Alva Myrdal – and Gun Kessle.

Myrdal and Kessle, who must have been among the very first Western Hoxhaists, define Albanian socialism specifically in opposition to the more established, staid models of socialism. Other countries had lost their revolutionary spirit, but in Albania that flame was still burning (Myrdal and Kessle 1976: 174–75):

> In the revisionist countries technocracy, along with [...] bureaucracy, has become an important means whereby the working class has been deposed from leadership [...] The economy in these countries, which the revisionists persist in calling 'socialist' [...] is operated by, serves, and

works for the new bourgeois bureaucratic and techno-cratic class [...]

[The Albanian] developmental model [...] is wholly unlike any being used by any other country. [...] The Albanians have analyzed what has happened in such countries as the Soviet Union, and [...] they are trying to build socialism in a way that cannot lead to the growth of new privileged social strata.

The authors warn that there is no guarantee that Albania will always remain a people's state, but they are optimistic (ibid.: 176–77):

The Albanian people [...] are [...] building a new type of society. [...] [F]ailure can be envisaged. The Albanian Communists are well aware of this. Their state can become bureaucratic, the people can lose control over it. [...] To implement the workers' power in a state is not easy; it is not easy to ensure that the people will always have control [...] What is so hopeful about Albania is that the Albanians can see clearly, and are openly discussing, all these possibilities of an evil development. For in this way they can be overcome.

They dispute the claim that Albania is a dictatorship (ibid.: 182):

The party does not stand above the people. The working class is in power; the party serves the working masses. It is not the party that is in power over the working class.

Enver Hoxha has many times taken up this question of working-class control and of rendering accounts to the masses of people.

Nor is Enver Hoxha a dictator, and what *seems* like a personality cult is, in truth, no such thing (ibid.: 183–84):

Enver Hoxha [...] is one of the great working-class leaders and Marxist-Leninists of our time. It is natural that much popular feeling has concentrated on him. [...] [H]e is respected and beloved. But he is not the subject of a cult of personality; he does not stand above or outside the people. [...] [H]e is applauded not as a personality but as the founder and servant of the party.

The principles of workers' democracy permeate all areas of economic life, especially the workplace. Myrdal and Kessle visit a mine and report (ibid.: 173–74):

At a meeting [...] the workers [...] criticized the manager and the administration. Management had tried to avoid doing heavy work in the mines; they had tried to get themselves easy work during their days in production. [...] They had been criticized as comrades. [...] Now those who had made these errors in management had improved. They had seen the error of their ways. Now they were working as ancillary workers.

The authors see the Albanian economy as a huge success story (ibid.: 178–79):

> The planned economic development has been rapid. [...] The economic base of socialism has been built [...] Socialism is possible. Centralized planning democratically controlled by the working people makes the even development of the whole country possible. [...]
>
> When the market no longer rules, the people are able to shape their own future with their own work. [...] Life is better, social development is rapid.

Albania Defiant drives home two of the leitmotivs of this book. Firstly, it shows, once again, that the this-time-is-different claim is not remotely new. The idea that previous models of socialism were bad, but that the model which is currently in vogue represents a complete break from that, has a long history. Ever since Soviet socialism fell out of fashion, Western socialists have always explicitly defined the socialist model *du jour* in opposition to previous models. This time is always different – until it turns out that it was not so different after all.

Secondly, the book shows how little it sometimes takes to construct a this-time-is-different claim. Throughout the book, Myrdal and Kessle constantly repeat the assertion that while the established socialist countries are run by self-serving bureaucratic elites, Albania is run by 'the working class'. They never explain how 'the working class' supposedly does that, in practice. They never identify any institution, or any decision-making mechanism, which Albania has, and which the Warsaw Pact countries or the non-aligned socialist countries lack. It is as if they believed that repeating the assertion often enough was enough to make it so, and that public displays of hostility towards Warsaw Pact countries were enough to guarantee a different outcome.

Albania was never a popular pilgrimage destination. Hoxhaism was never remotely as popular among Western intellectuals as Maoism was. It remained the preserve of stranded Maoists, who were especially impatient to find a new cause when Maoism fell out of fashion. And unlike Maoism, remnants of which can still be found, Hoxhaism disappeared almost without a trace. The programme of the Revolutionary Communist Party of Britain (Marxist–Leninist) still states (RCPB-ML 1995: 4):

> [T]he Soviet Union of Lenin and Stalin and Albania under the leadership of Enver Hoxha [...] were states where the working class was in power, which were run in the interests of the working people and where the political processes ensured representation in the interests of the working class and people. These were the most advanced examples to date of states with democratic political processes.

But such fringe groups aside, Hoxhaism has vanished without leaving any legacy.

8   EAST GERMANY UNDER THE SED: 'THE ORGANISED MIGHT OF THE WORKING CLASS'

East German socialism

If an economic model fails once, twice, three times or four times, the claim that it was a good idea in principle, which has just been badly implemented, need not be implausible. Poor implementation can ruin the best economic policy ideas.

If it fails for an eighth, a ninth and a tenth time, without there being a single positive counterexample, the claim begins to lose its plausibility. In this respect, socialists were lucky that during the Cold War, Western media representation tended to emphasise the commonalities, not the policy variations, between the different members of the Warsaw Pact. Their economic models were not treated as socialist experiments in their own right, but as carbon copies of the Soviet model. This is already reflected in our language: we talk about a 'Soviet Bloc', a 'Soviet sphere of influence' or even a 'Soviet empire'. Conveniently for socialists, this has the effect of reducing the number of failed socialist experiments. The failure of many different variants of socialism becomes the failure of one single model, which just happened to fail in a number of places at around the same time.

But most Warsaw Pact countries had their own home-grown Marxist traditions. When they were occupied by the Red Army, the Soviet Union simply made sure that an already existing socialist party (or a merger of several of them) would gain and retain power. Once in power, these parties implemented the same policies that they would probably also have implemented if they had come to power in other ways.

The most clear-cut case has to be the German Democratic Republic. The Socialist Unity Party of Germany (SED), which governed the GDR throughout its existence, was a direct successor of the old Communist Party of Germany (KPD).[1] The KPD had been formally established as a party just after World War I, but its roots stretch back much further: communist organisations had existed as early as in the 1830s (Conway 1987: 146–61). This was a homegrown tradition of Marxism – literally so, since Karl Marx himself had been personally involved – which long predated the Soviet Union.

The SED could never have risen to power without the backing of the Soviet Union. We can see this from the fact that its West German counterparts remained electorally insignificant throughout. But if it *had*, in whatever way, come to power independently of the Soviet Union, it is hard to see what it would have done differently, at least in

---

1 Technically, the SED was the product of a forced merger of the Communist Party and the Social Democratic Party, but it was a merger under commu-nist terms.

terms of economic policy. The SED simply created the kind of economy that the Weimar-era KPD had always said it would create. The KPD's election manifestos demanded the nationalisation of industry, of banking and finance, of wholesale trade, of large landholdings, of parts of the housing stock, and of personal wealth above a certain level (KPD 1922; KPD 1930). That is exactly what the SED then did.

Soviet apologists had often blamed the Soviet Union's repressive character on the country's backwardness. Laski (1946: 52), for example, claimed:

> [W]e must be clear about the conditions its [the Soviet Union's] makers confronted. They were dealing with a barely literate and semi-Westernized country, accustomed only to [...] despotism. The industrial middle class was a tiny fragment of the population; and the urban proletariat was only a small proportion of the vast peasant mass [...]
>
> Those who made the Revolution intended to apply Marxist principles. They assumed a necessary period, on the Marxist model, of iron dictatorship. [...] [T]hey were confident that the necessity of dictatorship would be transitional only

According to this view, socialism would have turned out completely differently if it had been introduced in a country with a more advanced economy, a more educated population, and a working class with more experience in democratic self-organisation.

It is hard to think of a better test case for this view than East Germany. Germany had already achieved near-universal adult literacy in the mid nineteenth century (Graff 1991: 375). There was a strong culture of working-class self-organisation, comprising hundreds of independent working-class associations. In the German states, and later, the German Empire, working-class people used to run adult education centres, libraries, provident societies, building societies, and all kinds of mutual aid and mutual insurance associations comparable to British Friendly Societies (Habermann 1994). While this working-class culture had been suppressed by the Nazi regime, it quickly bounced back after the war – or at least it did in West Germany. It was the self-proclaimed Workers' and Farmers' State which was not too keen on independent working-class organisations.[2]

East German socialism started under immensely difficult conditions, given the extent of wartime destruction. But while it probably did not seem that way to people who lived through that period, rebuilding something that was already there once is easier than building something new

---

2   A good example is the *Naturfreunde* ('Friends of Nature'), an organisation which grew out of the labour movement in the late nineteenth century. The *Naturefreunde* aimed to make the recreational and health benefits of nature accessible to people on low incomes, mainly by providing low-cost board and lodging in self-built, self-managed forest chalets. Under the Nazis, the organisation was banned and their forest chalets expropriated. After the war, they quickly reconstituted themselves in the West and their property was restituted. In East Germany, their property was transferred to state-controlled organisations, and the *Naturfreunde* was not re-established as an independent organisation until the end of 1989. See: Chronik der Naturfreunde (https://www.naturfreunde.de/chronik-der-naturfreunde).

from scratch. Around the time the Soviet Occupation Zone became the GDR, industrial production had already recovered to about two thirds of the pre-war level (Steiner 2010: 51).

In terms of the outcomes it produced, GDR socialism was, indeed, different from Soviet socialism. It avoided the worst excesses. There were no Gulags, no famines and no mass executions. The exact death toll is unknown, but we are talking about hundreds or thousands, not hundreds *of* thousands (Borbe 2010).[3] There was no cult of personality around any particular leader figure. Economically, the GDR was the richest country in the Eastern bloc,[4] and thus presumably the richest socialist country that has ever existed. As far as socialism goes, the GDR is probably as good as it gets.

And yet, the relevant control group is not the Soviet Union, but the Federal Republic of Germany (FRG), and compared to this benchmark, the GDR comes up short. The regime may not have killed its opponents in droves, but it was nonetheless a notorious police state, where arbitrary arrests and imprisonment were commonplace. There was an extensive spy and surveillance network, and pervasive

---

3   However, it has to be said that the Soviets did a lot of the 'dirty work' for them. The worst excesses occurred between 1945 and 1949, in the Soviet Zone of Occupation. Technically, these killings were the deeds of the Soviet regime, not the East German regime. And yet, it is fair to say that if the GDR regime had had to carry out the collectivisations and initial neutralisation of political opponents themselves, its death toll would have been substantially higher.

4   The convergence dream 25 years on, *Bruegel*, 6 January 2015 (http://bruegel .org/2015/01/the-convergence-dream-25-years-on/).

censorship. Its secret police, the State Security Service, has gained almost proverbial status: to this day, we talk about 'Stasi methods' when we criticise infringements of civil liberties.

On some measures, the East–West gap – the cost of socialism – can be quantified. Just after reunification, GDP per capita in East Germany was just one third of the West German level, with other indicators of economic performance showing similar gaps (Röhl 2009: 1–3).[5] The poorest West German region, Schleswig-Holstein, was still two and a half times as rich as the richest East German region, Saxony (Burda and Weder 2017: 4). There was also a three-year gap in life expectancy (ibid.: 20).

The cost of reunification to date has been colossal. Net transfers from West to East Germany over the period from 1990 to 2016 add up to €1.88 trillion in today's prices.[6] Annual net transfers from West Germany still account for about 15 per cent of East Germany's GDP (Burda and Weder 2017: 23–24).

---

5   The figures are from 1991, the first year for which we can truly compare like with like, because in the course of reunification, the East German economy had also become part of the Federal Republic's system of national accounts. Living standards are hard to compare between a market economy and a planned economy. Measures such as GDP per capita rely on market prices, which a planned economy, by definition, does not have. It was only with the introduction of market prices in East Germany that living standards in East and West became truly comparable.

6   To be fair, it was not an *inevitable* cost of reunification, but the result of a political choice, namely the choice to try to close the gap quickly. The government could, in theory, have decided to just accept the gap, and allow it to persist.

The ultimate test of a system's success, of course, is whether or not people want to live in it. On those terms, the outcome of the experiment was decided long before it formally ended. Between the founding of the GDR and the construction of the Berlin Wall, more than 2.7 million people migrated from the GDR to the FRG (Bade and Oltmer 2005). The 2.7 million figure is an absolute lower bound: it comes from the registries of refugee camps in the FRG, so it would not include people who, for example, stayed with friends or relatives.

The quasi-natural experiment, then, has produced a conclusive result. It is now clear which system was superior. But it was not always so clear.

Western admirers of the GDR: the early years

The GDR never inspired pilgrimages of the kind that the Soviet Union, Maoist China and Cuba inspired during their honeymoon periods. It lacked the crucial ingredient of a popular pilgrimage destination: the promise of a complete fresh start. It was too closely, and too obviously, aligned with the Soviet Union.

Thus, it was never admired as an earthly paradise. But it did have a range of relatively prominent supporters in Western countries such as Britain and the US (far less so in West Germany). In the early years, a lot of that support stemmed from the GDR's self-portrayal as an 'anti-fascist' state.

In a Marxist interpretation, fascism was not a system and an ideology in its own right, but simply an especially savage and brutal form of capitalism. As Kostas Papadakis, a Marxist MEP, puts it:

> [F]ascism is a form of capital's power in specific conditions. In Germany, Nazism constituted the ideal form to support capital in the conditions of the military preparations for the conquest of new markets, in the conditions of a very deep capitalist crisis [...] It was supported politically and financially by sections of German capital, it identified with monopolies (Krupp, I. G. Farben, Siemens etc.), it collaborated with the colossi of the 'democratic' capitalist states (General Motors, General Electric, ITT, Ford, IBM).[7]

This was exactly the view that the East German government took. They believed that by overcoming capitalism, 'their' part of Germany – and *only* their part – had also overcome the structural cause of Nazism. Of the two Germanies, then, only one could claim to have truly rooted out Nazism once and for all. In this way, anti-fascism became the founding myth of the GDR, a message which appealed to some Western observers.

Berger and LaPorte (2008 and 2010) analyse British attitudes towards the GDR in the 1940s and 1950s. They find that while 'there was little interest in the GDR among the British general public, [...] this was not always so on the British Left' (Berger and LaPorte 2008: 537).

---

7   The equation of Communism with Nazism is unacceptable and provocative, *In Defense of Communism* blog, 30 August 2017 (https://communism gr.blogspot.co.uk/2017/08/kostas-papadakis-equation-of-communism .html).

The authors identify two groups of people who were sympathetic to the GDR. The first group, unsurprisingly, was the Stalinist left, which simply extended its pro-Soviet sympathies to the Soviet Union's sister states. But at that time, Stalin-mania was already past its prime, and the Stalinist left was losing relevance. What is more noteworthy is that the authors also find support for the GDR among the wider labour movement, and thus among people who would have been indifferent or hostile to the Soviet Union. This means that support for the GDR was a phenomenon in its own right. Every Soviet sympathiser was also a GDR sympathiser, but not every GDR sympathiser was also a Soviet sympathiser.

Berger and LaPorte (2008: 537) explain:

[I]t was among Communist and left-Labour trade unionists and left-wing Labour Party supporters, including several MPs, that the GDR found perhaps its most unwavering supporters. Within the wider British labour movement, interest was driven by [...] curiosity about 'really existing socialism', but, above all, by the perception of the GDR as an antifascist state. [...] [W]hat precisely motivated not only the small pro-Soviet Left, but also wider Labour Party circles, to accept this image as a basis of support for the 'other Germany'?

And elsewhere (ibid.: 73–74):

The Labour left had considerable sympathies for the socialist Germany [...]

[T]he CPGB on balance proved a reliable ally of the GDR [...]

Communist trade unionists [...] sought to counter the official anti-communist stance of the General Council of the TUC. Whereas the latter cooperated closely with the West German unions to defeat communism, communist unions took up the FDGB's [the Free German Trade Union Federation of the GDR] offer of mutual exchanges. Relations between the British labour movement and the GDR could be justified on grounds of ideological proximity.

According to John Green, a British journalist and filmmaker (quoted in Berger and LaPorte 2008: 540):

Many of those who had occupied leading positions in Hitler's Germany found little difficulty in slipping into similar positions in the new FRG [...] In the East it was those who had resisted fascism who formed the leadership of the new state and party apparatus. [...] [S]o many antifascist resistance fighters freely identified with [the GDR.]

The Electrical Trades Union published a booklet about the GDR, which stated (ibid.: 543):

[T]he difference between East and West Germany is that Nazism has been completely liquidated in the Eastern part and that the government consists of those who had suffered under Nazism. In the Western part, the government is composed of those who were actually fascists.

The bureau chief of Reuters' News Agency in Berlin, John Peet, wrote in his 'Democratic German Report' that 'in the GDR anti-nazis run things, and an ex-nazi in public life is the rare exception; in West Germany the former Nazis are back in power, and a man with an anti-nazi record is a rarity' (ibid.: 543).

After a visit to Stalinstadt (formerly, and now again, Eisenhüttenstadt) in 1953, Emry Hughes, the MP for South Ayrshire, described the city as 'an overpowering example of what a socialist Germany can achieve' (quoted in Berger and LaPorte 2010: 67). After another visit in 1960, he described the GDR as the 'better Germany' (ibid.: 95).

To its supporters, the GDR was a People's State, even if it superficially *looked* like a dictatorship. A socialist state, they argued, could never function unless it was supported by the vast majority of the population; hence, its very existence was proof that it had mass support. William Gallacher, the MP for West Fife, argued in a House of Commons debate (Hansard 1949):

> There has been talk in this Debate of the Communists being only 5 per cent in Germany and in other countries. [...] It [...] would never have been possible for the Irish Republican Army to carry on the fight against the British Forces but for the fact that the mass of the people were sympathetic to them. In the same way it would be utterly impossible [...] to carry on the struggle [...] unless the mass of the people were sympathetic [...]

> The Eastern [European] countries are free and independent. [...] Why will men blind themselves to the truth? [...]
>
> It is impossible for the Communist Party in this or any other country to break the power of the capitalist class. The only force which is strong enough to do that is the organised might of the working class, and sooner or later the organised working class [...] will overcome the capitalist class. There will be one party representing the people.

From this perspective, the mass uprisings of 1953, which were brutally crushed by the GDR regime with the aid of Soviet troops, represent a problem. How can there be a workers' uprising in a Workers' State? Under socialism, 'the working class', as a whole, is in power, and logically, the working class cannot rise up against itself. Once again, there was a mismatch between actual people and 'The People' as a romanticised abstraction, and socialists had to find a way of explaining it away.

John Peet, the aforementioned chief of Reuters Berlin, claimed that the uprising had been led by 'fascist agents of foreign powers' and 'SS criminals' (quoted in Berger and LaPorte 2008: 544).

The *Daily Worker* magazine blamed 'a CIA sponsored [...] West German pro fascist organisation' (ibid.: 544).

Stephen Owen Davies, the MP for Merthyr Tydfil and the former Chief Organiser of the South Wales Miners' Federation, asserted that 'Nazis and agent provocateurs from the West Zone of Berlin have been bribed [...] to join in and help create disturbances in the Eastern Zone' (ibid.: 544).

Jack Grahl, the Assistant General Secretary of the Fire Brigades Union, also justified the crushing of the uprising, claiming that the strikers had been fascist sympathisers (Berger and LaPorte 2010: 68).

Bertolt Brecht,[8] a German playwright and theatre director, also initially sided with the GDR government. In a letter to Walter Ulbricht, the General Secretary of the SED, Brecht wrote (quoted in Deutscher Bundestag 2006: 6; translation mine):

> History will pay its respect to the revolutionary impatience of the Socialist Unity Party of Germany. The great debate with the masses about the speed of socialist construction will lead to [...] a safeguarding of the socialist achievements. It is my desire [...] to express my solidarity with the Socialist Unity Party of Germany.

And elsewhere (ibid.: 7):

> Organised fascist elements tried to instrumentalise [...] dissatisfaction for their own gory aims. For several hours,

---

8 This book is about Western intellectuals idolising socialism from afar, so technically, Brecht should not qualify, because, by then, he had permanently settled in East Berlin. But he was originally a West German (Bavarian), who had later acquired Austrian citizenship. He had moved to East Germany voluntarily, and he was under no obligation to write those words.

> Berlin was on the verge of a Third World War. It is only thanks to the rapid intervention of the Soviet troops that these attempts could be thwarted. [...]
>
> I now hope that the provocateurs have been isolated and their communication networks destroyed.[9]

However, such explanations were not widely believed. The crushing of the 1953 uprising constituted a serious blow to the GDR's international standing, which subsequent events did not exactly improve. At the same time, pro-GDR sympathies had, to some extent, fed on hostility towards West Germany, which eventually began to wear off.

Berger and LaPorte (2008: 552) conclude that:

> The crude dichotomy between an antifascist GDR and a neo-fascist FRG proved less and less convincing to younger British observers. [...] As the FRG made strenuous efforts to come to terms with its Nazi past, the GDR's wild accusations that West Germany was a bulwark of fascism seemed increasingly wide of the mark. The GDR had lived on the credit of antifascism for too long.

---

9 Brecht must have changed his mind drastically soon afterwards. It was in response to the uprising that he wrote his poem 'Die Lösung', which ended with the famous lines:

'Would it not be easier
In that case for the government
To dissolve the people
And elect another?'

Western admirers of the GDR: the later years

In the 1960s, the American Civil Rights Movement developed a more militant wing, which had a strong socialist streak. Various senior figures of this movement flirted with the GDR for a while (Werner 2015).

Perhaps the most prominent example was Angela Davis, a professor at the University of California and director of the Feminist Studies Department. Davis was a leading figure in the Civil Rights Movement, and, later, its socialist breakaway. She was involved with the Black Panther Party, and later became the leader of the Communist Party USA.

In the GDR, news reporting about Western countries tended to focus on social problems, such as homelessness and drug addiction. Their main target, naturally, was West Germany, but racial tensions in the US also provided them with plenty of material. When Angela Davis was briefly imprisoned, the GDR organised a high-profile solidarity campaign for her. In 1972, she was invited on an official visit, where she met party leaders Walter Ulbricht and Erich Honecker, was granted an honorary doctorate from Karl Marx University (formerly, and now again, the University of Leipzig), and awarded the Star of People's Friendship.

Those American GDR admirers did not put their impressions into writing. It is therefore hard to reconstruct what exactly they saw in the GDR.

Meanwhile, in the UK, there was an academic community which saw the GDR in a generally favourable light. Searle (2011) reviews a number of standard references on the GDR from British authors, published in the 1970s and

1980s, and finds them to be predominantly well-disposed towards it (ibid.: 20):

> British writing on the GDR between 1973 and 1989 moved [...] towards a more positive portrayal which embraced its economic and welfare achievements, along with its community spirit and traditional values. [...] [M]any of the authors set out to counter [...] Cold War stereotypes [...] [I]n concentrating primarily — and often solely — on the positive aspects of life and society which could be found, they went to another extreme, thus contributing to the illusion that the SED was a much more permissive and tolerant leadership than it actually was. [...]
>
> One motivation was often the presence of sympathies with the Socialist ideal. There was a well-known contingent of GDR supporters among the British political left.

Similar to Bruce Cumings's defence of North Korea (see Chapter 5), these accounts can be seen as an illustration of the 'Golden Mean Fallacy', the idea that when there are competing positions on an issue, the truth must always be 'somewhere in between'. (In this case, this would mean somewhere in between the regime's self-presentation, and the negative perception prevailing among the general public.)

In *Socialism with a German Face*, published in 1977, Jonathan Steele claimed that it was 'no longer possible to argue that the system is both politically inacceptable [*sic*] and in any way economically inefficient' (quoted in Searle 2011: 7).

The GDR, Steele claims, had experienced its 'own economic miracle' (ibid.). He acknowledges the system's authoritarian character, but sees it as excusable (ibid.: 8):

> The excesses of [the GDR's] political way of life and the lack of travel possibilities for its people are the product of special conditions, and the continuing confrontation with West Germany. But its overall social and economic system is a presentable model of the kind of authoritarian welfare state which East European nations have now become.

In 1983, Martin McCauley published *The German Democratic Republic since 1945*, in which he argued that 'economic success is the foundation of stability in the GDR and the source of legitimacy of the party'. He acknowledges that the '1980s will be a difficult decade', but maintains that there is 'not enough [discontent] to threaten the stability of the state' (ibid.: 17).

In *German Democratic Republic: Politics, Economics and Society*, released in 1988, Mike Dennis argued that (ibid.: 15):

> [W]hile the human cost of the Berlin Wall cannot and should not be denied, the simple dichotomy of totalitarian communism and free democracies glosses over the complexities of political life in both West and East. The GDR cannot be reduced to one simplistic ideological construct.

He speaks of a 'social contract', which consists of (ibid.):

a tacit and somewhat uneasy compromise between regime and populace: a relatively widespread acknowledg-
ment of the SED's political primacy is complemented by
the regime's greater sensitivity to many of the needs and
wishes of the population, including a tolerable standard
of living.

Dennis concedes that critics of the regime 'may still be
subjected to arbitrary treatment by the instruments of
coercion', and that this creates 'a climate of uncertainty'
(ibid.: 16).

None of these authors are in the same league as Hollander's pilgrims. These are not starry-eyed utopia-seekers. They are academics who try hard to be 'balanced'
and 'nuanced', eager to stress positive achievements, and
reluctant to condemn totalitarian aspects or economic
failures. They practise the inverse of damning with faint
praise: they praise with faint damnation. The shoot-to-
kill order at the Berlin Wall becomes a 'lack of travel
possibilities', police state repression becomes 'a climate
of uncertainty', etc.

But while their assessments are not nearly as absurd as
those of Stalin's, Mao's or Kim Il Sung's pilgrims, with the
benefit of hindsight, it is clear that they were still widely off
the mark. The authors characterised East German socialism as a system which had some downsides, but which was
economically relatively successful, and which people were
ultimately quite content with. Especially in the case of
those books that were published just a few years before the
fall of the Berlin Wall, these assessments did not age well.

The pattern of support for the GDR was different from that for other socialist experiments. It did not quite follow the conventional three-stage pattern described elsewhere in this book (a honeymoon period of enthusiastic support, followed by a period of excuses, denial and whataboutery, and then finally the stage of retroactive disowning). Rather, different groups of people praised the GDR at different times for different things. Support for the GDR was never enthusiastic and never widespread, but, such as it was, it lasted for an unusually long period.

But while the GDR does not fit the three-stage pattern as neatly as other examples, what is clear is that as soon as the Berlin Wall was open, it fully and unequivocally entered the not-*real*-socialism stage. During this period, the idea that GDR socialism was not 'real' socialism played a major role in the GDR itself.

After the fall of the Berlin Wall, the SED was forced to allow a free democratic election. Some of the parties that ran for that election argued that GDR socialism was not *real* socialism. The solution they advocated was not re-unification with West Germany and the introduction of a market economy, but a reformed, democratised GDR with *real* socialism.

The manifesto of the United Left (VL), which had grown out of the GDR's democratic protest movement, stated (Vereinigte Linke 1990; translation mine):

> For too long, our country has been at the mercy of self-aggrandising bureaucrats [...] One of the most devastating consequences of Stalinist politics is that many people

in our country have begun to associate socialism with Stalinism. [...] We say: The alternative is [...] SOCIALISM; a socialism of freedom and democracy [...] It has not failed, because it has not begun yet.

Similarly, the Spartacist Workers' Party of Germany (SpAD) argued:

The Stalinist bureaucracy of [East Germany] [...] discredited the idea of socialism. We, the Spartacists, say: Socialism, under the *real* leadership of the working class, has not even begun yet.[10]

Even the SED tried, with some credibility, to give itself a reformist image. It had renamed itself the Party of Democratic Socialism (PDS), expelled several high-profile Stalinist hardliners, and promoted democratic reformers within its own ranks to top positions. Its 1990 election manifesto said:

The democratic fresh start in our country is also a fresh start with a Party of Democratic Socialism, which will lead the process of the definitive rejection of Stalinist structures, mechanisms, dogmas [...] all the way through to the end [...]

We must not give up on the social values and achievements of the GDR, among which we count [...] cooperative

---

10 DDR Wahl 1990 – Spartakist Arbeiterpartei Deutschlands Wahlwerbespot (https://www.youtube.com/watch?v=5SILGjR2p6E). Translation mine.

and public ownership in industry, agriculture and other sectors of our economy.[11]

A handful of British parliamentarians took a similar view. They believed that what they were witnessing was not the end of socialism in the Warsaw Pact countries, but, on the contrary, the beginning of 'true' socialism. In December 1989, an Early Day Motion in the House of Commons, signed by Ken Livingstone and Jeremy Corbyn, read:

[T]his House [...] recognises that this outburst of discontent and opposition in East Germany and Czechoslovakia, in particular, reflects deep anger against the corruption and mismanagement of the Stalinist bureaucracy; sees the movement leading in the direction of genuine socialism, not a return to capitalism; [...] and considers that the only way forward for the peoples of the Soviet Union and Eastern Europe is on the basis of a return to the principles of genuine workers' democracy and socialism which formed the basis and inspiration for the October revolution.[12]

This, needless to say, did not come to pass. In the March 1990 election, the pro-reunification parties won an overwhelming victory. This sealed the fate of the GDR and of East

---

11 Demokratische Freiheiten für alle – soziale Sicherheit für jeden. Wahlprogramm der PDS (https://www.wir-waren-so-frei.de/index.php/Detail/Object/Show/object_id/565/set_id/46). Translation mine.

12 Workers' Democracy in Eastern Europe, Early Day Motion 210 (http://www.parliament.uk/edm/1989-90/210).

German socialism more broadly. Six months later, the GDR was no more, and none of its major institutions survived.

But the *idea* of socialism very much did. Surveys show that a few years later, the idea that socialism was a good concept, which had just been 'badly implemented' in the GDR, had become the conventional wisdom (Stöcker 2016: 202).

Remnants of GDR apologetics today

Support for the GDR has never completely disappeared. Seumas Milne still defends the systems of the Eastern Bloc, and the GDR in particular. In Milne's version of events, the popular uprisings of the late 1980s, which brought these regimes down, never happened. He sees these events as a counterrevolution initiated from above, in which the general public were just passive bystanders, who now regret it. In a radio interview with the former Respect Party MP George Galloway, Milne explained:

> [T]here was a group of people in power who saw that they stood to benefit from the restoration of capitalism, and many ordinary people who benefited in many ways from the form of socialism there was in Eastern Europe didn't really feel ownership of the system, and they didn't necessarily see what was happening, or what they could do to stop it.
>
> But [...] most people in a good number of those countries regret the loss of [...] the positive aspects of that system [...] 1989 was an important shift, and an important

loss, for many millions of people. As well as some gains. [...]

In eastern Germany most people today have a positive view of the former East Germany, the GDR, and regret its passing [...] [T]he huge social benefits that have been lost, not only in Eastern Germany but across Eastern Europe and in the Soviet Union are mourned by the people of those countries.[13]

He sees the Berlin Wall and other repressive features of the GDR as lamentable, but ultimately excusable by the circumstances of the time:

A particular form of socialism grew up in the post-war period in the conditions of the Cold War [...] East Berlin was absolutely at the front line of the Cold War. That's what the Berlin Wall was. It was a front line between two social and military systems and two military alliances, and a very tense one at that. It wasn't just some kind of arbitrary division to hold people in, it was also a front line in a global conflict. And that conditioned a lot of the things that happened.

His interviewer, George Galloway, added:

There was no unemployment. Everyone had a house. Everyone had a free school. A free hospital. A free

---

13 George Galloway and Seumas Milne discuss the fall of the Berlin Wall, *Talksport*, 7 November 2009 (https://www.youtube.com/watch?v=ZSGISHyrCVc).

university. Free access to sports and cultural lives that ordinary working people in most societies like ours wouldn't even dream of [...] [E]specially in the GDR, there was the pioneering of education and an involvement of women in the society.[14]

In 2015, journalist and film-maker John Green and UNISON representative Bruni de la Motte published the book *Stasi State or Socialist Paradise? The German Democratic Republic and What Became of It.* They see the GDR as (Green and de la Motte 2015: 7–9):

an idealistic attempt to build a democratic and socialist state [...] which, for a variety of reasons, fell far short of that ideal. [...]

The GDR did, despite all the warts, represent the germ of a better form of society to that existing in most capitalist countries. It was based on solidarity, people were united by a common purpose, the collective good came before individual egoism and personal wealth, consumerism played a minor role in people's lives

The authors portray the GDR as the victimised underdog (ibid.: 20–21):

Throughout its existence the GDR found itself in a permanent state of siege and subject to an economic war, not unlike that suffered by Cuba. [...]

14 Ibid.

> Right from [...] its foundation [...] there was a determi-
> nation in the West [...] to 'strangle it at birth', to ensure
> that an alternative social model to Western capitalism
> would not survive. Various kinds of chicanery were used
> to make life for the GDR impossible, including sabotage.

These circumstances make the construction of the Berlin
Wall excusable (ibid.: 21):

> [T]he open border in Berlin was a focus of Cold War
> tensions [...] It was also a Mecca for spies and for acts of
> sabotage against the GDR. There is little doubt [...] that
> the building of the Wall in August 1961 contributed to
> reducing tensions.
>
> The early years of the GDR, until 1961, with its still open
> border to West Berlin, were marked by acts of sabotage
> by those opposed to it as well as infiltration by Western
> spy agencies.

The GDR's travel restrictions in general are seen as perfectly reasonable measures: 'There were a number of valid
reasons for the GDR's travel restrictions, not least [...] the
fear of the country losing key professionals' (ibid.: 73).

The authors admit that the GDR had political prisoners,
but present the sentences as lenient (ibid.: 78):

> Over the years, several people were convicted and im-
> prisoned for political activities, but most of the sentences
> were for several months or a few years, rarely for very
> long periods. A number of these prisoners also had their

prison sentences curtailed when they were exchanged for GDR agents imprisoned in West Germany or for hard currency.

The Stasi sometimes exaggerated a little, but was ultimately a security service like any other (ibid.: 77, 81):

> The central role of all security agencies, and the GDR was no different, was to protect the state from attempts to undermine or destabilise it. [...]
>
> If, as a GDR citizen, you were not a dissident [...] you would probably have had little or no contact with the Stasi throughout your life. [...] [T]he Stasi was hardly the monstrous all-seeing, omnipotent vicious organisation it has been depicted. What is also certainly true, is that the Stasi was not a corrupt force in the sense that the British police were recently shown to be.

Economically, the GDR was, in this version of events, a phenomenal success story (ibid.: 50–51):

> According to [...] a former member of the GDR's State Planning Commission, the real German economic miracle took place in the 'little GDR', and this is hardly an exaggeration, given what was achieved [...]
>
> [T]he GDR was among the leading 20 industrialised countries of the world.

What explains this success? According to the authors (ibid.: 35):

> [E]veryone knew that the profits they created by their work would go into the 'social pot' and would be used to make life better for everyone, not just for a few owners or shareholders who would pocket the surplus. Most people recognised that the surplus they created helped increase what was called the 'social wage'.

The GDR may not have been a democracy if we use the term in the narrow, Western sense, but very much so once we use it in a broader, richer sense (ibid.: 70–71, 8–9):

> In the West, freedom and democracy have always been largely defined as the right to vote within a multi-party system and to act and speak relatively unrestrained [...] However, freedom and democracy cannot be adequately defined or encapsulated in such a simplistic manner. [...]
>
> While democratic rights, as understood in the West, were limited in the GDR, there was wide participation in democratic processes at grassroots level.
>
> [W]here its strengths lay was in the field of economic democracy. As Tony Benn so often quite rightly emphasised: democracy is about much more than voting for a choice of parties every four years or so. The whole question of economic democracy – rights in the workplace, egalitarian fiscal and taxation measures, gender equality and empowerment of communities – is rarely discussed in western societies.

'True' freedom means things like the absence of stress caused by advertising (ibid.: 25–30):

The absence of mass advertising and sex misused as a sales tool meant that women were not objectified as in the West and this helped mitigate psychological pressures on individuals. [...]

[T]he absence of mass advertising [...] meant that women were not continually confronted with impossible role models to aspire to in terms of physical beauty or possessions, and their sexuality was not exploited for promoting sales.

If the GDR was such a wonderful place, why did it ultimately fail? According to the authors, it happened more or less by accident. East Germans just wanted a reformed socialism – but once the Wall was open, they were duped by the West German establishment (ibid.: 86–87):

People's confidence in being able to create a separate reformed socialist state was systematically undermined by a mixture of lurid exposure stories and disinformation about the GDR's former rulers. In addition, the (West German) media began a propaganda war claiming that the GDR economy was near collapse [...]

[Kohl] saw his chance of fulfilling an old dream, namely [...] banishing the spectre of a socialist alternative [...]

The powerful West German political parties [...] donated large sums of money, printed election propaganda and provided a free service of 'advisers' to their designated partners in the East.

The foreword to the book, unsurprisingly, is written by Seumas Milne (2015: 4–5):

> The GDR was home to the Stasi, shortages and the Berlin Wall. But it was also a country of full employment, social and women's equality [...], cheap housing, transport and culture, one of the best childcare systems in the world, and greater freedom in the workplace than most employees enjoy in today's Germany. [...]
>
> 1989 unleashed [...] free-market shock therapy, commercial robbery dressed up as privatisation, vast increases in inequality, and poverty [...]
>
> Reunification in Germany meant annexation, the takeover and closure of most of its industry, a political purge of more than a million teachers and other white collar workers, a loss of women's rights [...]
>
> 1989 opened the door to a deregulated model of capitalism that has wreaked social and economic havoc across the world.

A note on pro-GDR revisionism

Since the fall of the Berlin Wall and the end of the Cold War represent such a crucial watershed moment in the history of socialism – a severe but ultimately temporary setback for the socialist cause – it is worth taking a closer look at revisionist interpretations of those events.

Seumas Milne's claim – that members of the ruling elites deliberately worked towards a 'restoration of capitalism', that the general public were just passive bystanders in that process and that a silent majority still supported socialism – is patently absurd.

As described above, the GDR's fate was not sealed on 9 November 1989, but on 18 March 1990, the day of its first-ever (and only) democratic election. The question whether the GDR should remain a sovereign socialist country, or whether it should join the Federal Republic and adopt its version of the market economy, was a central question during the election campaign. The turnout was 93 per cent, and the pro-market/pro-reunification parties won around 80 per cent of the popular vote between them (BPB 2014). So East Germans did not exactly sleepwalk into this.

But that was then. What about Milne's claim that *today*, a majority of East Germans have 'a positive view of [...] the GDR, and regret its passing'?

One can find evidence either way. According to a survey by Emnid, a polling company, 57 per cent of East Germans believe that the GDR had 'more positive sides than negative sides'.[15] According to a survey by Infratest Dimap, another polling company, 74 per cent of East Germans believe that reunification had brought them personally 'more advantages than disadvantages'.[16] Either way – at least a significant minority claim to miss the GDR, or substantial aspects of it. GDR-nostalgia, or *Ostalgie*, is a real

---

15 Mehrheit der Ostdeutschen bewertet DDR positiv, *Rheinische Post Online*, 26 June 2009 (http://www.rp-online.de/politik/deutschland/mehrheit-der-ostdeutschen-bewertet-ddr-positiv-aid-1.2299138).

16 Infratest Dimap (2014) 25 Jahre Mauerfall: Systemvergleich BRD / DDR Eine Studie im Auftrag der Sendereihe des MDR, Exakt – So leben wir!

phenomenon.[17] Does this confirm Milne's claim that East Germans suffer from a form of buyer's remorse?

Not necessarily. Nostalgia for the GDR does not automatically mean nostalgia for socialism. It seems natural to presume that somebody who expresses a positive view of the GDR must share the political values of the (far-)left: the GDR was, after all, a socialist country. However, the GDR was also, in a lot of ways, a very socially conservative country.

So we need to look, more specifically, at what it is that these people claim to miss about the GDR. This is where the above-mentioned Infratest Dimap survey is helpful, because contains a more detailed breakdown by policy area, asking people to benchmark East Germany against West Germany (or the reunified Germany).[18] The pattern that emerges is this: in those areas that are most clearly related to the economic system, namely 'economy', 'living standards' and 'opportunities for professional self-realisation', the FRG enjoys a clear lead. (The same is true for all areas related to political freedoms and civil liberties, although presumably, even Seumas Milne would not dispute the FRG's superiority in those categories.)

The GDR does best in the categories that are least related to the economic system, namely 'school system' and 'protection from crime'. Since the school system and the

---

17 '*Ostalgie*' is a portmanteau of *Osten* (East) and *Nostalgie* (nostalgia).

18 Ibid. More precisely, it is a mix of a relative and an absolute evaluation. A policy area can be classified as 'a strength of the GDR' or as 'a strength of the Federal Republic', but respondents who are dissatisfied with both systems have the option of picking neither.

criminal justice system were, of course, also state run in West Germany, this tells us nothing about the perceived relative merits of socialism and capitalism. It probably does tell us something about the GDR's social conservatism: the school system was highly discipline-focused, and the criminal justice system was tough and punitive.

Not least, there was very little immigration and little exposure to foreign cultures in general. The above survey does not specifically ask about immigration, but given the large and persistent East–West gap in support for anti-immigration parties, it is not a huge stretch to argue that some of today's *Ostalgie* is about that – not socialism.

None of this is to say that socialism is not popular in East Germany: it is extremely popular. But like in so many other places, it is popular *as an abstract ideal*, when explicitly divorced from the socialism that actually existed (Stöcker 2016: 202).

Milne's claim that the Berlin Wall was primarily an instrument of defence, rather than 'an arbitrary line to keep people in', is equally absurd. Neither the Berlin Wall nor the Inner-German border fence had any military relevance; neither could have served any useful defence purpose if the Cold War had turned hot at any point. But they did one thing very effectively: hold people in. Before the Wall was built, well over 200,000 people moved from the GDR to the FRG per year. Once it was built, this figure abruptly dropped to about 20,000 (based on Bade and Oltmer 2005).

But people's desire to leave never ebbed. When the border fence between Hungary and Austria was opened in September 1989, about 15,000 East Germans escaped to

Austria via Hungary in just one day (Deutsche Botschaft Budapest n.d.). This – not 'counterrevolutionaries' at the top – was always the GDR's main problem. It simply could not convince its own citizens to stay.

The Berlin Wall was not an aberration. As mentioned in Chapter 1, planned economies typically restrict people's freedom of movement, including domestically, because large-scale movements of people would make a mess of the Five-Year Plans. A ban on emigration is a logical extension of that.

East Germany was the richest country in the Warsaw Pact. It was probably the most successful, or, rather, least unsuccessful socialist economy that has ever existed. Socialism is not going to get any better than this. And yet, it still depended on a heavily fortified border and a pervasive secret police for its very survival. Emigration is, ultimately, the most honest feedback people can give about a system. It is the ultimate show of 'revealed preferences' as opposed to 'stated preferences', such as expressing a positive view of socialism in an opinion survey.

9   VENEZUELA UNDER HUGO CHÁVEZ: 'A DIFFERENT, AND A BETTER WAY OF DOING THINGS. IT'S CALLED SOCIALISM'

Socialism of the twenty-first century

The socialist experiments which were most popular with Western intellectuals were the ones that were least tainted by associations with earlier, now discredited, experiments. Intellectuals had to be able to convince themselves, and others, that they had found a genuinely novel model of socialism, which had nothing in common with those earlier ones. It was not enough for a country to just adopt socialism: it had to contain the promise of a fresh start, a promise that 'this time will be different' (see Hollander 1990: 277).

Mao-mania started at the time of the Sino-Soviet split. Hoxhaism started at the time of the Sino-Albanian split. The Cuban revolution was popular because it was home-grown. The same was true of the Sandinista revolution in Nicaragua. Pilgrims of a more romantic disposition were drawn to politically isolated places such as North Korea and Cambodia, because isolated places could not be tainted by associations with earlier, now discredited, attempts to build a socialist society. The German Democratic

Republic, in contrast, received some praise, but it never inspired starry-eyed enthusiasm.

'Venezuela-mania' is an extension of this pattern. It took off around the time that the Venezuelan government started to brand its policies internationally as a new model of socialism. It defined this new model not just in opposition to capitalism, but also, crucially, to earlier socialist models. In 2005, President Hugo Chávez was a keynote speaker at the World Social Forum, an annual conference of various anti-capitalist groups from around the world. Chávez said:

> [T]here is no doubt in my mind [...] that it is necessary to transcend capitalism [...] through socialism, true socialism, with equality and justice. [...]
>
> We have to re-invent socialism. It can't be the kind of socialism that we saw in the Soviet Union, but it will emerge as we develop new systems that are built on co-operation, not competition [...]
>
> We must transcend capitalism. But we cannot resort to state capitalism, which would be the same perversion of the Soviet Union. We must reclaim socialism as a thesis, a project and a path, but a new type of socialism, a humanist one, which puts humans and not machines or the state ahead of everything.[1]

Chávez's catchphrase – 'Socialism of the 21st Century' or '21st Century Socialism' – quickly caught on. A few months

---

1   Venezuela's Chávez closes World Social Forum with call to transcend capitalism, *Venezuela Analysis*, 31 January 2005 (https://venezuelanalysis.com/news/907).

later, it was used in headlines in the *New York Times*.[2] It turned out that adding '21st century' was all it took to cleanse the term 'socialism' of its associations with earlier attempts.

And that was, of course, the whole point. The phrase had originally been coined by Heinz Dieterich, a German-born, now Mexican, sociologist. In 1996, Dieterich had published the book *Der Sozialismus des 21. Jahrhunderts*. As he explains:

> The term [socialism] comes with a lot of baggage, and that was a problem when I wrote my book [...] If you use the term, it evokes the experience of the GDR and of the Soviet Union. If you leave it out, you exclude a lot of people whose heart still beats on the left. I wanted to illustrate the continuity of an alternative to the market economy, but I also want to make clear that it has nothing to do with the socialism of the 20th century. Hence 'Socialism of the 21st Century'.[3]

Among Western admirers of the Chávez government, the term quickly developed a life of its own. Although Dieterich was an advisor to Chávez for a while, most Western Chavistas will never have heard of him, or his

---

2   Chávez restyles Venezuela with '21st-Century Socialism', *New York Times*, 30 October 2005 (http://www.nytimes.com/2005/10/30/world/americas/chavez-restyles-venezuela-with-21stcentury-socialism.html).

3   Wir Sozialisten. Heinz Dieterich, Ex-Wirtschaftsberater südamerikanischer Staatschefs, über die Wiederkehr einer alten Ideologie. *Zeit Online*, 15 December 2011 (http://www.zeit.de/2011/51/Interview-Dieterich). Translation mine.

specific version of Marxist theory. In practice, 'Socialism of the 21st Century' simply meant 'Socialism, but without the negative connotations', or 'Socialism, but somehow different'.

It worked. A few months later, Venezuela-mania was in full swing. In 2006, a Chávez speech in Vienna attracted a crowd of about 6,000 supporters.[4] And Venezuela had become a popular pilgrimage destination. *The Guardian* reported:

> To sceptics they are naive westerners seduced by hype [...]
>
> Meet the revolutionary tourists, a wave of backpackers, artists, academics and politicians on a mission to discover if President Hugo Chávez really is forging a radical alternative to neoliberalism and capitalism. From a trickle a few years ago there are now thousands, travelling individually and on package tours, exploring a leftwing mecca which promises to build social justice in the form of '21st century socialism'.[5]

But what had actually happened in Venezuela?

Chavismo was not a complete break with Venezuela's prior economic history. Take the following description:

---

4 Successful screening of new Hugo Chávez documentary in London, Hands off Venezuela, 16 April 2015 (https://www.handsoffvenezuela.org/success ful-screening-of-new-hugo-chavez-documentary-in-london.htm).

5 Welcome to Chávez-land, the new Latin mecca for the sandalistas, *The Guardian*, 15 January 2007 (https://www.theguardian.com/world/2007/ jan/15/venezuela.rorycarroll).

Venezuela's new leaders concentrated on the oil industry as the main source of financing for their reformist economic and social policies. Using oil revenues, the government intervened significantly in the economy. [...] [T]he government addressed general social reform by spending large sums of money on education, health, electricity, potable water, and other basic projects. [...]

Increased public outlays manifested themselves most prominently in the expansion of the bureaucracy. [...] [T]he government established hundreds of new state-owned enterprises and decentralized agencies as the public sector assumed the role of primary engine of economic growth. [...] In addition to establishing new enterprises in such areas as mining, petrochemicals, and hydroelectricity, the government purchased previously private ones.

This could easily pass as an account of *Chavismo*. But it actually refers to the 1960s and 1970s (Haggerty 1990). Opponents of *Chavismo* like to point out that before Chávez, Venezuela was the richest country in Latin America. This is technically true. Before Chile overtook it in the early 2000s, Venezuela had the region's highest GDP per capita (PPP) (IMF 2017) (see Figure 9).

But it was nonetheless not an economic success story. It was a petrodollar economy, built on the world's largest proven oil reserves. In the 1960s and 1970s, Venezuela was awash with oil money, which the government spent lavishly on social programmes, public works projects, asset purchases and subsidies. Venezuela became a patronage economy, and the Venezuelan state became a client state. It was an economic model that was built on high and rising oil prices.

Figure 9   GDP per capita (PPP) in Chile and Venezuela, 1980–2016

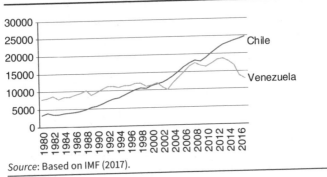

Source: Based on IMF (2017).

The 1970s therefore became the country's golden age. But in 1980, global oil prices peaked, and entered a nearly two-decade-long period of steady decline (Macrotrends n.d.). During that period, the country's economic performance became volatile and erratic. The government tried to maintain the high public spending levels that the population had grown accustomed to by borrowing and printing money. Between the early 1980s and the mid-1990s, government debt increased from less than 30 per cent of GDP to around 70 per cent (Restuccia 2010: 21). Inflation increased from about 10 per cent to over 60 per cent (ibid.: 26).

Successive governments tried to come to grips with these macroeconomic imbalances, but found it politically impossible. Adjustment packages were initiated, but never seen through. As Corrales (1999) explains:

Venezuela has been stuck in an ax-relax-collapse cycle of reform. Each cycle begins with [...] harsh cutbacks and adjustments – the 'ax.' After some initially positive results, the reforms soon lose momentum, becoming either haphazardly implemented or prematurely abandoned – the 'relax' stage. This culminates in yet another economic crisis – the 'collapse.' [...] Venezuela is thus neither a case of reform avoidance nor of neoliberal transition, but rather of reform non-consolidation.

It is in these conditions that the left-wing populism, of which *Chavismo* would become the most extreme variant, was born. Both of Hugo Chávez's predecessors had campaigned on an explicitly anti-'neoliberal' platform. Both had blamed external forces for the country's woes, and promised a return to the old, free-spending ways of the 1970s. Once in office, both of them quickly had to U-turn, simply because denying the existence of economic constraints does not make those constraints go away. Venezuela had become the perfect illustration of Thomas Sowell's dictum that 'the first lesson of economics is scarcity: There is never enough of anything to satisfy all those who want it. The first lesson of politics is to disregard the first lesson of economics'.

Had oil prices remained constant after Chávez's election, his presidency might well have followed the same pattern: some initial populist grandstanding, then a U-turn with spending cuts and adjustment measures. This might well have been followed by the emergence of the next populist, who would have denounced Chávez as a neoliberal sell-out.

But Chávez was exceptionally lucky. Oil prices reached their historic trough a few weeks before he took office, and then rose steeply and almost constantly for the next fifteen years, surpassing even their 1970s levels (Macrotrends 2018). Even today, oil prices are not particularly low by historical standards. They have merely fallen back to where they were in the mid-2000s, i.e. at around the time Venezuela-mania started (see Figure 10).

Figure 10 Oil prices in current $US, 1989–2017, by presidency

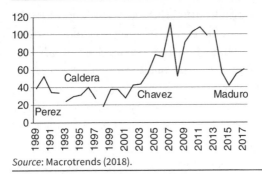

Source: Macrotrends (2018).

Due to the oil price boom, Venezuela's oil revenue more than quintupled in real terms (Mahoney 2017: 5–6). Chávez had promised a return to the free-spending ways of the 1970s. The oil price explosion meant that he could actually deliver that. Government spending increased from under 30 per cent of GDP to over 40 per cent (Quandl 2018).[6]

---

6   See also: How Chávez and Maduro have impoverished Venezuela, *The Economist*, 6 April 2017 (http://www.economist.com/news/finance-and-econ omics/21720289-over-past-year-74-venezuelans-lost-average-87kg-weight -how).

The spending splurge was not entirely without precedent – it was a turbocharged version of what had happened in the 1970s – and something similar would probably have happened under any other government as well. What made Chavismo different was the copious use of microeconomic interventions, such as price controls and exchange rate controls,[7] which then begat further interventions. When the initial interventions did not produce the desired effect, or when private sector actors did not behave in the way the government wanted them to behave, the government railed against the industry in question, and intervened in more heavy-handed ways. This often culminated in 'revenge nationalisations'.[8]

For example, in 2009, *The Economist* reported:

> A rice plant belonging to Cargill, an American company, was seized [...] Two plants owned by Empresas Polar, Venezuela's largest private conglomerate, were taken over 'temporarily' to enforce production of price-controlled rice. Like other companies, Polar argues that controls force it to sell at a loss. [...] Mr Chávez rejects this argument, and threatened to expropriate all Polar's businesses[9]

---

7   Meat, sugar scarce in Venezuela stores, *Washington Post*, 8 February 2007 (http://www.washingtonpost.com/wp-dyn/content/article/2007/02/08/AR2007020801240.html).

8   Venezuela's nationalizations under Chávez, *Reuters*, 1 December 2011 (https://www.reuters.com/article/venezuela-nationalizations/factbox-venezuelas-nationalizations-under-chavez-idUSN1E79I0Z520111201).

9   Feeding frenzy, *The Economist*, 12 March 2009 (http://www.economist.com/node/13278245).

Thus, under the Chávez government, nationalisations were not led by strategic considerations. The government did not have a recognisable theory about which sectors ought to be state run and in which sectors private ownership was tolerable. Instead, nationalisations were used as a disciplining tool, a way to punish recalcitrant private sector actors. In this sense, 'Socialism of the 21st Century' was an ad hoc 'revenge socialism'.

Previous Venezuelan governments had been interventionist, but they had remained broadly within the rule of law. The Chávez government was different in that it rode roughshod over the rule of law. This can be seen in the decline of various key governance indicators (Figure 11).

Figure 11 Key governance indicators, 2000–2015

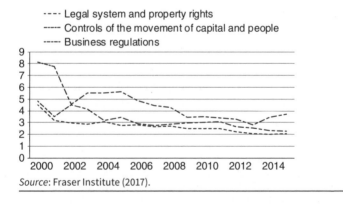

Source: Fraser Institute (2017).

One need not be a believer in free markets to realise that Chavismo could never have been a workable economic model. The fact that price controls lead to shortages is not Friedmanite or Hayekian economics – it is just GCSE-level economics. The fact that a predatory government, with no respect for the rule of law, deters economic activity is not even economics at all – it is just basic common sense. Nor does it take a lot of imagination to see that a rapid expansion of public spending programmes increases the scope for corruption, patronage and nepotism.

And indeed, the problems we currently associate with Venezuela long predate the drop in oil prices. They were already in evidence at the height of the boom. In 2007, *The Guardian* reported:

> Welcome to Venezuela, a booming economy with a difference. Food shortages are plaguing the country at the same time that oil revenues are driving a spending splurge [...] Milk has all but vanished from shops. Distraught mothers ask how they are supposed to feed their infants. [...] [E]ggs and sugar are also a memory. [...] When supplies do arrive long queues form instantly. Purchases are rationed and hands are stamped to prevent cheating. The sight of a milk truck reportedly prompted a near-riot last week. Up to a quarter of staple food supplies have been disrupted[10]

Over time, such shortages became more severe, and affected a wider range of products. In 2013, when oil prices were still abnormally high, *The Guardian* reported:

---

10 Venezuela scrambles for food despite oil boom, *The Guardian*, 14 November 2007 (https://www.theguardian.com/world/2007/nov/14/venezuela.inter national).

> [C]ertain items long gone from the shelves are hitting a particular nerve with Venezuelans. Toilet paper, rice, coffee, and cornflour [...] have become emblematic of more than just an economic crisis. [...]
>
> For Asdrubal Oliveros, an economist at Ecoanalítica, [...] this [...] is the result of [...] price controls and [...] the decrease in agricultural production resulting from seized companies and land expropriations. 'More than 3m hectares were expropriated during 2004–2010. [...] That's a perverse model that kills off any productivity,' he says.
>
> Venezuela's central bank, which has been publishing a scarcity index since 2009, puts this year's figure at an average [...] similar to countries undergoing civil strife or war-like conditions.[11]

But for as long as the oil price boom lasted, many other economic and social indicators looked very positive. Western admirers of Chavismo attributed all of those gains to Chávez's policies.

As mentioned, Chávez defined his version of socialism explicitly in opposition to previous models. This was not empty rhetoric. Under Chavismo, there were genuine attempts to create alternative models of collective ownership and democratic participation in economic life. In particular, the formation of worker cooperatives and various

---

11 Venezuela food shortages: 'No one can explain why a rich country has no food', *The Guardian*, 26 September 2013 (https://www.theguardian .com/global-development/poverty-matters/2013/sep/26/venezuela-food -shortages-rich-country-cia).

forms of social enterprises was heavily promoted. Exact figures are hard to come by, but, according to Piñeiro Harnecker (2009: 309), the number of worker-run cooperatives increased from fewer than 1,000 when Chávez was first elected to well over 30,000 in less than a decade. By the end of Chávez's second term, cooperatives accounted for about 8 per cent of Venezuela's GDP and 14 per cent of its workforce (ibid.).

Venezuelan socialism would later show many of the negative features associated with earlier forms of socialism, but it was never government policy to replicate any of those earlier models. When Western Chavistas insisted that the Venezuelan government was trying to create a different model of socialism, they were not deluding themselves.

Data on the economic performance of this state-created cooperative sector are scarce, but it is safe to say that the sector never became self-supporting. It remained dependent on government subsidies throughout. But then, its primary purpose was never an economic one. The social sector was seen as a training ground where workers could develop a socialist mindset, and thus an incubator for a more advanced stage of socialism. The government believed that working in an economic environment characterised by cooperation, sharing and joint democratic decision-making would instil socialist values and habits in them (ibid.: 313–14). This was part of their programme of building socialism from below, rather than imposing it from on high.

It did not work out that way. Piñeiro Harnecker (2009) conducted a study into the attitudes of Venezuelan cooperative workers, based on interviews and surveys. Although the tone of the paper suggests that the author is strongly sympathetic to the Chavista government, she concludes, with barely concealed disappointment, that the cooperative sector has not had that effect. She notes (ibid.: 316–17):

> It soon became clear to Venezuelan policy makers that many cooperatives were behaving like capitalist enterprises, seeking to maximize their net revenue [...] For example, rather than supplying their products to local markets [...] some have chosen to export them to other countries where they can sell them at higher prices [...] Also, many cooperatives have refrained from accepting new members. [...] [T]hey fear that including new members is going to affect their income. [...]
>
> [M]any members I interviewed were against having to start paying taxes [...] They asserted that [...] they are already contributing enough to their local communities. [...]
>
> All this has occurred despite President Chávez's frequent calls for solidaristic behaviour.

To her great dismay, the cooperative workers she interviews often sound very small-c conservative (ibid.: 324):

> [T]he most common argument used to oppose contributing to neighboring communities was the claim that their cooperatives' economic success was the result of their own efforts alone. Ignoring the inadequate capabilities

that some have [...] some workers claimed that community members 'were not trying hard enough' and had to 'help themselves like we are doing in the cooperatives' [...] Others stated that their revenue was not large enough to be redistributed, as if only they were entitled to it.

Many cooperative workers were, of course, engaged in their communities in various ways. But so are many people who do *not* work for cooperatives, and Piñeiro Harnecker provides no evidence that cooperative membership made a difference. She does, however, find that cooperatives' social engagement remained limited to their own local areas. Some were happy to support their communities, but that 'community' was not the nation as a whole and 'there were only a few instances where cooperative members' solidarity towards distant communities had materialized' (ibid.: 325–26).

Realising that cooperatives were not a stepping stone towards socialism, the Chávez government grew increasingly disillusioned with them. As Chávez himself said (ibid.: 331–32):

'The model of cooperatives [cooperativismo] does not guarantee socialism because a cooperative is collective private property; that is, if we are 20 in a cooperative, we are going to work for the benefit of us 20, and that is merely capitalism. Cooperatives need to be impelled towards socialism'. [...]

Chávez suggested that an enterprise is only 'socialist' or of 'social property' if it is controlled by society, thus

> satisfying social needs. An enterprise of social property, he elucidated, 'belongs to the entire community and [...] operates under a direction, a plan; it produces in accordance with the interests not only of the cooperative members but of the entire community'.

This is also Piñeiro Harnecker's conclusion. Capitalism, she laments, cannot be overcome via the formation of co-operatives, because these fail to promote socialist norms. They are just a different business model under capitalism. What is needed, instead, is planning at a higher level, a level which takes the needs of the whole community, not just of one organisation, into account.

Despite the emphasis on how Venezuelan socialism was supposed to be incomparably different from Soviet socialism, this sounds suspiciously like the Soviet Union again.

Chávez's pilgrims

When a country seems to be making rapid economic and/ or social progress, it is bound to attract some positive media coverage. Other Latin American countries, such as Mexico and Brazil, were growing at comparable rates, and their progress was duly noted in the international press as well.

But favourable coverage of Venezuela was different. Other countries were praised for specific policies. Venezuela was praised in more abstract terms; it was praised, first and foremost, as an economic and social *model*, with specific policies (for example, public housing programmes) being an afterthought. Indeed, one can find lengthy articles waxing lyrical about Venezuela without really saying anything about what that country actually did, other than being 'an inspiration' and 'an alternative to global capitalism'.

In 2007, Naomi Klein, arguably the trendiest Western intellectual of the 2000s (and beyond), wrote:

> The staunchest opponents of neoliberal economics in Latin America have been winning election after election. [...] [C]itizens had renewed their faith in the power of democracy to improve their lives. [...]
>
> Latin America's mass movements [...] are learning how to build shock absorbers into their organizing models. [...] [T]he progressive networks in Venezuela are [...] highly decentralized, with power dispersed at the grassroots and community levels, through thousands of neighborhood councils and co-ops. [...]
>
> The new leaders in Latin America are also becoming better prepared for the kinds of shocks produced by volatile markets. [...] Surrounded by turbulent financial waters, Latin America is creating a zone of relative economic calm and predictability, a feat presumed impossible in the globalization era.[12]

In 2009, Noam Chomsky, perhaps the archetype of the Western intellectual, travelled to Venezuela, and said:

---

12 Latin America's shock resistance. Recent events in the region show how societies can recover from extreme capitalism, *The Nation*, 8 November 2007 (https://www.thenation.com/article/latin-americas-shock-resistance/).

[W]hat's so exciting about at last visiting Venezuela is that I can see how a better world is being created [...] The transformations that Venezuela is making toward the creation of another socio-economic model could have a global impact.[13]

In 2012, journalist and author Owen Jones went on a pilgrimage to Venezuela as well, and reported that 'Venezuela is an inspiration to the world, it really does show that there is an alternative. I met so many people who told me how their lives had changed since the election of President Chávez' (Venezuela Solidarity Campaign 2012).

In the *Independent*, Jones elaborated further:

Chávez [...] is the first Venezuelan president to care about the poor. [...]

Venezuela's oligarchs froth at the mouth with their hatred of Chávez [...] Why do they despise him? As Chávez's vice-minister for Europe [...] puts it to me, it's because 'the people who clean their houses are now politically more important than them'. Under Chávez, the poor have become a political power that cannot be ignored [...]

[H]e has proved it is possible to lead a popular, progressive government that breaks with neo-liberal dogma. Perhaps that is why he is so hated after all.[14]

---

13 Noam Chomsky meets with Chávez in Venezuela, *Venezuela Analysis*, 27 August 2009 (https://venezuelanalysis.com/news/4748).

14 Hugo Chávez proves you can lead a progressive, popular government that says no to neo-liberalism, *Independent*, 8 October 2012 (http://www

One of the key themes of Venezuela-mania was that Venezuela was not just a huge success story in its own right, but also a model to be learned from. In Owen Jones's words: 'It's so important to me that we don't look at Latin America as something that's just happening elsewhere, but as something which gives us all hope'.[15]

Seumas Milne went on a pilgrimage to Venezuela as well in 2012. He saw the 'transformation of Latin America' as 'one of the decisive changes reshaping the global order'. Milne spoke of a 'tide of progressive change', which had brought governments to office that have:

> redistributed wealth and power [and] rejected western neoliberal orthodoxy [...] In the process they have [...] demonstrated to the rest of the world that there are, after all, economic and social alternatives in the 21st century. Central to that process has been Hugo Chávez and his Bolivarian revolution in Venezuela. It is Venezuela [...] that has spearheaded the movement of radical change [...]
>
> To visit any rally or polling station during the election campaign was to be left in no doubt as to who Chávez represents: the poor, the non-white, the young, the disabled – in other words, the dispossessed majority [...] Euphoria at the result among the poor was palpable.

.independent.co.uk/voices/comment/hugo-Chávez-proves-you-can-lead -a-progressive-popular-government-that-says-no-to-neo-liberalism-82 02738.html).

15 Corbyn and hard-left fawning over Socialist Venezuela (prior collapse) (https://www.youtube.com/watch?v=VSIQAKpaR20).

Milne sees Venezuelan socialism not just as admirable in itself, but specifically as an alternative to European social democracy:

> Venezuela's [...] innovative social programmes, experiments in direct democracy and success in bringing resources under public control offer lessons to anyone interested in social justice and new forms of socialist politics in the rest of the world. [...] Venezuela and its Latin American allies have demonstrated that it's no longer necessary to accept a failed economic model, as many social democrats in Europe still do.[16]

The General Secretary of Unite the Union, Len McCluskey, commented on Chávez's re-election in 2012 (Venezuela Solidarity Campaign 2012: 5):

> We welcome this result which is a clear endorsement of Hugo Chávez's progressive social policies. Venezuela shows that governments that put the needs of ordinary working people first can expect strong support at the ballot box. [...] Europe might want to learn the obvious lessons from Venezuela.

Andy Slaughter, the MP for Hammersmith, added that 'This is a great result for the people of Venezuela, progressive politics, and the democratic process' (ibid.).

---

16 The Chávez victory will be felt far beyond Latin America, *The Guardian*, 9 October 2012 (https://www.theguardian.com/commentisfree/2012/oct/09/Chávez-victory-beyond-latin-america).

Chávez's death in 2013 triggered an avalanche of statements celebrating his legacy and lessons for the rest of the world. Owen Jones wrote:

> Chávez became an icon for Venezuela's long-suffering poor. [...] [H]is policies transformed the lives of millions of previously ignored Venezuelans. [...] Chávez was a democratically elected champion of the poor. [...] He demonstrated that it is possible to resist the neo-liberal dogma that holds sway over much of humanity. He will be mourned by millions of Venezuelans – and understandably so. [17]

The General Secretary of the Communication Workers Union (CWU), Bill Hayes, said 'Hugo Chávez helped to inspire a new socialism for the 21st century and provided the spark that lit up the whole South American continent' (Venezuela Solidarity Campaign 2013: 7).

The General Secretary of UNISON, David Prentis, believed that 'Hugo Chávez will be remembered for his continuous struggle to raise up the poor, his commitment to social justice and his dedication to fairness and equality' (ibid.: 7).

The General Secretary of the Trades Union Congress (TUC), Frances O'Grady, thought that 'Hugo Chávez saw

---

17 Hugo Chávez was a democrat, not a dictator, and showed a progressive alternative to neo-liberalism is both possible and popular, *Independent*, 6 March 2013 (http://www.independent.co.uk/voices/comment/hugo-cha vez-was-a-democrat-not-a-dictator-and-showed-a-progressive-alterna tive-to-neo-liberalism-is-8522329.html).

the implementation of an impressive and highly progressive programme, lifting millions out of poverty and providing citizens with healthcare and education' (ibid.: 7).

Gabi Zimmer MEP, the chair of the European United Left – Nordic Green Left Group in the European Parliament, said 'His fight for the oppressed, hit by an insatiable and ruthless economic system, earned and continues to earn him the enmity of the powerful, but also the unwavering support of his people and the oppressed' (ibid.: 6).

Jon Trickett, the MP for Hemsworth, called Chávez 'a titan of a man. Progressive, democratic, garrulous. In turbulent times he made change happen for the poorest' (ibid.: 6).

Two Early Day Motions were tabled in the UK parliament. One of them, signed by 25 MPs from four different parties, read:

> [T]his House [...] acknowledges the huge contribution he [Chávez] made to conquering poverty in his country and region [...] and the way he spoke for the poorest and most marginalised people in Latin America.[18]

The other one, signed by nine MPs from three different parties, read:

> [T]his House [...] notes that he [Chávez] led the Bolivarian Revolution which lifted millions of people out of abject

---

18 President Chávez of Venezuela, Early Day Motion 1154, 6 March 2013 (http://www.parliament.uk/business/publications/business-papers/commons/early-day-motions/edm-detail1/?edmnumber=1154&session=2012-13).

poverty in Venezuela; further notes that he was a steadfast and unflinching opponent of Western imperialism and a supporter of the poor and oppressed everywhere; and believes that his memory will long survive his death through his extraordinary achievements.[19]

At a pro-Chávez rally in London, Jeremy Corbyn said 'Chávez [...] showed us that there is a different, and a better way of doing things. It's called socialism [...] [I]n his death, we will march on, to that better, just, peaceful and hopeful world'.[20]

In an interview, Diane Abbott MP said 'Chávez is so important [...] because he showed another world is possible. He put helping the poor, raising the living standards of the very poorest, at the top of his agenda'.[21]

At a pro-Venezuela event in the UK, Abbott said:

[H]e showed the region that it was possible to do things differently [...] the Chávez regime had the best results in fighting poverty and increasing the living standards of the very poorest of any regime in the region. And that's one of the reasons why I feel particularly passionate about defending the revolution of Venezuela and the Chávez legacy.[22]

---

19 UK Parliament: Early Day Motion 1153: Death of President Hugo Chávez, 6 March 2013 (http://www.parliament.uk/edm/2012-13/1153).

20 British MP Corbyn Praises Chávez at London Vigil, 7 March 2013 (https://www.youtube.com/watch?v=iYEfYsZ8SaA).

21 Corbyn and hard-left fawning over socialist Venezuela (https://www.youtube.com/watch?v=VSIQAKpaR20).

22 Ibid.

In a documentary called 'Chávez: a portrait from Europe', John McDonnell MP, now the Shadow Chancellor of the Exchequer, said:

> [Chávez] lit a spark that really started a firebrand [...] Venezuela and the Bolivarian Revolution became an item on the agenda for all socialists [...]
>
> The Bolivarian Revolution [...] came at a time as well when capitalism went into yet another one of its crises. So here you had capitalism in crisis, demonstrating that it would always be crisis-ridden [...] And then in contrast with that you had the Bolivarian Revolution going on in Venezuela, where [...] poverty was being addressed, employment was being raised, public services were being invested in [...]
>
> So here you had the contrast between capitalism in crisis, and socialism in action.[23]

This was the zenith of the Bolivarian Revolution's popularity among Western commentators.

After the zenith

In March 2013, Javier Corrales, a Latin America expert, wrote in *Foreign Policy* magazine:

---

23 Hugo Chávez: un retrato desde Europa – a portrait from Europe. Telesur documentary directed by Pablo Roldán (https://www.youtube.com/watch?v=dpNrh-u3S78).

[Chávez's] designated successor, Vice President Nicolás Maduro, [...] will find himself commanding a remarkable store of political capital. Yet Maduro [...] will also inherit one of the most dysfunctional economies in the Americas – and just as the bill for the deceased leader's policies comes due.[24]

This turned out to be an understatement. Soon after, Venezuela's economic woes turned into a full-blown crisis. The crisis provoked widespread discontent, in response to which the government increasingly resorted to authoritarian measures. Venezuela's international reputation suffered. Venezuela ceased to be a showcase that Western socialists would triumphantly hold against their opponents, and turned into an anti-showcase which their opponents would hold against *them*.

At that point, the tone among Western Chavistas changed noticeably. Pro-Venezuela articles, which had so far tended to be hopeful and optimistic, became angry and defensive. The emphasis shifted from the supposed achievements of *Chavismo* to whataboutery, and to questioning the motives of *Chavismo*'s critics both in Venezuela and internationally.

In 2014, Owen Jones wrote an article for the *Independent* entitled 'Socialism's critics look at Venezuela and say, "We told you so". But they are wrong'. Jones acknowledges the existence of 'recent economic troubles', but the emphasis

---

24 The house that Chávez built, *Foreign Policy*, 7 March 2013 (https://foreign policy.com/2013/03/07/the-house-that-chavez-built/).

of the article is on the problems of the pre-Chávez era ('let's have some context'), and on the violence committed by parts of the opposition. It culminated in the claim that '[t]hose who relish using Venezuela's troubles for political point-scoring have no interest in the truth'.[25]

Seumas Milne took this logic several steps further. After going on another pilgrimage to Venezuela in 2014, Milne wrote an article entitled 'Venezuela shows that protest can be a defence of privilege – Street action is now regularly used with western backing to target elected governments in the interests of elites'. In his account, the people who were protesting against shortages of food and medicines were a coalition of foreign stooges funded by 'imperialist' governments, and old elites trying to reclaim their privileges:

> US-linked opposition leaders [...] launched a campaign to oust Maduro [...]
>
> [The] protests have all the hallmarks of an anti-democratic rebellion, shot through with class privilege and racism. Overwhelmingly middle class and confined to wealthy white areas, the protests have now shrunk to firebombings and ritual fights with the police [...] Support for the government, meanwhile, remains solid in working class areas. [...]

---

25 Socialism's critics look at Venezuela and say, 'We told you so'. But they are wrong, *Independent*, 28 February 2014 (https://web.archive.org/web/20140302210757/http://www.independent.co.uk/voices/comment/owen-jones-socialisms-critics-look-at-venezuela-and-say-we-told-you-so-but-they-are-wrong-9155295.html).

It's hardly surprising in the circumstances that Maduro regards what's been going on as Ukraine-style US-backed destabilisation, as he told me. [...] Evidence for the US subversion of Venezuela [...] is voluminous.[26]

We can see parallels here with earlier pilgrimage accounts from the utopias of yesteryear (see Hollander 1990: 160–67). Pilgrims had always struggled with the idea that there could be discontent in a People's State (except maybe insofar as the construction of socialism was still unfinished business). Under socialism, The People are in charge. So how could there be protests? Logically, The People cannot protest against themselves. So dissenters had to be defined as a group apart from (and hostile to) The People, such as class enemies, counterrevolutionaries, foreign spies, etc.

After its zenith, Venezuela-mania turned into something quite similar, and 'Socialism of the 21st Century' started to look suspiciously like socialism of the 20th century again.

Seumas Milne was in good company. Mark Weisbrot, the co-director of the Center for Economic and Policy Research (CEPR), also found:

Venezuela's poor have not joined the right-wing opposition protests [...] it's not just the poor who are abstaining

---

26 Venezuela shows that protest can be a defence of privilege – Street action is now regularly used with western backing to target elected governments in the interests of elites, *The Guardian*, 9 April 2014 (https://www.theguard-ian.com/commentisfree/2014/apr/09/venezuela-protest-defence-privilege-maduro-elites).

> – in Caracas, it's almost everyone outside of a few rich areas [...] where small groups of protesters engage in nightly battles with security forces, throwing rocks and firebombs [...]
>
> I came away skeptical of the narrative [...] that increasing shortages of basic foods and consumer goods are a serious motivation for the protests. [...]
>
> The class nature of this fight has always been stark and inescapable [...] Walking past the crowd that showed up for [...] the anniversary of Chávez's death, it was a sea of working-class Venezuelans [...] What a contrast to the disgruntled masses of Los Palos Grandes, with $40,000 Grand Cherokee Jeeps bearing the slogan of the moment: SOS VENEZUELA.[27]

Neil Findlay, a member of the Scottish Parliament, also claimed 'There is a seismic shift that the corporations and their US allies detest. [...] They hate the fact that the people are in control and not them' (Venezuela Solidarity Campaign 2014: 9).

Bethan Jenkins, a Member of the National Assembly for Wales, believed 'Venezuela is an oil rich country. Of course America are [sic] going to be looking to Venezuela to destabilise the situation. Look at what happened in Iraq' (ibid.: 8).

Fernando Perez MEP, a member of the Party of European Socialists, also claimed 'The chaos, destabilisation

---

27 The truth about Venezuela: a revolt of the well-off, not a 'terror campaign', *The Guardian*, 20 March 2014 (https://www.theguardian.com/commentis free/2014/mar/20/venezuela-revolt-truth-not-terror-campaign).

and violence by the Right and the oligarchy are an attempt to illegitimately overthrow Nicolás Maduro' (ibid.: 8).

Writing for *Jacobin Magazine*, George Ciccariello-Maher asserted that:

> [T]hose seeking to restore the feudal privileges of the deposed Venezuelan *ancien régime* have attempted to harness largely middle-class student protests to depose the Maduro government [...] Well-heeled domestic elites (whose English shows no trace of an accent) have taken to Twitter and the international media [...] [T]he reactionary opposition takes to the streets, fueled by a racial and class hatred.[28]

He vaguely acknowledged the government's increasingly authoritarian character, but saw it as justifiable:

> If we are against unnecessary brutality, there is nevertheless a radically democratic form of brutality that we cannot disavow entirely. This is the same brutality that 'dragged the Bourbons off the throne' [...] This was not brutality for brutality's sake [...] It is instead a strange paradox: egalitarian brutality, the radically democratic dictatorship of the wretched of the earth. Those smeared today [...] are in fact the most direct and organic expression of the wretched of the Venezuelan earth.

---

28 Venezuelan Jacobins. Only the Venezuelan sans culottes can save the Bolivarian Revolution, *Jacobin Magazine*, 13 March 2014 (https://www.jacobin mag.com/2014/03/venezuelan-jacobins).

Jeremy Corbyn also saw sinister forces at work. At an event organised by the Venezuela Solidarity Campaign in 2015, he accused the US of trying to destabilise Venezuela and undermine its government. It never became clear which specific actions Corbyn was referring to, but he evoked historical examples of US involvement in military coups (especially in Chile in 1973), and then asked, as a rhetorical question, whether today's situation was really that different.[29]

By then, Venezuela's economy was in freefall, but Corbyn still celebrated its 'successes':

> When we celebrate – and it is a cause for celebration – the achievements of Venezuela, in jobs, in housing, in health, in education, but above all, its role in the whole world as a completely different place, then we do that because we recognise what they have achieved, and how they're trying to achieve it.[30]

A few weeks later, Corbyn wrote an article (now deleted) for his website, in which he claimed:

---

29 This was certainly in line with the rhetoric of the Maduro government itself. For example, after Chávez's death, Nicolás Maduro raised the question of whether US agents might have been responsible, by deliberately infecting him with cancer. See: Scientists will study possible Chávez poisoning, Venezuelan leader says, *CNN*, 13 March 2013 (http://edition.cnn.com/2013/03/12/world/americas/venezuela-Chávez-death-investigation/index.html).

30 British MP Jeremy Corbyn Speaks out for Venezuela, *Telesur*, 6 June 2015 (http://www.telesurtv.net/english/news/British-MP-Jeremy-Corbyn-Speaks-Out-For-Venezuela-20150605-0033.html).

[H]istory is being played out to its fullest extent in Venezuela, where the Bolivarian revolution is in full swing and is providing inspiration across a whole continent. [...] Venezuela is seriously conquering poverty by emphatically rejecting [...] Neo Liberal policies [...]

Success for radical policies in Venezuela is being achieved by providing for the poorest, liberating resources, but above all by popular education and involvement. As with Cuba the threat to the USA by Venezuela is not military [...] It is far more insidious, a threat by example of what social justice can achieve.[31]

In this, Corbyn was a bit behind the curve. By then, most Western Chavistas had simply fallen silent on the issue. The remaining ones, however, doubled down.

Coming full circle

As shown above, after the zenith, Western Chavistas convinced themselves that there was no legitimate discontent in Venezuela – just CIA-funded stooges and disgraced oligarchs. At some point, they took this narrative several steps further.

Initially, the 'stooges and oligarchs' had been accused of cynically taking advantage of an economic crisis, in order to further their own political agenda. This soon morphed into accusations of actively *causing* that same economic

---

31 Venezuela, 27 July 2015 (https://web.archive.org/web/20150727072253/http://jeremycorbyn.org.uk/articles/venezuela/).

crisis. They were now no longer just opportunists who tried to instrumentalise the country's problems for their own ends. They were the ones who had *created* those very problems in the first place.

Western Chavistas began to sound a lot like Soviet propagandists from the 1930s, railing against 'saboteurs', 'wreckers', 'hoarders', 'speculators', 'profiteers', etc.[32]

The Venezuela Solidarity Campaign argued (2016: 2):

Right wing forces have waged an economic campaign reminiscent of the destabilisation of Allende's government in Chile in the 1970s. [...] [T]his economic war has attacked the poorest in society through artificially created shortages, price speculation, and black marketeering in basic necessities, while blaming the government for the resulting hardship.

Peter Bolton, a Research Fellow at the Council on Hemispheric Affairs, wrote:

[B]usiness sectors friendly to the opposition are waging an aggressive and protracted campaign of economic sabotage to deliberately stir up social unrest to destabilize and discredit the governing Chavista bloc [...] [T]hese hostile sectors have been engaging in acts such as hoarding and price speculation and have purposely generated scarcity in pursuit of calculated chaos. [...]

---

32 Although this was partly a compositional effect: the mainstream left had fallen silent on Venezuela, leaving only the hardliners behind.

Problems inevitably arise because this elite already holds the reins and can aggressively resist a recalibration of economic and social power. In 1998, the highly corrupt business class controlled almost every economic structure imaginable [...] [T]heir ability to throw a wrench in the government's efforts for reform has been formidable. [...]

By creating [...] scarcity, the elite were essentially trying to starve the public into rejecting the revolution, a tactic influenced by the United States' economic blockade against Cuba.[33]

Writing for MintPress News, Caleb Maupin argued:

The problems plaguing the Venezuelan economy are not due to some inherent fault in socialism, but to artificially low oil prices and sabotage by forces hostile to the revolution. [...] [P]rivate food processing and importing corporations have launched a coordinated campaign of sabotage. This [...] has resulted in inflation and food shortages.[34]

John Wight, a writer and journalist who has written for *The Guardian*, the *Independent*, the *Huffington Post*, etc., wrote for *Russia Today*:

---

33 The other explanation for Venezuela's economic crisis, Council on Hemispheric Affairs, 24 March 2016 (http://www.coha.org/the-other-explanation-for-venezuelas-economic-crisis-2/).

34 US-led economic war, not socialism, is tearing Venezuela apart, MintPress News, 12 July 2016.

Since Maduro came to office, the global economic climate has combined with a determined campaign conducted by the [...] oligarchs and their supporters to plunge Venezuela into an economic, social and political crisis [...] [T]here is a shortage of basic goods on supermarket shelves, which Maduro has blamed on an orchestrated policy by his political opponents of hoarding food supplies in order to foment social unrest.[35]

Eva Maria, a Venezuelan-born writer, believed that Chavismo had simply not gone far enough on the road to socialism, and that this timidity enabled capitalist 'saboteurs' to undermine the economy:

[S]ocialism did not cause the crisis, but the opposite: the popular measures enacted during the most prosperous years of the revolution were never socialist, but rather attempts to fix capitalism [...] From the beginning, long-established local capitalists worked with the new bureaucracy to take advantage of the system. [...] This situation, when combined with [...] right-wing tactics to sabotage any progressive measures, gave rise to a crisis [...] [H]esitance to go all the way against capitalism as a system has stalled the process [...] [U]nless a system takes the levers of power away from capitalists and

---

35 Venezuela, South America, and the return of the oligarchs, *Russia Today*, 16 May 2016 (https://www.rt.com/op-edge/343201-venezuela-south-amer ica-oligarchs/).

puts in the hands of workers, gains will always be rolled back.[36]

Writing in *Jacobin Magazine*, George Ciccariello-Maher blamed the crisis on 'capitalist sabotage of production', and on an opposition that 'has sought to stoke crisis, destabilize the government, and to make the country ungovernable'. He was convinced that 'The situation that prevails is not the result of too much socialism, but too little'. The solution, then, was to go the whole hog:

> There is no coherent understanding of revolution that doesn't involve defeating our enemies as we build the new society. [...] We cannot defeat such dangers without weapons [...]
>
> No one would claim that the Venezuelan masses are in power today, but the past twenty years have seen them come closer than ever before. Their enemies and ours are in the streets, burning and looting in the name of their own class superiority [...]
>
> The only path forward is to deepen and radicalize the Bolivarian process [...] The only way out of the Venezuelan crisis today lies decisively to the Left: [...] in the construction of a real socialist alternative[37]

---

36 Why 'twenty-first-century socialism' failed, *Jacobin Magazine*, 4 August 2017 (https://www.jacobinmag.com/2016/08/venezuela-chavez-maduro-pink -tide-oil-bureaucracy).

37 Which Way Out of the Venezuelan Crisis?, *Jacobin Magazine*, 29 July 2017 (https://www.jacobinmag.com/2017/07/venezuela-elections-chavez -maduro-bolivarianism).

This style of thinking was brought to its logical conclusion by Ken Livingstone, the former Mayor of London, who told *The Times*:

> Hugo Chávez did not execute the establishment elite, he allowed them to continue so they're still there. I think there's a lot of rumours they've been blocking the important food and medicines and things like that because they control a lot of the companies. And America has got a long record of undermining any leftwing government as well.[38]

Livingstone later told *Talk Radio*:

> One of the things that Chávez did when he came to power, he didn't kill all the oligarchs. [...] He allowed them to live, to carry on. I suspect a lot of them are using their power and control over imports and exports to make it difficult and to undermine Maduro.[39]

---

38 Livingstone backs Maduro and blames US meddling for Venezuela collapse, *The Times*, 1 August 2017 (https://www.thetimes.co.uk/article/living stone-backs-maduro-and-blames-us-meddling-for-venezuela-collapse -kr5wjkh2h).

39 Ken Livingstone: Venezuela crisis due to Chávez's failure to kill oligarchs, *The Guardian*, 3 August 2017 (https://www.theguardian.com/politics/2017/ aug/03/ken-livingstone-venezuela-crisis-hugo-Chávez-oligarchs). This is not the same as saying that the Venezuelan government *should* kill 'the oligarchs'. Livingstone did not literally call for mass murder. But he clearly does think that these ill-defined 'elites' are the cause of the crisis, and it follows that killing them would be one possible solution to it (whether or not it is Livingstone's preferred solution).

This was when things had come full circle. At this point, the illusion that Venezuelan socialism was completely different from any of the discredited previous attempts evaporated.

The aftermath: not real socialism – again

At the time of writing, Venezuelan socialism is transitioning from stage two to stage three. The emerging consensus is that Venezuela's economy never had much to do with socialism, and that holding this example against socialists is intellectually lazy and ignorant.

Mentioning Venezuela is already widely considered a cheap shot, a cue for eye-rolling and scoffing.

John Prescott, the former First Secretary of State and Deputy Prime Minister, recently wrote:

> Venezuela is being used as another stick to beat Jeremy Corbyn [...] Not just by the Tory Government but also by a small band of his own MPs who actively campaigned to remove Corbyn over a year ago. None of these Bitterite [a portmanteau of 'bitter Blairite'] MPs have raised the issue of Venezuela in the House of Commons before.[40]

Brian Wilson, the former Minister of State for Foreign and Commonwealth Affairs, as well as Minister of State for Trade, wrote that 'Those who gloat over its [Venezuela's]

---

40 Venezuela used as another stick to beat Jeremy Corbyn but he will survive regime change call, *Daily Mirror*, 12 August 2017 (http://www.mirror .co.uk/news/politics/john-prescott-venezuela-used-another-10976707).

tragedy, in pursuit of a domestic political point should be called on to answer questions as well as asking them'.[41]

Mary Dejevsky, a columnist for *The Independent* newspaper, talked about a 'Venezuela fixation' and asserted:

> The fact is that many of those now decrying the crisis in Venezuela across the UK media are doing so less out of concern for that country and its people than because it provides them with a new stick to beat Jeremy Corbyn with.[42]

There are exceptions. A few former Chávez admirers have simply admitted that they had been wrong, and moved on.

Asa Cusack, the managing editor of the LSE's Latin America and Caribbean blog, wrote in *The Guardian*:

> [D]id his [Chávez's] good intentions blind me and others to dangerous failings in his government? Did I think centralisation of power was a price worth paying? [...] Did I downplay abuses I would have denounced with a more rightwing government? [...] I suspect that I did. If it's true that 'the left outside Venezuela can help rebuild the movement by participating in an honest accounting

---

41 Venezuela is a tragedy, not an opportunity to score domestic political points, *The Scotsman*, 11 August 2017 (http://www.scotsman.com/news/opinion/brian-wilson-venezuela-is-a-tragedy-not-an-opportunity-to-score-domestic-political-points-1-4528573).

42 Most politicians decrying the crisis in Venezuela don't care about its people – they care about a stick to beat Corbyn with, *Independent*, 10 August 2017 (http://www.independent.co.uk/voices/venezuela-jeremy-corbyn-why-wont-he-condemn-chavez-general-election-a7886931.html).

of what went wrong', then admitting and learning from our own failures is a necessary first step.[43]

James Bloodworth, a left-wing journalist, had already said in early 2014, when the worst was yet to come:

> There was a time when the so-called Bolivarian Revolution in Venezuela appeared to hold great promise. I remember [...] being mesmerised by what I saw [...] Looking back, I have no trouble remembering which side I was on. More than a decade on, however, the picture is far less encouraging. [...]
>
> Anyone who is genuinely concerned about the poor (rather than simply interested in sloganeering on their behalf) is obliged to recognise just how bad the situation in Venezuela is becoming as a result of the policies pursued by the government.[44]

Three years later, Bloodworth made the same point more forcefully. He was especially critical of the complete lack of soul-searching on the British left in the wake of Venezuela's implosion:

---

43 What the left must learn from Maduro's failures in Venezuela, *The Guardian*, 2 August 2017 (https://www.theguardian.com/commentisfree/2017/aug/02/left-learn-maduros-failures-in-venezuela-bolivarian-revolution-chavismo).

44 The left has a blind spot on Venezuela. When will it acknowledge that Chávez's socialist dream has turned into a nightmare?, *Independent*, 19 February 2014 (http://www.independent.co.uk/voices/comment/the-left-has-a-blind-spot-on-venezuela-when-will-it-acknowledge-that-chavezs-socialist-dream-has-9138930.html).

> Berating those who got Venezuela wrong would be point-less. But it is fair to ask whether any lessons have been learned from the tragedy. [...]
>
> *[W]hy* have opposition voices been silenced? *Why* did production collapse in several Venezuelan sectors soon after industries were nationalised? Has a mighty state with its tentacles in every area of Venezuelan life really given the country's poor more control over their destiny?
>
> Or perhaps to even ask such questions on the British left is to automatically consign oneself to the camp of reaction. Nevertheless, there is something distasteful in celebrating a movement when times are good but dis-owning it when its unpleasant features come to the fore.[45]

This latter sentence, of course, is exactly what Western in-tellectuals have been doing for a century.

Cusack and Bloodworth are the exception. A more common response was to downplay the socialist aspects of Venezuela's economy, and to present its crisis as a gen-eral case of 'mismanagement', 'poor leadership', etc. Mary Dejevsky, for example, wrote:

> [T]he reasons why [...] Venezuela is now in the perilous state it is, cannot be ascribed only, or even largely, to dogma – Marxist, socialist, populist or whatever. The dominance of one charismatic leader always carries

---

45 Hugo Chávez was a hero to many on the left. Where are they now Vene-zuela is collapsing?', *International Business Times*, 4 July 2017 (http://www .ibtimes.co.uk/hugo-chavez-was-hero-many-left-where-are-they-now-ven ezuela-collapsing-1628929).

dangers; corruption, incompetence, the decline in global oil market, the country's social structures all played their part.[46]

Meanwhile, the disputing of Venezuela's socialist credentials is also already well underway.

Ryan Beitler, a journalist, fiction writer and musician, writes:

[T]he corruption, greed, and elitism [...] is directly at odds with everything socialism represents and everything the people of Venezuela long for. [...] [S]ocialist ideas are not what has led the country to starvation and commodity shortages [...]

From a long history of [...] Red Scare brainwashing, socialism is equated with tyranny [...] despite the central goal of the ideology being an equitable, classless society. [...]

[W]hy do we blame socialism? It is not the ideology that is at work here, just like socialism wasn't practiced during the Soviet Union [...]

---

46 See, for example: Don't blame socialism for Venezuela's woes. We explain why blaming only socialism for Venezuela's political and economic crisis doesn't make sense, *Al Jazeera*, 17 June 2017 (http://www.aljazeera .com/programmes/upfront/2017/06/don-blame-socialism-venezuela -woes-170617080851514.html). See also: Most politicians decrying the crisis in Venezuela don't care about its people – they care about a stick to beat Corbyn with, *Independent*, 10 August 2017 (http://www.independent.co.uk/ voices/venezuela-jeremy-corbyn-why-wont-he-condemn-chavez-general -election-a7886931.html).

> If Maduro and his government truly fulfilled the stated values of egalitarian democratic socialism, people wouldn't be starving, there wouldn't be bread lines, there wouldn't be medicine shortages, there wouldn't be inflation, and there wouldn't be riots.[47]

Shadow Chancellor John McDonnell said at the World Economic Forum summit in Davos:

> It's not that the issue is socialism vs capitalism. [...]
>
> All the objectives of Chávez [...] would have been successful if they had mobilised the oil resources to actually invest in the long term [...]
>
> I think in Venezuela they took a wrong turn, a not particularly effective path, not a socialist path.[48]

A few months later, McDonnell said on the *Sunday Politics* show, 'I don't think it [Venezuela] is a socialist country. [...] I don't think they have been following [...] socialist policies [...] And as a result of that they're experiencing problems'.[49]

---

47 What's the matter with Venezuela? It's not socialism, it's corruption, *Paste Magazine*, 19 June 2017 (https://www.pastemagazine.com/articles/2017/06/whats-the-matter-with-venezuela-its-not-socialism.html).

48 John McDonnell says hard-left Venezuela collapsed because they weren't socialist enough, *The Sun*, 26 January 2018 (https://www.thesun.co.uk/news/5429849/john-mcdonnell-says-hard-left-venezuela-collapsed-because-they-werent-socialist-enough/).

49 John McDonnell says Venezuela is failing because it is 'not a socialist country', *City AM*, 20 May 2018 (http://www.cityam.com/266141/john-mcdonnell-says-venezuela-failing-because-not-socialist).

Noam Chomsky, who had once hailed Venezuela as an example of how 'a better world is being created', now claims:

> I never described Chávez's state capitalist government as 'socialist' or even hinted at such an absurdity. It was quite remote from socialism. Private capitalism remained [...] Capitalists were free to undermine the economy in all sorts of ways, like massive export of capital.[50]

Slavoj Žižek asks:

> [W]hy was there no Venezuelan left to provide an authentic radical alternative to Chávez and Maduro? Why was the initiative in the opposition to Chávez left to the extreme right which triumphantly hegemonised the oppositional struggle, imposing itself as the voice of the ordinary people who suffer the consequences of the Chavista mismanagement of economy?[51]

So once again – it was not *real* socialism. *Real* socialism has never been tried.

---

50 Chomsky's Venezuela lesson, *Creators*, 31 March 2017 (https://www.crea tors.com/read/john-stossel/05/17/chomskys-venezuela-lesson).

51 The problem with Venezuela's revolution is that it didn't go far enough, *Independent*, 9 August 2017 (http://www.independent.co.uk/voices/vene zuela-socialism-communism-left-didnt-go-far-enough-a7884021.html).

10 WHY SOCIALIST IDEAS PERSIST

Haidt's social intuitionist model and Caplan's theory of 'rational irrationality'

When reading the accounts of socialist pilgrims, one cannot help wondering how so many highly educated, highly intelligent, well-informed and well-meaning people can be so colossally and persistently wrong. Of course most of us are not experts on the economy, political system or social structures of a foreign country, and it is easy for an outside observer to come up with a wrong assessment. But socialist pilgrims were not just wrong in the way in which, say, a finance journalist who mistakes a short-lived boom for a genuine increase in prosperity, is wrong. Those pilgrims travelled to some of the most hellish places in the world and came back convinced that they had seen paradise.

Hollander's (1990) work leaves no doubt that pilgrims were not simply being naive. A naive person does not *want* to be deceived – they are just not good at spotting deception. Being a socialist pilgrim, in contrast, requires a deliberate effort of self-manipulation and reality-filtering, of selective seeing, not-seeing and un-seeing. Being a socialist pilgrim is hard work.

Haidt's social intuitionist model

This is where Jonathan Haidt's (2012) research into how our faculties for moral and political reasoning have evolved, and how they work, is insightful. Haidt shows that a lot of our moral and political reasoning is post-hoc rationalisation. Its primary purpose is not to *arrive* at a conclusion, but to *justify* a conclusion *after* we have reached it. We often arrive at a broad conclusion quickly and intuitively, and then selectively look for arguments to back it up retrospectively. Haidt sums this up in the formula 'Intuitions come first, strategic reason comes second'.

Thus, our mind does not work like a judge, who studies evidence, weighs it, interprets it, and only then comes to a conclusion. It works more like a lawyer, who settles for the broad position they want to take in court early on (for example, 'my client is innocent') and then builds a case for it. That case can be perfectly logical, coherent and persuasive. But it is not the reason why the lawyer arrived at that position. The lawyer started from that position and then 'reverse-engineered' a case for it. If that case breaks down (say, if their client's alibi turns out to be false), the lawyer will not discard their position. They will keep the position and just justify it in a different way. They will build a new case that will arrive at the same conclusion. If evidence against it is so overwhelming that there is no way the position can be maintained, they will settle for the smallest concession they can possibly get away with.

For example, Haidt runs a series of interviews, in which participants are asked for their moral judgement on some hypothetical action X, and to explain their reason(s) for that judgement. When participants claim to oppose X, on the grounds that it can lead to negative outcome A, the interviewer changes the setup (it is just a thought experiment, so the interviewer can change it at will) in such a way that X could not possibly cause A. But rather than softening their stance on X in response, most participants simply reach for a different line of attack: if X does not cause A, then surely it causes the equally undesirable outcome B. When the interviewer then takes that argument away as well (by changing the setup again to rule out B), most interviewees jump straight to attack C. And so on. This shows that neither A nor B nor C were ever the reasons why the interviewees opposed X. They were post-hoc justifications for an intuitive and visceral dislike of X.

This has important implications (Haidt 2012: 48):

> The social intuitionist model offers an explanation of why moral and political arguments are so frustrating: *because moral reasons are the tail wagged by the intuitive dog.* A dog's tail wags to communicate. You can't make a dog happy by forcibly wagging its tail. And you can't change people's minds by utterly refuting their arguments.

We often think of emotion and reason as forces that are independent of each other, which can pull in opposite directions. The emotional part of our mind supports a particular policy because it feels good and is based on good intentions; the rational part of our mind opposes it because the policy has been tried elsewhere and failed. Haidt's research shows that this is not the way it works. Emotion and reason are not antagonists. The relationship between them is more like an employer–employee relationship. The emotional, intuitive part of our mind settles for a position and then 'employs' the reasoning part to come up with good arguments for it.

It is, as Haidt also points out, not a master–slave relationship. If the employer comes up with completely unreasonable requests, the employee can refuse to do it. Most of us could not persuade ourselves that the world is ruled by humanoid lizards or that the Holocaust never happened, even if we had a desire to believe that. But conspiracy theorists who do hold such beliefs are not outliers who lack 'normal' reasoning skills. Rather, they show tendencies which we all show and just take them to extremes. It is a difference in degree, not a qualitative difference. Conspiracy theorists are able to reach the conclusion they want to reach even when all the evidence is unambiguously against them, whereas most of us need at least *some* ambiguity. But since there is almost always some ambiguity, and it is almost always possible to find support for a range of positions, we usually find reasons to reach the conclusion that we want to reach.

This tendency can manifest itself in various ways. One is 'confirmation bias' – our well-documented tendency to magnify evidence which supports what we already believe and to overlook or dismiss evidence to the contrary.

A related, often more sophisticated, form of post-hoc rationalisation is 'motivated reasoning'. As Haidt (2012: 84) explains:

Psychologists now have file cabinets full of findings on 'motivated reasoning', showing the many tricks people use to reach the conclusion they want to reach. When subjects are told that an intelligence test gave them a low score, they choose to read articles criticizing (rather than supporting) the validity of IQ tests. When people read a (fictitious) scientific study that reports a link between caffeine consumption and breast cancer, women who are heavy coffee drinkers find more flaws in the study than do men and less caffeinated women.

A motivated reasoner does not completely ignore or deny evidence that contradicts their beliefs, rather, they will try to pick holes in it. They may, for example, demand impossible standards of accuracy from sources of inconvenient information, usually coupled with lax standards for sources of convenient information.

Haidt's findings are not as pessimistic as they may sound at first. Haidt does not say that we cannot reason our way to the truth. He just highlights the strength of intuitions in moral and political arguments. This is not always a problem.

On many issues, most of us do not have strong intuitions one way or another. We may feel strongly that Britain should leave the EU or remain in the EU. But most of us will not have strong feelings on, say, whether Britain should remain part of the Single European Sky agreement. Reasoned argument prevails when its findings do not run up against strong intuitions.

More importantly, our intuitions will often be conflicted. We may feel strongly that Britain should consolidate its public finances and keep government debt under control. But we may also feel strongly about protecting people who rely on government support. If we just see 'austerity' as pointless cruelty (that is, if we do not have conflicting intuitions), we will not be receptive to arguments about the dangers of runaway deficits. But if our intuitions give us mixed messages, there is no reason why we should not go wherever the best evidence leads us.

Haidt emphasises that very simple things, such as being friends with people with opposing political views, can change political intuitions, because it takes the hostility and bitterness out of political disagreement. We may still disagree, but we are more likely to give opposing arguments a fair hearing. It is very difficult to concede that a political opponent may have a point when we feel resentment towards them. This is why Haidt emphasises the dangers of political self-segregation and hyper-tribalism, of the kind that we currently see on social media or in university campus culture wars. In such environments, people with similar political views cease to be just a loose alliance and become a moral tribe which commands loyalty and punishes dissent. People with opposing views, meanwhile, cease to be just political opponents and become an enemy tribe; their views cease to be just wrong and become actively malicious.

The tendency to use reasoning as a tool for justifying and confirming existing beliefs, rather than for finding the truth, exists at the best of times – but some settings counteract that tendency, while others magnify it. Turning politics into a moral crusade turbocharges it. We can see this process in action when opposing views, or the people holding them, are described in the same terms we would use to describe rotten food or milk: 'disgusting', 'repugnant', 'repulsive', 'sickening', etc. If this is our visceral response to a point of view, the reasoning part of our mind will immediately switch into 'lawyer-mode'.

Haidt's research is not specifically about intellectuals, but he cites a study which investigates how reasoning skills vary by education level and intelligence (ibid.: 80–81). Study participants were asked to pick a side in a contemporary policy debate, to write down the case for their own position, and to write down the case for the opposing position. This latter task is about testing people's ability to put themselves into the mind of a political opponent and to argue as an opponent would argue. When it comes to defending one's own position, the study results are as one would expect: reasoning skills are positively correlated with education and intelligence. But on the second task – arguing from the perspective of an opponent – there was no such correlation (ibid.: 81):

> Smart people make really good lawyers and press secretaries, but they are no better than others at finding reasons on the other side. Perkins [the study's lead author] concluded that 'People invest their IQ in buttressing their own case rather than in exploring the entire issue more fully and even-handedly'.

Haidt's research does not lead us to a fatalistic position; it does not suggest that rational inquiry and persuasion are impossible and that we should just give up trying. But it shows that it takes an extraordinary amount of intellectual self-discipline to discard a political/moral position that we are emotionally comfortable with, and to embrace a position that we are emotionally uncomfortable with instead, purely on the basis of superior evidence in support of the latter.

Caplan's theory of 'rational irrationality'

Bryan Caplan's (2006) research on 'rational irrationality' provides additional insights. Caplan shows that there are a lot of economic policy ideas that are demonstrably wrong and rejected by economists of virtually all political persuasions and methodological schools – but that nonetheless remain widely popular. He does not look at socialism (although some of the policies he refers to could be reasonably described as socialist) and he does not specifically look at attitudes among intellectuals. But it is not a huge stretch to extrapolate from his findings.

Caplan explains (ibid.: 14–16):

Economists usually presume that beliefs are a means to an end, not an end in themselves. In reality, however, we often have cherished views, valued for their own sake. [...] Outside of economics, the idea that people like some beliefs more than others has a long history. [...] Few dispassionately accept their religious teachings as the 'current leading hypothesis.' [...] Like the adherents of traditional religion, many people find comfort in their political worldview, and greet critical questions with pious hostility.

Thus, holding on to a demonstrably wrong belief can be entirely rational, if that belief is a source of pleasure, pride, emotional comfort and perhaps even a sense of identity. It only seems irrational if we erroneously assume that the person holding that belief is motivated solely by a desire to know the truth. Beliefs that are emotionally appealing confer a benefit on the person holding them, irrespective of whether or not they are true.

What about the costs? According to Caplan, there is a huge difference between holding (or rather, acting upon) irrational beliefs in our personal lives and holding irrational beliefs in political life. We bear the full cost of the former, but there is no cost associated with the latter. If we bear the cost of holding an irrational belief, there is a strong incentive to revise it, or at least, to find an excuse for not acting upon it. This is why we often see, for example, people who hold xenophobic beliefs, but who would not hesitate to buy a foreign product, hire a foreign worker or work for a foreign employer, etc., if this makes them better off than buying a domestic product, hiring a compatriot or working for a compatriot, etc. They may still cherish their irrational beliefs, but they act *as if* they hold rational beliefs.

Irrational political beliefs, of course, also come at a cost if they turn into irrational policies. But that cost is not borne specifically by the people holding those beliefs. It is shared across the whole population, and no single member of the public has a perceptible impact on political outcomes. Unlike in the sphere of personal choices, there is therefore no correlation between the political beliefs we hold individually and the politics we get. There is no need to be careful what we wish for, because there is no relationship between what we wish for and what we actually get.

We could fervently advocate a policy which, if it were ever enacted, would quickly ruin the country, including ourselves. Holding that view comes at no cost to us.

Economists have long known the concept of 'rational ignorance': it is rational not to be well-informed about politics (unless we find the subject interesting in its own right) because we cannot change its outcomes anyway. Caplan proposes an alternative, or rather, an extension to the concept of rational ignorance, namely rational irrationality (ibid.: 2):

> [I]rrationality, like ignorance, is selective. We habitually tune out unwanted information on subjects we don't care about. In the same vein [...] we turn off our rational faculties on subjects where we don't care about the truth. Economists have long argued that voter ignorance is a predictable response to the fact that one vote doesn't matter. Why study the issues if you can't change the outcome? I generalize this insight: Why control your knee-jerk emotional and ideological reactions if you can't change the outcome?

If a false belief is emotionally satisfying, and if there is no cost associated with holding it, we would expect it to be widely held: 'we should expect people to "satiate" their demand for political delusion, to believe whatever makes them feel best. After all, it's free' (ibid.: 18).

In Caplan's model, political irrationality is the result of a straightforward (implicit) cost–benefit analysis. Discarding a cherished political belief is painful. It involves an emotional cost. But there are no corresponding gains. So why do it? It is rational to stick to a cherished belief, even if it is refuted by all the evidence. It is rational to be politically irrational.

Applying Haidt's and Caplan's findings to socialist intellectuals

Haidt's and Caplan's research is not specifically about socialism or intellectuals, so drawing inferences is necessarily a bit speculative. But it is a starting point.

Confirmation bias, for example, is written all over practically every pilgrimage account. Pilgrims constantly see people who 'seem happy' or 'seem content'. It is as if pilgrims suddenly acquire telepathic abilities as soon as they touch socialist ground. They 'sense' the enthusiasm of the masses. They are 'struck by' a pervasive spirit of solidarity and community. They 'cannot help but notice' how dedicated to the revolution everyone is.

In the same vein, completely ordinary observations that one could also see in any Western country acquire a different meaning in a socialist country. An unremarkable sight like a train station becomes a marvellous achievement by virtue of being located in a People's State; it becomes a

People's Train Station, built by The People, for The People. Luise Rinser sees a child in Pyongyang smile at her, and attributes this child's happiness to socialism, and to the genius of Kim Il Sung. Carla Stea sees a North Korean woman wearing high heels, and marvels about how 'a woman's shoes, especially high heels, are very often an expression of her self-esteem'. Seumas Milne and George Galloway marvel about how East Germany offered free healthcare and free schooling, even though this was equally true of West Germany.

These are all peculiar forms of confirmation bias. To see why, one only need to imagine somebody writing in a similar vein about a Western country. Take a random passage by Luise Rinser, describing a completely ordinary observation, such as a smiling child. Replace 'Pyongyang' with 'Munich' (Rinser's home town), 'the Democratic People's Republic of Korea' with 'the Free State of Bavaria', 'President Kim Il Sung' with 'Governor Franz Joseph Strauß', and 'the Workers Party of Korea' with 'the Christian Social Union'. The absurdity would be self-evident.

All the techniques of motivated reasoning are in evidence as well. When somebody raises allegations of human rights abuses and/or economic failure in the socialist paradise *du jour*, pilgrims ask what the people who make those allegations might have to gain from it – cui bono? If they can find one critic who might indeed have some ulterior motive, it is reason enough to dismiss all criticism as a fabrication. The Orwell quote that 'some things are true even though the *Daily Telegraph* says they are true' is lost on the motivated reasoner. Seumas Milne, for example, finds two

German historians and one Austrian philosopher, whose work on Stalinism was indeed widely construed as an attempt to relativise the Nazi holocaust.[1] Milne goes on to imply that this is the 'true' motivation of all critics of socialism. For the motivated reasoner, a few atypical cases, combined with guilt by association, is all it takes.

For others, the tainting associations can be even more tenuous. In Noam Chomsky's account, everything that appears in 'the Western media' becomes by definition suspicious, because 'the Western media' – a homogeneous block – is part of 'the Western propaganda system'.

One of the pilgrims' favourite techniques is whataboutery. What about Western colonialism? What about American foreign policy interventions? What about the UK's relationship with Saudi Arabia? What about racism in Western countries? It is never fully spelt out what the point of this exercise is supposed to be, especially given that most critics of socialism would *not* defend Western colonialism, or US foreign policy interventions or the UK's relationship with Saudi Arabia. Whataboutery seems to have no purpose other than to raise a counter-accusation (even if it is a false one), and to reclaim the moral high ground in this way.

Pilgrims also demand impossibly high standards of rigour and accuracy from critics, but quickly relax those

---

1   Stalin's missing millions, *The Guardian*, 10 March 1990 (https://shirazso cialist.wordpress.com/2012/09/29/seamas-milne-on-stalins-missing -millions/). We are not in a position to judge whether that really was their agenda, but they were controversial in their respective home countries at the time.

standards when a source of convenient information comes along. When evidence of mass murder in Cambodia emerged, Western Khmer Rouge apologists demanded chapter and verse, which was impossible to provide at the time, given that the regime would obviously not show its mass graves to the Red Cross or Amnesty International. Unverifiable statements from the odd sympathetic foreign observer, however, were taken at face value.

If anti-capitalism is mainly visceral, and anti-capitalist arguments mainly post-hoc attempts to rationalise that visceral dislike of capitalism, we would expect anti-capitalists to quickly replace one line of attack with another, if it is convenient to do so. This has indeed happened many times. Capitalism has always been under attack, but not always for the same reasons. For example, during the post-war boom, the criticism quickly shifted from 'capitalism immiserates the workers' to 'capitalism promotes a vulgar consumerist culture and shallow materialism'. In the late 1990s and early 2000s, the anti-globalisation movement, which saw 'globalisation' as the exploitation of poor countries by rich countries, was extremely fashionable on Western campuses. Then Western perceptions of countries such as China changed: they were no longer seen as poor sweatshop economies, but as emerging markets, and as serious competitors. As a result, the anti-globalisation movement lost prominence – but it never engaged in any soul-searching. It simply shifted its focus to more generic left-wing causes, such as opposition to welfare cuts, privatisation, tax avoidance, etc., and was absorbed by other movements.

Haidt highlights how moral tribalism turbocharges the tendency to go with our gut feelings and use reasoning purely for post-hoc rationalising. The anti-capitalist left is a clear example of a moral tribe. One of the most successful anti-capitalist books of the last decade was Naomi Klein's *The Shock Doctrine*. The main message of that book was not that free-market economics produces bad outcomes, but that its proponents are malevolent, demonic figures, who are happy to cause human suffering on a massive scale. The book became an instant bestseller and award-winner. Although all the major claims made in the book are wrong (see, for example, Norberg 2008),[2] it was a tremendous success because it arouses the righteous rage of a moral tribe. It is the ideal book for a reader who starts with a strong emotional dislike of the market economy and who seeks validation for it. This is the climate in which Venezuela-mania took off.

Pilgrims also show a tendency to talk themselves into the role of a victimised minority. They frequently insist that 'the mainstream media' relentlessly attacks socialist countries, while turning a blind eye to human rights abuses in Western-allied, non-socialist countries. The Khmer Rouge's apologists were probably the ones who took this line of argument furthest. But it was never remotely true. Ear (1995: 69–71) references a study which analyses the coverage of human rights abuses in the US's leading newspapers and news channels. It contains a breakdown of such

---

2   See also: Shock Jock, *New York Sun*, 3 October 2007 (http://www.nysun.com/arts/shock-jock/63867/).

coverage by country, which shows that in 1976 South Korea was mentioned more than five times as often as Cambodia, while Chile was mentioned more than eight times as often. (Cuba and North Korea were barely mentioned at all.) Yet Khmer Rouge apologists such as Noam Chomsky saw themselves as the lone voices in the wilderness, speaking truth to power. This self-perception is bound to amplify moral tribalism and motivated reasoning tendencies.

Last but not least, it is worth noting that most pilgrim statements are not so much wrong as *unfalsifiable*. They are unfalsifiable because they are too abstract to be falsified. A frequent claim is that the socialist utopia *du jour* may *look* like a system of autocratic rule, but in reality The People are in charge. The dictator, or the ruling party, is just a medium through which The People exercise their collective will. This cannot, strictly speaking, be refuted. How would you 'prove' that this is not true?

Perhaps the best example is Jan Myrdal's book *Albania Defiant*. Myrdal repeatedly asserts that Albania is different from the Warsaw Pact countries, because the latter are run by a bureaucratic elite, while Albania is run by the Albanian working class. He never quite explains what this is supposed to mean in practice. How does Myrdal know that 'the Albanian working class', as a whole, is 'in control'? How does he know that there is such an entity as 'the Albanian working class', and how does he know that Enver Hoxha's policies are in line with the desires of that entity? How does this hypothetical entity exercise that control? Myrdal would have a hard time proving his assertion to a sceptic – but a sceptic would have an equally hard time proving Myrdal wrong.

The same goes for the idea that repressive measures are just a response to external threats. Pilgrims tend to think of socialist regimes as one would think of a teenage bully who is not genuinely malicious, but who feels insecure, and who overcompensates for that insecurity through aggressive behaviour. Give them the respect and recognition that they crave and their behaviour will change. In some cases, this has been refuted by events, because the external threats identified by apologists later disappeared, but the character of the regime in question never changed. But most of the time, the threats they identify are much more intangible. A hostile comment from a US politician, diplomat or civil servant becomes evidence of efforts to 'undermine' a socialist government, which, in the eyes of Western pilgrims, makes all kinds of repressive measures excusable.

Finally, the Caplanite cost–benefit analysis is different for pilgrims than it is for the 'Average Joe'. Caplan argues that it is often rational to stick to a demonstrably false, but cherished, political belief, because the (emotional) cost of discarding it outweighs the benefits. Caplan's work focuses on the median voter. A pilgrim is, almost by definition, much more strongly invested in the ideas they cherish than the median voter could ever be. Those ideas may be part of their very identity.

This is especially true in the case of public intellectuals, whose ideas are the defining feature of their public persona. Imagine if a public figure such as Owen Jones wrote an article with a title like 'I remain committed to social justice, but after Venezuela I have finally given up on socialism', or 'Let's be honest with ourselves: Yes, it WAS socialism that ruined Venezuela'. They would disappoint a fan base of hundreds of thousands of people. They would be called sell-outs and traitors. They would endanger their very position as a public intellectual. For them, the cost of giving up on a wrong idea would be infinitely greater than for the Average Joe.

Being wrong, however, has no cost whatsoever. With the exception of Malcolm Caldwell, it is hard to find an example of a Western pilgrim who suffered negative consequences for being wrong. The pilgrims did not have to live under the systems they admired from afar. They did not go hungry while they denied or made excuses for food shortages. They did not have to toil in the forced labour camps they romanticised or rationalised. They did not even suffer reputational consequences in their home countries. The Webbs and George Bernard Shaw remain highly regarded figures to this day. Noam Chomsky remains a 'rock star intellectual', while the people who had been right about Cambodia have been largely forgotten. At least in his native Sweden, Jan Myrdal, who idolised Mao Tse-Tung, Enver Hoxha and Pol Pot, remains an anti-capitalist icon. After writing a book glorifying North Korea, Luise Rinser could still become a presidential candidate in West Germany. After idolising Mao's Cultural Revolution, Maria-Antonietta Macciocchi went on to a successful career as a parliamentarian, both in her native Italy and at the EU level. After Venezuela fell off a cliff, some of Britain's most eager Chavistas went on to become some of the most senior political figures in the country.

With this in mind, the question 'How can so many highly educated people be so completely and so consistently wrong?' becomes a bit moot. Why would they *not* indulge in their favourite fantasies, given that there is absolutely no incentive to be right?

Intuitive anti-capitalism, or anti-capitalism as a default position

Most reasoning is post-hoc rationalisation. We often start with a gut feeling and then seek out reasons to justify it. Given a little bit of ambiguity, we will find those reasons. Those tendencies are there at the best of times, but hyper-tribalism and hyper-moralism amplify them.

This still leaves an elephant in the room: why are our gut feelings so anti-capitalist? Why do we not start off with the hunch that capitalism might be a good thing? This is not such an outlandish idea. It is fashionable to hate capitalism, but capitalism is infinitely better than its reputation. Where it has been practised, and *to the extent* that it has been practised, its results have not been too shabby. If you reduce the record of the market economy to food banks and zero-hours contracts, then yes, you will reach an unfavourable verdict. But a look at the bigger picture gives a rather different impression.

For hundreds of thousands of years – almost all of human history – people's living standards were essentially static, or increased only at an imperceptibly slow pace. If a Saxon settler in sixth-century Britain had fallen into a wormhole and travelled a thousand years into the future, they would have blended in quite easily, at least as far as economic life is concerned. They would have been confused by the changes in language, religion, etc., but they would not, for example, have encountered technologies they would not understand. The society they would have arrived in would not have seemed futuristic to them. For most people, living standards and everyday life would have been mostly the same. In contrast, if a time traveller from a hundred years ago arrived in our day and age, they would be overwhelmed. Our society would seem unbelievably prosperous, and unbelievably advanced, to them.

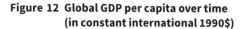

Figure 12 Global GDP per capita over time (in constant international 1990$)

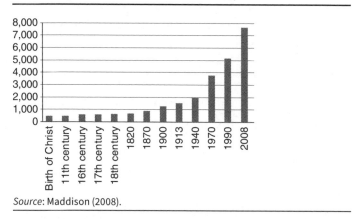

Source: Maddison (2008).

We take it for granted that living standards rise over time. For most of history, they did not. This trend only really began with the advent of industrial capitalism, which was a game changer in world history (see Figure 12). It was initially confined to a few regions in Western Europe and its overseas offshoots, and then began to spread to other parts of the world, *to the extent* that they allowed it to happen.

Before the advent of industrial capitalism, virtually the whole of the world's population lived in abject poverty. Before the mid nineteenth century, it would not even have made sense to *measure* poverty, because such a measure would not have shown anything interesting. Its long-term average would have been close to 100 per cent, and it would only have shown random fluctuations, not a systematic trend over time. It is not a coincidence that poverty measurement started in Britain in the late nineteenth century (see Niemietz 2011: 23–25, 56–58). Britain had reached a stage of development at which poverty was no longer the norm and no longer static. Later, other countries went through the same process, when and *to the extent* that they embraced free markets.

Figure 13 Global population and global poverty, 1850–2010

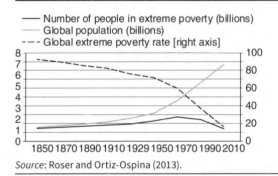

Source: Roser and Ortiz-Ospina (2013).

In the mid nineteenth century, there were only about 1.3 billion people in the world, virtually all of whom lived in poverty. Today, there are about 7 billion people and the global poverty rate has fallen to below 10 per cent for the first time in history (Figure 13).

For most of history, average life expectancy was below 30 years. This was partly the result of extremely high infant mortality rates, but life expectancy among those who survived infancy was still well below 50 years (Roser 2017). It was only with the spread of industrial capitalism that life expectancy began to rise systematically over time, at first only in the Western world and then elsewhere. Globally, the average life expectancy is now over 70 years (Figure 14).

Figure 14 Global average life expectancy at birth (years), 1870–2015

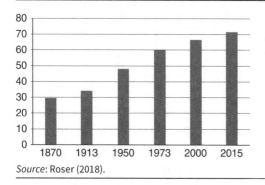

Source: Roser (2018).

For most of history, life really was 'nasty, brutish and short', consisting mainly of backbreaking labour. The concept of 'leisure' only arose with industrial capitalism. In the 1870s, non-agricultural labourers in what was then the industrialised part of the world still worked for an average of around 60 hours per week. The length of the average working week then dropped to under 50 hours by the mid twentieth century. Combined with increases in holiday time, this led to a decrease in the annual number of hours worked per employed person. Legislation and pressure from trade unions played a role, but Roser (2017) finds a strong negative correlation between productivity and working hours (Figure 15).

Figure 15 Annual number of hours worked per worker

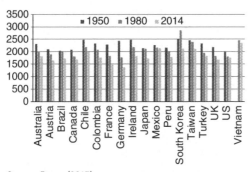

Source: Roser (2017).

There is poverty in the UK, but it is not comparable to the kind of poverty that existed in the Victorian age, let alone in the pre-industrial age. Virtually every single household in the UK can afford an indoor bathroom, central heating or a functional equivalent, a TV, a telephone and a washing machine. Over 95 per cent of UK households can afford meals with meat, chicken and/or fish at least every other day. People in the bottom decile of the income distribution can still afford to spend almost one fifth of their household budget on restaurants, hotels and other leisure activities (Niemietz 2011: 85–87). Food bank use is, in the vast majority of cases, a stop-gap solution rather than a long-term state of affairs.

One can pick almost any economic or social indicator at random, and bet that it will indicate a long-term improvement. Some of these improvements happened, or *could* have happened, in socialist countries as well, but on the whole, economic freedom scores are strongly positively correlated with indicators of economic and social development (Fraser Institute 2017: 22–26). One can always find exceptions, but, by and large, people become more prosperous, and better off in all kinds of ways, *to the extent* that their governments adopt free-market policies.

So why does the system which has produced, and which keeps producing, all those benefits, arouse such widespread and such passionate hatred? Why do we so easily dismiss all the massive gains that capitalism delivers and obsess over its shortcomings? Why are we so desperate for an alternative that we are prepared to give the most horrendous systems a free pass (at least for a while), provided they are not capitalist? Why are (or were) so many well-meaning observers willing to turn a blind eye to Gulags and Laogai, but incandescent with rage when large companies earn a profit, or when some people earn a lot more money than others?

The first thing to note here is that anti-capitalist sentiments are not new. In 1942, Joseph Schumpeter (1976 [1943]: 63) wrote:

The atmosphere of hostility to capitalism [...] makes it [...] difficult [...] to form a rational opinion about its economic and cultural performance. The public mind has by now so thoroughly grown out of humor with it as to make condemnation of capitalism and all its works a foregone conclusion – almost a requirement of the etiquette of discussion. Whatever his political preference, every writer or speaker hastens to conform to this code and to emphasize [...] his aversion to capitalist and his sympathy with anti-capitalist interests. Any other attitude is voted not only foolish but anti-social.

But even then, hostility to capitalism was far from new. As Hayek (1988: 90) explains:

[D]istrust and fear have, since antiquity and in many parts of the world, led ordinary people as well as socialist thinkers to regard trade [...] not only as chaotic and superfluous [...] but also as suspicious, inferior, dishonest, and contemptible. Throughout history merchants were objects of very general disdain and moral opprobrium [...] [A] man who bought cheap and sold dear was fundamentally dishonest. [...] Merchant behaviour violated patterns of mutuality that prevailed within primary groupings [...] The hostility, in particular of the scribe, towards the merchant is as old as recorded history.

Anti-capitalism, in short, is older than capitalism itself. But where does it come from?

Hayek believed that anti-capitalist impulses were a legacy from a prehistoric age. Drawing on more recent insights from evolutionary psychology, Peter Foster (2014) has recently elaborated further on this idea. Foster's argument could be summarised as follows.

Our minds, and especially our moral intuitions, have evolved over hundreds of thousands of years, during which our ancestors lived in small tribes of hunter-gatherers. Our minds are therefore, in many ways, poorly adapted to a modern environment, and this is particularly true in the economic sphere. They are adapted to the economic life of a tribal society – *not* to an economy based on the division of labour and coordinated by anonymous mechanisms.

In a hunter-gatherer tribe, all economic activity is purposeful and consciously directed. It is a group effort. The members of the tribe share common aims and means. There is not much of a division of labour, and certainly not between strangers.

In this setting, *intentions* matter a great deal. Individuals who want to promote the welfare of the group end up promoting the welfare of the group; individuals who want to enrich themselves end up enriching themselves at the expense of the group. There is no 'invisible hand', which makes selfish individuals inadvertently promote the welfare of others. It therefore makes perfect sense for group members to police each other's motives, to be highly sensitive to signs of selfish behaviour, and to punish the individuals who engage in it.

In a hunter-gatherer society, economic activity is mostly a zero-sum game. The sharing of the spoils is an inherently political act, and the way the spoils are divided reflects power dynamics within the group, as well as moral judgements and notions of desert. The group must work out who 'deserves' how much.

If Foster is right, our economic intuitions are a legacy of the tribal age. Most anti-capitalist arguments, then, no matter how much complex-sounding sociological jargon they may use, are really just sophisticated rationalisations of primitive urges.

Of course, nobody would literally argue that we should organise a modern society in the same way as a hunter-gatherer tribe. We all know that a modern economy is infinitely more complex than a mammoth hunt. But, in essence, that is what socialism is: it is an attempt to turn economic life, once again, into a consciously directed group effort. The tribe gathers around the camp fire, its members work out what their common needs and priorities are, they agree on a way to fulfil them, and put it into action. The drafting of a Five-Year Plan, then, is just a more sophisticated version of the camp fire gathering.

All of this is, of course, informed speculation, not hard science. Evolutionary psychology is not (yet) that far advanced. But whether anti-capitalism really is hardwired into us, or whether it has other origins, it is safe to say that anti-capitalism comes easily, effortlessly and naturally to us. It is a default opinion, which we can arrive at long before we give the issue much thought. We do not have to read the collected works of Marx and Engels first. Appreciation of the market economy, in contrast, is an acquired taste. It is hard to think of a prominent free-market thinker who was already a free-market thinker at the beginning of their career. F. A. Hayek, of all people, was initially sympathetic to socialism. So was James Buchanan, a co-founder of the Public Choice School. Milton Friedman was initially sympathetic to Keynesianism and New Deal–type economic interventionism. These economists certainly understood their opponents' moral intuitions, because these had once also been their own. This understanding was rarely mutual.

The Gary Lineker fallacy

The sports broadcaster and former footballer Gary Lineker once jokingly defined football as a game in which 22 men chase a ball for 90 minutes, and, in the end, the Germans win.

The joke works at more than one level, one of them being that it invokes a logical fallacy of sorts (a variant of the No True Scotsman fallacy[3]): Lineker mixes a possible

---

3   The No True Scotsman fallacy is the logical fallacy of retrofitting one's definition of X around an assertion about X one has made before. For example, somebody claims that no Scotsman would do Y. They are then presented with a counterexample, i.e. a Scotsman who *does* do Y. In response, they change the statement to 'No *true* Scotsman would do Y', where the definition of a 'true' Scotsman includes the fact that they would not do Y. The statement therefore becomes tautological. ('Someone who does not do Y does not do Y'.) Arguably, though, this is not the best example of the fallacy. There is nothing wrong with defining Scottishness, or any regional identity, in terms of habits, attitudes and eccentricities that are deemed typical of that region (as opposed to defining it in terms of, say, ancestry). The No True Scotsman fallacy is then only a fallacy insofar as the statement is too absolutist (although in practice, when we talk about a 'true' Scotsman, we don't literally mean 'true' but *typical*). It is also a bad example insofar as there is no objective definition of a regional identity which the person committing the fallacy could deviate from.

outcome of a game into its *definition*. We can define a game by describing its rules, its process and its object, but any sensible definition must be outcome-neutral.

If we took Lineker's definition at face value, the German team could never lose a *real* football match, because as soon as they do, the match by definition ceases to be a *real* match. More, it was then never real in the first place. It retroactively becomes unreal.

This is, in essence, the fallacy that socialists commit in their definition of *real* socialism. They define 'real' socialism in terms of *outcomes* they would like to see. When a socialist experiment does not produce those outcomes, it retroactively becomes unreal. Since socialism *never* produces those outcomes, *all* socialist experiments sooner or later become unreal. This is the deeper meaning behind the old adage that '*real* socialism has never been tried'.

We can define a political and/or economic system in terms of institutional characteristics (and there is room for legitimate disagreement here). But any sensible definition must be outcome-neutral. Whether the system we favour produces the outcomes we would like to see remains to be seen. It may, or it may not. If it does not, we cannot claim that the system was therefore not 'real'.

Generally, the distinction between institutional characteristics of a system and observable outcomes is straightforward enough. Institutional characteristics are the features of a system over which policymakers have direct control. They can be introduced when the political will is there, and they can be abolished when the political will is there. 'Tariff-free trade' is an institutional feature. A government can introduce tariff-free trade, namely by abolishing tariffs. 'A high GDP per capita', in contrast, is an outcome. A government cannot 'introduce' a high GDP per capita, it can only implement policies that might *result* in a high GDP per capita. Similarly, 'private ownership of the main means of production' is an institutional characteristic. 'A high employment rate' is an outcome. 'Freedom of contract' is an institutional characteristic. 'A high life expectancy' is an outcome. 'Voluntary exchange of goods and services between consenting adults' is an institutional characteristic. 'A low rate of absolute poverty' is an outcome. 'Universal suffrage' is an institutional characteristic. 'A high level of voter engagement in politics' is an outcome. And so on.

But there is one outcome that socialists constantly mistake for an institutional characteristic: the idea that under 'real' socialism, 'the workers' are in control of economic life. Socialists seem to see working-class control as something that can be introduced any time given the political will. They seem to see it as akin to universal suffrage: if a government wants every adult citizen to have the vote, all they need to do is *give* every adult citizen the vote. And in a socialist worldview, if a government wants 'the working class' to be in control, all they need to do is *give* 'the working class' that control.

This assumption is never explicitly spelt out. But it is the only way to make sense of socialist think pieces such as the ones reviewed in Chapter 1. From this perspective, spelling out in detail *how* you would put 'the working class' in control would be just as tedious and unnecessary as spelling out the procedural and legal details of how you would introduce universal suffrage. You just do it. The rest is details.

If this were true, there would indeed be no need to explain what went wrong in the Soviet Union or other socialist experiments. The governments of those countries would be akin to a government that pays lip service to universal suffrage, but then fails to actually introduce it. There are no deeper reasons for this. If a government does not introduce universal suffrage, it is because it lacks the political will to introduce universal suffrage. That is all there is to know. The solution, then, is not to give up on the idea of universal suffrage, but to elect a government which does have that political will.

Ditto for 'real' socialism. The Soviet government, in this interpretation, was a government that paid lip service to empowering workers, but then failed to actually do so. There are no deeper reasons for this. If a government does not empower the workers, it is because it lacks the political will to empower the workers. That is all there is to know. The solution, then, is not to give up on the idea of empowering the workers, but to elect a government which does have that political will.

From this perspective, past failures of socialism can never prove anything, no matter how many failed attempts there may be. The fact that in the past, many governments were unwilling to introduce universal suffrage does not 'prove' that universal suffrage is impossible. All it proves is that, in the past, many governments were unwilling to introduce universal suffrage. And from a socialist perspective, the fact that socialism has failed more than two dozen times only proves that more than two dozen governments lacked the will to empower the workers.

The fundamental error that socialists make here is that they confuse an institutional characteristic, which a government can just introduce, with an outcome. But making public sector bureaucracies – and the political process in general – responsive to public demand is an outcome which is remarkably difficult to achieve.

This is not just true in socialist countries. For decades, and under successive governments, the language of 'empowerment' has permeated British politics. NHS reforms are about 'empowering' patients; education reforms are about 'empowering' parents; electoral reforms are about 'empowering' voters, and so on. If it were so easy to 'empower' people, how come that many of us do not feel all that empowered? Why is there such a widespread anti-politics mood?[4]

Large parts of our economy are already nationalised, or state controlled in other ways. Many more used to be nationalised, or state controlled in other ways, within living memory. Whatever the merits and demerits of that may be, it has never resulted in a sense of 'empowerment' among the general public. Even the keenest advocates of nationalisation admit this, which is why they often distance themselves from the forms of state ownership that currently exist, and that have existed in the recent past. Bhaskar Sunkara writes in the *New York Times* that 'A huge state bureaucracy [...] can be just as alienating and undemocratic as corporate

---

4   See, for example: Politicians remain the least trusted profession in Britain, *Ipsos MORI*, 30 November 2017 (https://www.ipsos.com/ipsos-mori/en-uk/politicians-remain-least-trusted-profession-britain).

boardrooms, so we need to think hard about the new forms that social ownership could take'.[5]

Similarly, Owen Jones writes about the state-owned industries of the 1970s (Jones 2014: 305):

> Thatcher was able to privatize [...] with little popular out-cry, because of the lack of a sense of shared ownership among the population. To many, once publicly owned assets [...] seemed remote, run by faceless apparatchiks.

In the same vein, when Jones called for the nationalisation of the British banking sector, he immediately distanced himself from those parts of the banking sector that were already state owned:

> [T]he British state technically owns a fifth of the retail banking industry because of its stake in Royal Bank of Scotland. [...] But the state's arms-length approach means RBS has failed both its customers and the broader economy.[6]

This is a small-scale version of the idea that *real* socialism has never been tried: real nationalisation has never been tried.

---

5   Socialism's future may be its past, 26 June 2017, *New York Times* (https://mobile.nytimes.com/2017/06/26/opinion/finland-station-communism-socialism.html).

6   British banks can't be trusted – let's nationalise them, *The Guardian*, 19 October 2017 (https://www.theguardian.com/commentisfree/2017/oct/19/british-banks-trusted-nationalise-city-profits-communities).

But if we cannot achieve 'real' public ownership with the size and scope that the state currently has, what hope is there that we can achieve it if we inflate the size of the state even more, and give it ever more power over even more areas of life?

Conclusion

Socialism has become fashionable again in Britain. Survey after survey shows widespread support both for socialism in the abstract and for a wide range of socialist policies.

And yet, that support for socialism as an ideal is not matched by a positive view of any particular example, contemporary or historical, of socialism in action. On the contrary: whenever any such example is mentioned, socialists invariably roll their eyes and dismiss it as a lazy straw man.

Socialists have largely succeeded in distancing themselves from previous attempts to build socialist societies. Holding a real-world example of socialism against a self-described socialist is considered a cheap shot today. The conventional wisdom is that people who associate socialism with the Warsaw Pact countries, Maoist China, North Korea or North Vietnam are simply not clever enough to understand the difference between an idea and a distorted application. Holding the Gulags or the Berlin Wall against democratic socialists is considered just as boorish as holding the atrocities of Al Qaida or the Islamic State against peaceful Muslims.

And yet, when asked what exactly was 'unreal' about previous variants of socialism, or what they would have done differently, contemporary socialists struggle to come up with a clear answer. When pressed, they escape into the abstract, talking about lofty aspirations rather than tangible characteristics. But the lofty aspirations that are usually cited are exactly the same old aspirations that have *always* been the aspirations of socialism. The idea that a socialist system should empower ordinary working people, rather than party apparatchiks, is not remotely as original as contemporary socialists think it is. That has *always* been the idea.

Contemporary socialists define 'real' socialism in terms of the outcomes they would like to see, rather than the institutional setup which is supposed to produce those outcomes. By mixing a desired outcome of a system into the very definition of that system, the idea that 'real' socialism has never been tried becomes unfalsifiable. It is as if we defined a rain dance as 'a dance that causes rainfall', as opposed to 'a dance that *aims* to cause rainfall'. Under the latter definition, it is possible to conclude, after a sufficiently large number of failed attempts, that rain dances cannot, after all, cause rain. Under the former definition, that is not possible. If an attempt at a rain dance does not cause rain, then by definition, it cannot have been a *real* rain dance. A real rain dance has never been tried. Those who claim that rain dances have 'failed' are just not clever enough to understand the difference between the *idea* of a rain dance and a distorted application.

Socialism in the sense in which self-identified democratic socialists define it, namely, a democratised economy planned collectively by 'the people', has never been achieved anywhere, and could not be achieved. Economic planning can only ever be done in a technocratic, elitist fashion, and it requires an extreme concentration of power in the hands of the state. It cannot 'empower' ordinary workers. It can only ever empower a bureaucratic elite.

But while this vision of socialism cannot be attained, it can be easily *projected* onto actually existing societies, by virtue of being so abstract and nebulous. For the same reason, that projection can just as easily be ended. This is what Western intellectuals have been doing for almost a century. Thirty years ago, Hayek (1988) wrote about 'intellectuals' vain search for a truly socialist community, which results in the idealisation of, and then disillusionment with, a seemingly endless string of "utopias"'. Since then, this string has only grown longer.

The reception of socialist experiments usually follows a three-stage pattern. Socialist experiments often go through an initial honeymoon period, during which they have, or at least seem to have, some initial successes, and during which their international standing is relatively high. During this honeymoon period, the experiment is usually showered with enthusiastic praise from Western intellectuals. It is held up as a role model of 'true' socialism, as 'proof' that socialism does work, and as an inspiring alternative to the morally bankrupt capitalist systems of the West.

This honeymoon never lasts forever. At some point, the model's failures become more widely known in the West, and the respective country's international standing deteriorates. During this period, Western intellectuals look frantically for excuses. There is still widespread support for the model in question, but language and emphasis change drastically: a hopeful and optimistic case is replaced by an angry and defensive one. Western socialists shoot the messenger; they act as if the critics of the system were somehow responsible for the system's failure. Outside forces and/or members of the old, discredited elites are accused of 'undermining' socialism. Western apologists engage extensively in whataboutery, raising counteraccusations and trying to shift attention to unrelated issues.

But there comes a point when the system's failures become so obvious, and its international reputation becomes so irreparably damaged, that defending it becomes a lost cause. This is the third and final stage. Small sects of true believers continue to defend the system, but mainstream intellectuals fall silent on the issue. After a while, the pilgrimages and eulogies fade from memory and Western intellectuals begin to dispute the system's socialist credentials. The new narrative becomes that the system was never truly socialist, that only a handful of extremists ever claimed it was, and that only a complete ignoramus would hold it against a self-described socialist. This narrative then becomes the conventional wisdom. The reputation of socialism, as an idea, survives unblemished.

The first example was the Soviet Union. In the 1930s, thousands of Western intellectuals travelled to Stalin's Soviet Union and returned full of praise. The 1930s were the most murderous period in Soviet history. They started with the forced collectivisation of agriculture and the liquidation of the Kulaks, which then gave rise to the – entirely avoidable – Soviet famine, followed by the Great Terror and the Moscow Trials. But in the accounts of Western pilgrims, Stalin's Soviet Union was the world's first workers' state, the harbinger of a new civilisation. Stalin-mania took a hit with the Molotov–Ribbentrop Pact, but it did not fully come to an end in the West until it came to an end in the Soviet Union itself.

It did not take long until new utopias replaced it. But from then on, every new socialist experiment had to be defined explicitly in opposition to the now discredited Soviet model, and where applicable, in opposition to other, now equally discredited models as well. In the 1960s, this was true of Maoist China, North Vietnam and Cuba.

In China, the Great Leap Forward led to what was probably the greatest famine in human history. In addition, millions were executed or worked to death in forced labour camps. But after the Sino-Soviet split, China became a popular pilgrimage destination for Western intellectuals. From California to West Berlin, Mao-themed 'fan merchandise' articles, such as the 'Little Red Book', became fashion icons during the student protests. Soviet socialism was discredited, but Maoist China represented the promise of a fresh start. Soviet socialism had just empowered a bureaucratic caste, but Maoist China was a true workers' and peasants' state. This time was going to be different.

Alas, it was not. After Mao's death, Mao-mania quickly disappeared in the West, and China's version of socialism retroactively ceased to be 'real' socialism.

In the 1960s, Cuba offered similarly high hopes. Cuba deviates from the conventional three-stage pattern, in that it seems to be permanently stuck somewhere in between phase two and phase three. One can still easily find relatively prominent supporters of the Cuban regime, who blame the country's economic underdevelopment and the regime's repressive character exclusively on external factors. But the initial enthusiasm has long gone, and today, even on the very far left, few would claim that Cuban socialism represents a model for the future.

Cambodia under the Khmer Rouge was almost completely closed off to foreign visitors until the regime's final year, ruling it out as a pilgrimage destination. But that did not stop a number of Western intellectuals from romanticising the regime from afar. In absolute terms, the Khmer Rouge's Western fan base was never huge. But it represented a large proportion of academics in the relevant fields. Western supporters saw Khmer Rouge socialism as an idyllic, quaint and rural version of socialism, built on community values and moral purification. Cambodia remained socialist after the Vietnamese invasion, but Vietnam, by that time, had already joined the club of countries with discredited versions of socialism: Vietnamese and Vietnam-aligned socialism was no longer 'real' socialism.

Once the Khmer Rouge's genocide could no longer be denied, Khmer Rouge socialism immediately ceased to be 'real' socialism as well, and, as always, this happened with retroactive effect. The conventional wisdom became that the Khmer Rouge were never socialist and that to suggest otherwise is a vicious smear, aimed only at discrediting the noble idea of socialism.

Just like the Sino-Soviet split had been the starting shot of Mao-mania, the Sino-Albanian split became the starting shot for Hoxhaism in the West. While China and the Warsaw Pact countries represented old, discredited versions of socialism, Albania became the new hope, a genuine workers' democracy which stayed true to its socialist ideals. Some disappointed Maoists transferred their hopes to Albania, and Hoxhaism became the new Maoism, if only on a much smaller scale. The country's self-imposed isolationism made it seem attractive to some Western intellectuals, because an isolated country cannot be tainted by associations with already discredited variants of socialism.

If mentioning the Soviet Union or Maoist China in the presence of a self-described socialist is considered déclassé today, mentioning North Korea is considered beyond the pale. Today, North Korea is seen as at best a grotesque caricature of socialism. But this was not always so. South Korea, against which North Korea is inevitably benchmarked, was not always the prosperous liberal democracy that it is today. As long as it was not quite so clear which of the two Koreas would become the more attractive one, some Westerners chose to project their idea of a workers' state onto the DPRK.

The German Democratic Republic is a case study that defies the three-stage pattern. There was no period of widespread enthusiastic support and hence no drastic reversal. Rather, this system was praised by different groups of intellectuals at different times for different things. In the early years, the GDR's self-image as an 'anti-Nazi state' was taken at face value by its admirers abroad. In the final phase, the emphasis shifted to the GDR's relative economic success, as the most advanced economy in the socialist bloc. These latter assessments were not nearly as delusional as those of Stalin's or Mao's pilgrims – but it is also clear that they did not age well.

Venezuela, the most recent example, followed the three-stage pattern to the letter. It started with the usual this-time-is-different rhetoric. Venezuela's nascent model of socialism was defined specifically in opposition to earlier models, both explicitly, for example in Hugo Chávez's speech at the 2005 World Social Forum, and via the catchphrase 'Socialism of the 21st Century' or '21st-Century Socialism'. The distancing from earlier forms of socialism was not empty rhetoric: the Chavistas tried really hard to build up new forms of social ownership and to find new ways of democratic participation. But ultimately, none of them got very far. Cooperatives, for example, became just subsidised private enterprises.

But the combination of socialist rhetoric and an oil-induced boom was enough to create the impression that Venezuela had found a way to make socialism work. Once again, Western intellectuals went on large-scale pilgrimages and came back convinced that they had seen the future. A leitmotif of Venezuela-mania was how Chavismo was not just a huge success story in its own right, but a model for the West to follow. When the country began to fall apart, Venezuela-mania turned angry and defensive. The emphasis shifted from the model's supposed achievements to the supposed motives of its critics. After a short period, most Chavistas simply fell silent on the issue.

For about a decade, Venezuela was the hobbyhorse of many Western intellectuals. Today, mentioning Venezuela is considered cheap political point-scoring. Venezuela's socialist credentials are being retroactively withdrawn. The emerging consensus is that Venezuela was never socialist and that only a person who is profoundly ignorant of socialism would claim otherwise.

And so, once again, what was once 'real' socialism has become retroactively unreal. Venezuela is the most recent example of its kind. It will not be the last. Socialism has ended in failure so many times, it is not as if two or three additional examples could make a difference.

The revival of socialism comes at a strange time. The global poverty rate is the lowest it has ever been in history. Global life expectancy, whether measured at birth or as remaining life expectancy at a given age, is the highest it has ever been in history. Global infant mortality rates are the lowest they have ever been in history. Global literacy rates are the highest they have ever been in history. One can pick almost any economic, social or even environmental indicator at random, and place a wager that it will have improved over the past 30 or 40 years. To a very large extent, these improvements must be attributed to capitalism. There are always exceptions and other factors at play, but on the whole, measures of economic freedom are a very good predictor of the extent of improvement. There is room for legitimate disagreement about what the best model of capitalism is. We can argue about whether we should be more like Sweden and Denmark, or whether we should be more like Hong Kong and Singapore. But it should have been clear a long time ago that the future cannot lie in Venezuela-style economic policies.

More than two dozen attempts at building a socialist society have ended in failure. But socialism is nonetheless here to stay. The reason is that most of us instinctively dislike the market economy. Anti-capitalism is a 'default opinion', which comes naturally and effortlessly to us. Whatever its achievements, capitalism *feels* wrong. It is counterintuitive. Even the most prominent free-market thinkers, such as F. A. Hayek, James Buchanan or Milton Friedman, did not *start* their careers as free-marketeers.

If we judge market economies primarily by their short-comings, while judging socialism primarily as an idea, and by the intentions of its proponents, then the market economy can never win. Motivated reasoning is a powerful force. We can *always* find an excuse to protect a cherished belief if we look hard enough. And we can always find flaws in ideas that we dislike if we look for them.

But this unicorn-chase is distracting us from finding workable solutions to the – very real – social and economic problems that Britain is currently facing. Whatever our political persuasions, few people would dispute that the past ten years or so have been a rough time for the UK. The economy contracted sharply during and after the financial crash, and the recovery has been torturously slow. Our productivity performance has been a joke. Real wages, as a result, have only grown imperceptibly slowly. Housing costs have continued to rise faster than incomes, as they have for more than two decades. Too many students leave university saddled with debt that exceeds the value of their degree. We still have a substantial budget deficit and our national debt keeps growing, when, given the demographic challenges ahead, the exact opposite is required. The health service lurches from one crisis to another.

But here is the crux of the matter: the reason why we know how bad these developments have been is that whichever problem we look at, we can always find comparable countries which have done considerably better in that regard. The fact that it is so easy to find better examples from otherwise similar countries shows that these problems are not inevitable and not intrinsic to market economies.

The solutions are not all in one place. But if we look for international best practice on a policy-area-by-policy-area basis, we can always find at least one decent real-world example in any given area. Learning from international practice in each policy area is, of course, easier said than done. Working out what exactly constitutes 'international best practice' in any given area, and whether that practice can be transferred to the UK, is anything but straightforward. But searching for solutions in this way would certainly be more fruitful than chasing after the next socialist utopia.

11 EPILOGUE
AN ALTERNATIVE HISTORY:
REAL SOCIALISM IS BEING TRIED[1]

The debate about whether socialism is a good idea that has just been distorted and/or badly implemented in practice, or whether the idea itself is flawed and could not have turned out very differently, is not new. It has been going on ever since the first sympathisers with the October Revolution fell out of love with the Soviet project.

It is fair to say that for now, proponents of the former view have won the debate. Where that question is explicitly asked in surveys, the results speak for themselves. Around four out of five East Germans, but also nearly every other West German, agree with the statement that socialism is a good idea which has just been badly implemented (Stöcker 2016: 202).

They are in good company. This interpretation is fully compatible with the two most famous critiques of actually existing socialism, namely George Orwell's *Animal Farm* and *Nineteen Eighty-Four*. Those two novels are not critiques

---

1   A previous version of this chapter was published in 2018 as IEA Discussion Paper No. 92.

of socialism per se. They are just critiques of the totalitarian socialism of the Soviet Union, leaving open (if not actively implying) the possibility that a different form of socialism could have turned out completely differently. In particular, neither novel contains an *economic* critique of socialism. There is no connection between the fact that the economies described in these novels are supposed to represent socialist economies and the fact that the societies are tyrannical societies. Nor are these economies in any way dysfunctional.

Animal Farm is fully compatible with the Trotskyite account of a betrayed revolution. Initially, everything works fine on Animal Farm. But then the pigs, who represent the Soviet Nomenklatura, gradually turn into a new ruling class. There is, however, nothing remotely inevitable about this. We could easily imagine a version of *Animal Farm* with a happy ending. We could remove the 'bad pig' Napoleon (= Stalin) from the story, or have the 'good pig' Snowball (= Trotsky) prevail over him. We could imagine the other animals being more vigilant and devising more effective safeguard mechanisms against the pigs' power grab. We could imagine the wise old boar Old Major (= Karl Marx), whose economic 'analysis' of the farm system inspires the revolution in the first place, living to see the revolution and keeping a watchful eye on how it evolves.

Had the pigs not taken over, there would be no economic problems in *Animal Farm* either. There is no indication in the book that the farm's output is, in any way, inadequate. The only reason why the animals' food rations keep being cut, and their workdays extended, is that the pigs appropriate all the surplus production.

In *Nineteen Eighty-Four*, it is not spelt out in detail how the dictatorship originally comes about, but it becomes clear that 'IngSoc' or 'English Socialism' is supposed to represent a perverted version of socialism. The main enemy of the state, Emmanuel Goldstein (probably inspired by Trotsky), is described as a former associate of Big Brother (probably inspired by Stalin), and a leading member of the party in its early days. This, too, hints at the idea of a revolution that has been betrayed and corrupted.

There is nothing wrong with Oceania's economy. Most of the population lives in poverty, but this is the result of a deliberate policy choice, rather than the inadequacy of a planned economy. The party keeps the population docile by ensuring that their daily struggles consume all their energies. They therefore wage a perpetual war they know they can never win, in order to destroy the surplus production and keep living standards close to subsistence levels.

In contrast, there have been two far less well-known novels which critique socialism from a classical liberal perspective. These are Eugen Richter's *Pictures of the Socialistic Future* (1891; English translation from 1893) and Henry Hazlitt's *Time Will Run Back* (1952, revised version from 1966) (see Makovi (2015) for a summary). Both novels describe a version of socialism under idealised conditions, assuming away many of the problems that socialist societies actually faced (or in Richter's case, *would* face in the future).

In particular, the abuse of power is not an issue at all. In both novels, socialist politicians are presented as genuine idealists, who use power reluctantly and who have the best of intentions. The usual excuses that socialists are fond of using are also assumed away: these fictional systems do not face any enemies, internal or external. There are no 'counterrevolutionaries' and no hostile foreign powers.

Yet even under those favourable conditions, socialism still leads to stagnation in the economic sphere and to authoritarianism in the political sphere. In both novels, the reasons are economic ones. Since economic activity cannot be coordinated by scarcity signals – i.e. market prices – the only substitute is command and control. When people do not behave in the way economic planners want them to behave, the state needs to use force to make them comply. Deviations from the government's economic plan cannot be allowed, because the different components of the plan depend on each other: the plan must be a coherent whole. Planners lack the relevant knowledge, so resources are misallocated and economic chaos ensues.

And so, socialism leads to tyranny and decline – not because it is 'badly implemented' and not because 'the wrong people' come to power, but due to features that are in the very DNA of socialism.

What follows below is a very minor addition to this strand of literature. It is an 'alternative history', which begins to diverge from 'our' version of history just after the fall of the Berlin Wall. In March 1990, the German Democratic Republic held its first-ever democratic election. In 'our' version of history, it was also its last-ever election, because the pro-reunification parties won with an overwhelming majority and six months later the GDR was no more. However, this outcome was not inevitable. As mentioned in Chapter 8, the question whether socialism had failed in the GDR, or whether the GDR had just deviated from 'true' socialism, was vividly discussed during the election campaign. Several of the parties that ran for that election took the view that the GDR was worth preserving as a sovereign socialist state, and that it could be democratised from within.

A small number of British parliamentarians shared this view. They believed that what they were witnessing was not the end of socialism in the GDR and its allies, but the very opposite: a return to 'true' socialism. An Early Day Motion in the House of Commons, signed by Ken Livingstone and Jeremy Corbyn, said:

> this House [...] recognises that this outburst of discontent and opposition in East Germany [...] in particular, reflects deep anger against the corruption and mismanagement of the Stalinist bureaucracy; sees the movement leading in the direction of genuine socialism, not a return to capitalism; [...] and considers that the only way forward [...] is on the basis of a return to the principles of genuine workers' democracy and socialism which formed the basis and inspiration for the October revolution.[2]

This obviously did not happen.

But what if it *had* happened? What would 'a movement leading in the direction of genuine socialism' and 'a return to the principles of genuine workers' democracy and socialism' have looked like?

---

2 Workers' Democracy in Eastern Europe, Early Day Motion 210 (http://www .parliament.uk/edm/1989-90/210).

'Socialism has not failed in East Germany – it hasn't been tried': Surprise victory of new socialist party in East German election

The Guardian, 19 March 1990

East Berlin is a city in shellshock today. Bonn, meanwhile, is a city of headless chickens. Forget everything you thought you knew about current affairs: after yesterday's surprise election result, all bets are off.

It was supposed to be a done deal. Until last night's exit poll, all pollsters and all pundits agreed on one thing: that the GDR's first-ever democratic election would also be its last. Whatever government would emerge from it would immediately start working towards its own abolition. Within less than a year, a Reunification Treaty was supposed to be signed and ratified by both Bonn and East Berlin. East Germany was supposed to accede to the Federal Republic and thereby cease to be a sovereign country. The GDR was supposed to be on its way out – and to take socialism with it.

Yesterday's election thwarted all those plans. The pro-market, pro-reunification parties have failed to win a majority. Whether the result represents a ringing endorsement of socialism, or whether it is primarily a rejection of a takeover by West Germany, is impossible to tell at the moment. But it is already safe to say that with the current political constellation, there will be no German reunification and no return to the market economy in East Germany any time soon. Socialism was supposed to be a dead man walking. Yesterday's election result has given it a new lease of life.

The pro-reunification Alliance for Germany, which had been predicted to win by a landslide, only came in second place. The Social Democratic Party (also pro-reunification, but at a slower pace), which the polls had down as the only serious contender, did even worse, coming fourth (Table 2).

Table 2   Distribution of seats in the new People's Chamber

United Left	137
Alliance for Germany	105
Party of Democratic Socialism	66
Social Democratic Party	59
Spartacist Workers' Party of Germany	13
Green Party	5
Alliance '90	4
Others	11
TOTAL	400

The surprise winner was the United Left (VL), a party which the polls had barely registered, and which had barely received any media attention during the campaign. So who are these new kids on the block?

The first thing to note about them is that they are not new. Most East Germans have been familiar with them for quite a while, if not under that name. The VL emerged out of the GDR's democratic protest movement, which played such an important role in the lead up to the opening of the Berlin Wall four months ago. In hindsight, it is tempting to assume that the anti-regime protesters must all have been staunch anti-socialists, but nothing could be further from the truth. The protest movement has always contained groups that explicitly described themselves as democratic socialists. Their opposition to the rule of the Socialist Unity Party of Germany (SED) was in no way an opposition to socialism. Rather, they saw themselves as the torchbearers of true socialism, and the SED leadership as power-hungry, careerist sell-outs. This is, perhaps, best expressed in the slogan 'Socialism yes – SED no'.

The VL is simply the party-political arm of this movement. Their aim was never to dismantle the GDR, but to democratise it from within. They want socialism – just not the hierarchical, Soviet-inspired socialism that the GDR has been practising so far. Their idea of socialism is socialism from below, a grassroots socialism, a socialism which empowers ordinary working people, not party apparatchiks or technocratic elites. It is a socialism with civil liberties, political rights and widespread democratic participation, a socialism which thoroughly democratises each and every aspect of life.

With 16 per cent of the vote, the Party of Democratic Socialism (PDS) also did better than expected. The PDS is the successor of the SED, which had ruled the GDR with an iron fist until just four months ago. Its critics see the PDS as no more than a slightly nicer version of the SED, but that criticism is unfair. The party has reinvented itself. It has expelled prominent hardliners and it has promoted intraparty reformers, whose democratic credentials are not in doubt. These reformers have a proven track record of criticising human rights abuses and authoritarian practices in the GDR from within the party, to the extent that this was possible for a party member. Some of them have been threatened with expulsion more than once.

In fifth place came the Spartacist Workers' Party, which stands for a romantic, back-to-the-roots vision of socialism. They want to go back to the original (and literal) meaning of a Soviet republic, namely, a semi-direct grassroots democracy, in which workers' councils form the main building blocks. This is the system that was beginning to take shape in Russia after the October Revolution in 1917. It was never completed because the experiment got corrupted at an early stage.

Could East Germany's current political constellation produce a socialist coalition? Arithmetically, it is possible. In practice, it is a tall order, given the substantial programmatic and cultural differences between the socialist parties.

And yet, a reformed, democratised socialism is the default option of East German politics at the moment. It will have to happen in one way or another.

The young VL voter we spoke to at a polling station in Berlin-Friedrichshain yesterday deserves to be quoted in full, because he no doubt spoke for many of his fellow countrymen:

> I was going to vote Alliance or SPD, but then I thought, hang on – this is throwing out the baby with the bathwater. I'm not opposed to socialism. I'm opposed to Stalinism. I'm opposed to the SED. I'm opposed to the Stasi. I'm opposed to being told what to think, what to say, what to do. I'm sick to death of the arrogant, out-of-touch elite that is running this country. But that's not socialism. That's the opposite of socialism.

> I want to live in a country where the economy exists to satisfy the needs of the people, not the other way around. That is socialism. Some say it has 'failed'. It hasn't. We've never had socialism here. It just hasn't been tried.

Indeed. Socialism, so defined, has never been tried. But it looks as though the GDR is about to try it now. We might be witnessing the beginning of a remarkable experiment.

'A socialism for the many': VL/PDS (+SpAD) coalition treaty signed in East Berlin

The Guardian, 28 April 1990

The first round of coalition talks was awkward. It was bound to be. The United Left (VL), the senior partner in East Germany's new coalition government, grew out of the GDR's democratic protest movement. The PDS, the junior partner in the new coalition government, grew out of the very party the protesters used to protest against. Some VL members had been imprisoned, beaten, spied upon and expelled from their jobs under the rule of the PDS's predecessor party. Some of them had friends who had been shot at the Berlin Wall. These wounds are still fresh.

But during the second meeting, the ice broke. And during the third meeting, they got on like a house on fire. Perhaps the reformers and the protesters have always had the same aims and just tried to achieve them in different ways: the latter through street protests, through pressure from outside and from below; the former through more subtle criticism from within, i.e. within the party and within the permitted parameters.

The Spartacist Workers' Party (SpAD) will not officially join the coalition, but it has signalled its intention to co-operate with the government on an issue-by-issue basis, and SpAD MPs have been given advisory roles in the new government. This makes the SpAD a kind of unofficial third member of the coalition.

All sides had to give and take a bit. The VL (and the SpAD) had to temper its revolutionary impatience some-what. The PDS had to accept bolder measures and a faster pace of reform than it would have chosen on its own. But make no mistake: this coalition treaty is internally consistent and profoundly radical.

Its civil liberties and human rights agenda alone is one of the boldest we have ever seen. The new GDR will guarantee complete freedom of conscience, freedom of the press, freedom of religion, freedom of speech, freedom of assembly, freedom to travel, a right to privacy, a right to due process and a right to a fair trial. The hated Stasi has already been dismantled and its former senior officials are now being prosecuted.

But the most interesting part of the coalition treaty is its economic agenda.

People-Owned Enterprises (VEBs), which account for the bulk of the GDR's economy, will be internally democratised. All major management functions will be passed on to democratically elected Workers' Councils (*Arbeiterräte*). The VEBs will become largely self-governing, autonomous entities, comparable to worker-run cooperatives.

What is even more ambitious is the agenda of democratising economic planning. At the moment, the State Planning Commission (SPK) – the GDR's equivalent of the Soviet Union's Gosplan – which drafts the Five-Year Plans, is the epitome of technocracy and elitism. It makes a complete mockery of the Marxist idea that 'the working class' is in charge of the economy. An ordinary worker has no more influence on the decisions of the SPK than an ordinary Catholic has on the proceedings of a Papal conclave. Five-Year Plans are drafted behind closed doors and then imposed upon the population from on high.

The promise of socialism has always been that it would give ordinary working people control over economic life. In practice, workers in socialist countries have even less control over such matters than workers in capitalist countries. The latter are at the behest of market forces, the former are at the behest of a technocratic elite. This is what the VL mean when they say that the GDR was never really socialist. And this is what they are now trying to change.

From now on, the head of the SPK will be democratically elected once every five years. The SPK will be obliged to consult extensively with external stakeholders, such as the above-mentioned Workers' Councils, and especially with newly established, democratically elected 'Consumer Councils' (*Konsumentenräte*). Every citizen of the GDR will be free to join as many consumer councils as they wish and to set up new ones. The SPK will be obliged to grant those councils unrestricted access to all economic data, including sensitive data. Some planning functions will be devolved to the regional or local level, where additional opportunities for public participation will be created.

In addition, the SPK will become a lot more transparent. It will have to publish the minutes of every meeting, as well as the early and intermediate drafts of the next Five-Year Plan. This will give the public a chance to monitor the process and to intervene where appropriate.

The key passage in the coalition treaty reads:

> In the past, we have had *state* planning of the economy, and *state* ownership of the means of production. This is not good enough. This is not socialism. In the future, *the people* will plan the economy, and *the people* will own the country's productive assets. The GDR used to call itself a Workers' and Farmers' State, but in truth, it was a bureaucrats' and politicians' state. This is where the GDR went wrong. And this is what we want to change.

After over forty years of nominal socialism, East Germany is finally discovering the true meaning of that term. What took you so long?

Four years on, has East Germany's programme of socialist renewal worked?
The Guardian, 19 March 1994

Four years ago, an unlikely coalition of former street protesters and reform-minded members of the GDR's former ruling party took office in East Berlin. Many predicted that it would fall apart immediately. The tenor in the West

German and the British press was that the GDR's days were numbered and that this desperate attempt to keep it on life support for a little longer would only delay the inevitable.

Four years on, the GDR is going from strength to strength. In yesterday's general election, the VL/PDS coalition has been confirmed in government with an increased majority in the People's Chamber. It enjoys popularity ratings that Mr Kohl's shambolic coalition, not to mention Mr Major's poor joke of a government, can only dream of.

The initially shaky coalition of revolutionaries (the VL) and reformists (the PDS) turned out to be a match made in heaven. The VL brought the energy, the enthusiasm and the zeal for radical change. The PDS brought the experience, the insider knowledge and the sense of continuity. Mixing those ingredients in a ratio of 2:1 turned out to be just right.

The coalition's hallmark is its programme of socialist renewal. State ownership has become public ownership. State planning has become public planning. The programme is still a work in progress, but it has already resulted in an unprecedented shift of power from unelected and unaccountable bureaucrats to ordinary working people and civil society.

But has it worked? Has socialist renewal been a success?

The answer is: it depends. For some, the main priority in 1990 was to close the huge East–West gap in economic output. If this is your only measure of success, then the answer to the above question is no. Despite the current recession in West Germany, the East–West gap remains as large as it has ever been. It might even have grown had it not been for a generous fiscal transfer from West Germany (not wholly motivated by altruism, but to prevent a flood of East German migrants, which would have put downward pressure on wages and upward pressure on rents). So in this respect, the government has yet to come up with a convincing solution.

But there is more to life than money, and there is more to a society's success than GDP figures. In many other respects, the transformation of the GDR has been impressive. The country has reinvented itself as a model of participatory socialism. In West Germany and Britain, millions of people work in dead-end jobs they do not enjoy, for companies with which they do not identify, in industries which they do not feel they have a stake in. They lack a sense of ownership, of empowerment, and of belonging.

Contrast this to the new GDR. East German workplaces are democratically run. Ordinary workers can elect their own company director – indeed, they can *become* their own company director, if they put themselves forward and persuade their colleagues to vote for them. Every East German worker has a right to attend and to speak at management meetings. West German and British workers are cogs in a machine. East German workers *own* the machine and *run* the machine.

But workplace democracy is just one of many layers of democratic control. In the GDR, the whole economy is democratically run. The State Planning Commission (SPK) is democratically elected and constantly holds public consultations on matters large and small. Expert planners are still involved, but civil society – represented by countless

Consumer Councils, Workers' Councils or just unaffiliated individuals participating in local planning meetings – is calling the shots.

The current Five-Year Plan is an outstanding democratic achievement. It is the first of its kind which has been drafted with mass public participation. Hundreds of planning meetings and planning consultations have been held up and down the country. Hundreds of thousands of people, from all walks of life, have been involved in its creation. It is the first genuine People's Plan in the history of socialism.

Net emigration has been much lower than expected, not least because, for the first time since 1949, migration between East and West Germany has become a two-way street again. Some East Germans have left, lured by the superficial attractions of a consumer society. But at the same time, many idealistic West Germans have been attracted by the promise of a different way of doing things. This appeal goes far beyond West Germany: the GDR is fast becoming a popular destination for democratic socialists from all over Europe. It is the place where Western Europeans who have given up on capitalism, and Eastern Europeans who have given up on top-down socialism, are coming together to create something genuinely new and exciting.

If you judge a country's success by GDP figures or productivity figures alone, then yes, you will find the West German economy more appealing. If you had to choose between an East German and a West German car or domestic appliance, you would probably choose the West

German one. But nobody finds West Germany 'inspiring'; nobody would look at West Germany thinking 'This could be the model for a better world'.

In contrast, the new GDR very much does inspire people. There are at least two dozen GDR study groups at British universities. There is a popular GDR Solidarity Campaign, whose members include the MP for Islington North, the MP for Glasgow Kelvin and the MP for Hackney North/ Stoke Newington.

The GDR is creating a new model of socialism – a socialism from below, a socialism of the people. It shows us that there is a different and a better way of doing things. In the weeks after the fall of the Berlin Wall, the dominant narrative in Britain was that socialism was finished and that the best we could hope for was a slightly modified version of Thatcherism. Few people would say that today. The new GDR has become a source of hope and courage for those of us who still believe that a better world is possible.

In this sense, the answer to the above question is an unqualified yes: East Germany's programme of socialist renewal has been a phenomenal success.

East German government re-centralises control over People-Owned Enterprises

The Guardian, 21 January 1995

'*People*-owned, not state-owned' is one of the GDR government's favourite slogans. 'Putting the *people* back into People-Owned Enterprises' is another. Workplace democracy is one of the cornerstones of the GDR government's programme of socialist renewal and one of its most widely admired achievements. And yet, the East German government now finds itself forced to put that project on hold for the time being. With effect from next month, the self-management rights of People-Owned Enterprises (VEBs) are going to be curtailed again and control over them partly re-centralised.

The East German government is at pains to point out that this does not represent a U-turn on policy. It is a temporary measure, which is meant to give the government the breathing space it needs to even out some of the new system's irregularities.

'We need to work out a more coherent system, in which incentives are better aligned', explains Jens Geißler, the Minister for Workplace Democratisation.

> After democratisation, in many of the large VEBs workers voted for substantial salary increases, or shorter workdays, or more paid holidays etc. Where they have voted for changes in working practices, this has often been with the aim of making them more convenient to the workforce, rather than more productive. There is nothing wrong with any of that, quite the opposite: The whole point of socialism is that the workers, not capitalists, reap the benefits of economic progress.
>
> But such measures need to be backed by productivity increases, and our productivity performance to date has simply not been good enough. The problem is that many of those VEBs are now behind on their production quotas. This has adverse knock-on effects on other parts of our

economy, jumbling our Five-Year Plan. If, for example, the production of tyres is behind schedule, the production of cars, motorcycles and bicycles falls behind schedule as well. And so on.

We could, of course, pay VEBs on a performance-related basis and give them responsibility for their own budgets. We could let some of them prosper and others go bust. But then we would be half way towards a market economy. That is not the way we want to do things here.

Geißler emphasises that the government remains fully committed to the principles of worker management and workplace democracy:

There is absolutely nothing wrong with those principles. We just need to remind ourselves that a VEB is jointly owned by *all* people, not just those who happen to work in them at any given time. Otherwise, they would just be capitalist enterprises. Maybe we have not made that sufficiently clear during the transition.

We are definitely on the right track, but we have probably rushed it a bit too much. We will pause some features of our workplace democracy agenda for the moment, until the backlogs in production have been cleared and until we have sorted out those inconsistencies.

Critics argue that even if this is not the government's intention, it is, in effect, a return to the old top-down model. What is the point of democratic governance structures in the VEBs if a VEB's management has no autonomy to do anything other than follow orders handed down from East Berlin?

But while the announcement is not popular, it has not provoked a backlash either. In practice, the initial enthusiasm for workplace democracy was already on the wane. Turnout at Workers' Council elections and workers' assemblies has already dropped sharply at VEBs across the nation.

We spoke to several workers at the VEB Kombinat Robotron in Dresden. Olaf Baumgarten, who works for the engineering department, told us:

> I like the idea in principle, but I find a lot of those meetings are just long-winded, boring and tedious. Look: I'm an engineer. I want to get on with my job. I don't want to sit in tedious committee meetings the whole time.

His colleague Hanna Hoffstädter agrees:

> Of course management should consult with the workforce. They do that in most West German companies as well, and for good reason. But whatever happened to specialisation? Whatever happened to the idea of letting people focus on what they're good at? Most of those committee meetings are about things that I don't have a clue about and that I'm not remotely interested in.

Franziska Krüger, who works in one of the assembly plants, is even more critical of what she calls the 'committee culture' (Komiteekultur):

> Ultimately, all those worker committees just get domin-
> ated by the sort of people who are good at networking
> and backscratching. The meetings, meanwhile, get dom-
> inated by those who are most enamoured with the sound
> of their own voice, and frankly, these are not always the
> people who have the most interesting things to say. Ei-
> ther way, you don't get a representative cross-section of
> the workforce – if there is such a thing.

The government's announcements, then, might not make
that much of a difference in practice.

VEB manager Heiko Kurz sees the changes as regret-
table, but remains optimistic overall:

> We will almost certainly see a revival of the workplace
> democracy agenda later this year. It is true that partici-
> pation has declined, but at least in the abstract, the idea
> remains hugely popular.
>
> Hopefully next time, there will be a greater focus on
> education and awareness. We need to make sure that
> people are properly prepared. You cannot expect a sys-
> tem like that to work overnight.

The return of the technocrats? East Germany quietly abandons 'People's Planning'

The Guardian, 4 March 1995

The system of participatory planning – or 'People's Planning' – is considered one of the proudest achievements of
the East German government. According to its supporters,

the democratisation of the planning process has given ordinary workers an unprecedented degree of control over economic life. If there is one policy area that symbolises the difference between the old top-down socialism inspired by the Soviet Union and the new bottom-up socialism of the GDR, it is this.

It therefore came as a surprise to some when the East German government announced that it would temporarily suspend important features of the new system. From next month, the State Planning Commission (SPK), the organisation which has the overall responsibility for drafting the Five-Year Plans, will see some of its former discretionary powers restored. By the same token, civil society stakeholders will see their influence reduced.

Why would the government put such a popular policy on hold? We met with Katrin Krause, a senior civil servant at the SPK, who told us:

> I'm not saying that the old system was great; believe me, I know its downsides better than anyone. But at least we used to get things done. The plans were usually finished on time and the production quotas mostly fulfilled.
>
> Now, it's just a nightmare. When the government told us to consult with 'the people', they assumed that 'the people' would all speak with one voice. Guess what – they don't. The supposed voice of the people sounds more like a cacophony of conflicting and mutually incompatible demands. This mythical entity called 'the people' actually consists of lots of different groups and different individuals with very different interests and preferences.

But weren't the new Consumer Councils supposed to for-
malise this process?

Most Consumer Councils are just lobbying for their own
pet projects. It's the same thing every day. We meet with a
Consumer Council which represents aficionados of product X. They tell us: 'X is supremely important. You need to
produce more X. You need to produce better X. West Germany is much better at X'. But when we ask them where
they think we should get the inputs from, they say, 'Oh,
we don't know. Just take them from somewhere. Produce
less Y, maybe. Y isn't that important'.

Then we contact the Consumer Council which represents Y-aficionados. They tell us: 'Y is supremely important. You need to produce more Y. You need to produce
better Y. West Germany is much better at Y'. But when we
ask them where they think we should get the inputs from,
they say, 'Oh, we don't know. Just take them from somewhere. Produce less X, maybe. X isn't that important'.

Surely, though, trade-offs are part and parcel of economic
life in any economic system, whether socialist, capitalist,
mixed, or anything else?

Of course they are. But that is exactly the problem: in our
system, we have no rational way of trading off these competing demands against one another. If we cannot simul-
taneously produce more of both X *and* Y, what should we
prioritise? Should we make it dependent on which group
shouts loudest? Is that socialism?

In West Germany, consumer demand is revealed through willingness to pay, and supply adjusts. I'm not saying we should go down that road, which would spell the end of socialism. But at least the West Germans have a method of rational economic decision-making. And we don't.

Krause and many of her colleagues at the SPK have been pointing out the flaws in People's Planning right from the start. They have been pleading with the government to restore some of the SPK's former discretionary powers for years. So far, their demands have fallen on deaf ears, because the VL/PDS government was convinced that they were self-serving. They believed that critics of People's Planning were just members of the old bureaucratic elite, who resented the loss of status and power that the new system meant for them. So the government replaced quite a few long-standing civil servants with new appointees who were more sympathetic to the project.

But when, after a short time in the job, most of those new appointees came to the same conclusions as the despised 'old bureaucratic elite', the government started to listen. When progress on the next Five-Year Plan stalled, the government was forced to act. It now seems to have settled for a halfway house, somewhere in between People's Planning and the old model of technocratic planning.

The SPK will still be obliged to consult with consumer and worker representatives. But when their demands are incompatible, the SPK will be allowed to revert to its old computer models for predicting consumer demand. The government insists that this is not a retreat from People's Planning. Stefan Bergmüller, the Minister of Economic Democracy, explains:

> People's Planning will remain the normal mode of economic planning in the GDR. Nobody wants to change that. But for the time being, we need to have a Plan B for those instances in which People's Planning does not produce a conclusive answer. We need a backup, a way to fill the remaining gaps.
>
> We will not need that backup forever. Once we have sorted out the inconsistencies in the current system, it will not be needed anymore. But we will need a better way to balance the needs of the whole community with the wishes of individual groups. Consumer Councils need to bear in mind that the Five-Year Plans are there to satisfy the needs of *all* people, not just selected groups. Perhaps we haven't made that sufficiently clear during the transition. Perhaps we have rushed the whole agenda a bit too much.
>
> We remain committed to People's Planning. We expect that over time, as the public's understanding of the system improves, we will need less and less SPK discretion. At some point, we may not need the SPK at all anymore.

This does not sound like a retreat at all. How important are those changes in practice? For Mrs Krause, the answer is: very.

They say that we should only use our old models when the demands of the Consumer Councils are incompatible. Here's the thing: they are *always* incompatible. If we wanted to produce everything the Consumer Councils ask us to produce, we would need an economy more than fourteen times the size of ours. We would need the whole economy of West Germany, basically. Plus a few Swiss cantons.

The minister's announcements have provoked surprisingly little criticism. In practice, East Germans were already falling out of love with People's Planning. Active participation in the planning process has dropped sharply over the last year. Annette Hartmann, who runs the SPK's Public Engagement Unit, tells us:

It is really hard to keep people involved. When we started these public consultations, there was a lot of enthusiasm. But most people just turn up for two or three meetings and then drop out.

I don't blame them. Once you get to the nuts and bolts, economic planning is, admittedly, a dry and technical matter. I can totally see why, after a long workday, most people would rather do something a little bit more entertaining or more relaxing. This is, ultimately, a very specialised job. Maybe the idea of mass involvement was never realistic.

The government remains optimistic that People's Planning will take off again once people become used to it.

Mass exodus: Over 240,000 people leave East Germany

The Guardian, 12 July 1995

When the Berlin Wall fell, demographers predicted a flood of East German migrants heading for West Germany. It turned out to be a rivulet.

This time, the demographers erred in the opposite direction. According to the record sections of West German municipalities, nearly a quarter of a million East Germans have settled in the Federal Republic over the past twelve months. Migration in the opposite direction, meanwhile, has come to an almost complete halt, meaning that for all intents and purposes, gross East–West migration equals net East–West migration.

This could be a one-off. But it could also mark the beginning of a return to the migration patterns we used to see in the decade before the Berlin Wall was built. In the 1950s, the GDR lost between 145,000 and 280,000 people every single year (which is, of course, the reason why the Berlin Wall was built in the first place).

Who are these new expats? Why are they leaving? What are they looking for? What could persuade them to return? We met a little GDR expat community in a beer garden in Munich.

Although most of them were reluctant to admit it, it quickly emerged that they mainly left for economic reasons. As Wolf Bauknecht, a car mechanic from Karl-Marx-Stadt, puts it:

I know you're not supposed to say that, because it's considered shallow and materialistic, but yes – I am here because of the higher living standards. I like the fact that I can afford a nice car here. I like the fact that I can go to nice restaurants. I like the fact that I can afford a holiday in Italy. I like the fact that the supermarket shelves are always full. I like the fact that there are plenty of leisure opportunities, plenty of interesting things to do.

His girlfriend Kerstin Karlsberg, a nurse, adds:

The GDR has changed for the better. They're not locking you up anymore for criticising the government. They're not bugging your phone anymore. You can vote in meaningful elections, not just the Mickey Mouse elections we used to have before 1990.

But what hasn't changed is the economy. The queues. The shortages. The monotony. The dreariness.

It's obviously great that the GDR has become a democracy. But our economic problems never had anything to do with the fact that we were not a democracy. It's the *economic* system, *not* the political system, which has created those problems, and which keeps creating them. If you only change the political system, without changing the economic system, then you're still going to have the same economic problems that you've always had.

But the economic system *has* changed. What about all those new opportunities for participating in economic planning which the GDR government has created? Why not use those avenues and try to improve the GDR, rather than just walk away from it? Ms Karlsberg is not impressed by them:

> I've been to a few of those planning meetings and found them completely pointless. Most of them aren't going anywhere, simply because the people who take part in them can't agree with each other. The only meeting I've ever been to which actually reached a conclusion was one which got hijacked by a group of single-issue cranks, who were completely obsessed with some niche topic. They took over, because everyone else just got bored and left.
>
> I prefer the way they do things here. You try to sell something. If people want it, you sell more. If people don't want it, you stop, and try something else. They have no endless debates about what 'the community' supposedly 'needs'. They just try different things. Some work. Some fail.

Will more East Germans follow? Most of the expats think so. Hans Stoltenberg, an electrician from Stralsund, thinks:

> There is a bit of a psychological barrier. We have been divided for so long, West Germany is a foreign country for us. I certainly found the idea of moving here daunting. But then a close friend of mine moved here, told me all about how it went – and that sort of took the edge off it. As more people have a similar experience, more people will move.

It remains to be seen whether he is right, but the macroeconomic situation certainly points towards more East–West migration. At the moment, the West German economy still suffers from the aftermath of a deep recession, which saw unemployment soaring to a post-war high. But leading indicators point towards recovery. If so many people are prepared to move when the economy is still in the doldrums, how many will come when the economy is picking up again?

East Germany reinstates border controls
The Guardian, 7 August 1995

Just over five years ago, Europe's hardest border suddenly became its softest almost overnight. The intra-German border, once the steel part of the Iron Curtain, became mere window dressing. With effect from next October, it is going to harden again. There will still be complete freedom to travel in both directions, but passport checks and customs inspections will make a comeback.

In 1990, the two Germanies did not bother to come up with a proper trade and customs agreement. It was deemed unnecessary. East German goods and services are generally not interesting to West German consumers and the average East German cannot afford much in West Germany anyway. In theory, the 1990 Brussels–East Berlin Amendment spells out the relationship between the GDR and the EU's Customs Union and its Single Market (of which the Federal Republic is a part). In practice, the agreement is full of holes and therefore often just ignored.

But over the past year, cross-border shopping has become a lot more common. It is true that the purchasing power of East Germans in West Germany is not huge. But

West German markets are characterised by a much higher degree of product differentiation than their East German counterparts. Where East Germany has two or three generic versions of a product, West Germany has at least a dozen, ranging from very basic no-frills versions to luxury versions with all the bells and whistles. West German products in the middle of the price range (let alone the top end) are generally unaffordable to East German consumers. But products in the no-frills segment, such as a supermarket's in-house brand, tend to be cheap even by East German standards. They are usually no worse than the generic East German product and unlike the latter they are always available.

In short, you will not hear many East German dialects in the *Kaufhaus des Westens*, West Berlin's luxury department store. But you will hear plenty of them at Lidl and Aldi. This is a huge problem for the East German economy, because once these cross-border shoppers have stocked up in West Germany, they are no longer interested in East German products.

Cross-border shopping in this sense is a one-way street. But in quite a different way, some East German products do end up in West Germany. East Germany provides a range of basic essentials at heavily subsidised prices which do not cover production costs. These are often in short supply, a problem which is far from new, but which has got a lot worse since the opening of the border. Some East Germans bulk-buy these products cheaply and then resell them on street markets in West Germany.

The new customs system will introduce tariffs on West German products, customs checks and limits on the quantity of goods that people can take with them in either direction. Re-manning and re-equipping this 1,400 km long border is a major feat, but the East German government is confident that at least a makeshift border infrastructure will be up and running by October.

Frederik Adler, the Minister of Trade, explains:

> The opening of the intra-German border was one of the most wonderful events in my lifetime. I will never forget how overwhelmed with joy I felt when I crossed it for the first time. It was a dream come true.
>
> And it is a dream that will remain true forever. The border between the two Germanies will be one of the most permeable borders in the world. It will not differ much from the border between, say, West Germany and Switzerland. A lot of people will barely notice it. We will introduce a fast lane, where people who are travelling on foot, bike or motorcycle, and without any bags, can go straight through.
>
> We are committed to keeping this border as open as it can possibly be, given the circumstances. But we also need to recognise that unlike the border between, say, West Germany and the Netherlands, the inner-German border is an interface between two very, very different economic systems. On one side you have an economic system based on profit-maximisation, and on the other side you have an economic system based on satisfying the needs of the people. This inevitably creates some tensions, which is why the interface between these two systems needs careful management. We cannot allow our subsidised products to leak out. And neither can we

expose ourselves to a competitive race to the bottom. It was therefore naïve to believe that this border could remain completely open forever.

One of the as yet unresolved issues is what will happen between East and West Berlin. The return of a border between these two cities, no matter how easily traversable, would inevitably bring back bad memories. And yet, this is where the economic problems identified by the minister are most acute.

East German government in row with West German press

The Guardian, 8 August 1996

As East Germany's brain drain intensifies, the government in East Berlin has accused several leading West German newspapers of adding fuel to the fire, by egging people on to leave. The Home Office speaks of a 'large-scale public disinformation campaign' and of a 'concerted effort to turn the public against the project of socialist renewal'.

The background to the row is this: with the West German economy picking up pace again, East–West migration has soared to levels not seen since the 1950s. The GDR is currently losing over 20,000 people every month, predominantly skilled workers in the prime of their careers.

A bloodletting on such a scale would be a problem for *any* economy, but it is an especially severe problem in a planned economy such as the GDR's. Katrin Krause of the State Planning Commission (SPK) explains:

You cannot plan an economy under those conditions. The current Five-Year Plan is based on workforce figures that are already completely out of date. It is, for all intents and purposes, worthless.

If people emigrated in a steady fashion, we could cope with it; we would factor it in when we draft the plans. But there are huge, unpredictable shifts in migration patterns. Over the past few months, we have suddenly lost lots of people who used to work for the railway. Fair enough – we have other mediums of transport. But the problem is that some of our other industries are heavily reliant on rail transport. Their activities are structured around the railway capacity that was forecast in the Five-Year Plan. Since that capacity is no longer there, many of them are now falling behind their production schedule. And if they fall behind, others, who rely on them, will fall behind as well. And then others... you get the point.

Don't get me wrong: I'm not saying we should put up the Wall again. As far as I'm concerned, everyone should be free to move to wherever they like, whenever they like, and as often as they like. Just don't expect me to plan an economy when the factors of production are moving around all the time.

Against this backdrop, earlier this year, the East German editions of two centre-right West German newspapers have started to explicitly encourage emigration. The *Bild* runs a series in which former East Germans, who have moved to the West, get to express how happy they are with their new lives. The *Welt* has been a bit subtler, but the message is the same: what are you waiting for? Come on over here and join us.

In addition, the East German edition of the *Frankfurter Allgemeine Zeitung* has begun to persistently and ruthlessly dissect the GDR's ongoing economic weaknesses.

Sven Holtermann, the GDR's Home Secretary, argues:

This is not journalism. This is just shoddy propaganda. If you read these articles, you would think that every West German is a millionaire, who lives in a mansion with a swimming pool and a private jet. It's so ludicrously biased. Why do they never mention the people who lose their jobs due to automation? Why don't they mention the disillusioned migrants, who end up returning to the GDR? Why don't they mention the rampant inequality? Why don't they mention the economic anxiety, the hyper-consumerism, the lack of community cohesion?

It's because their intention is not to inform. They have an agenda. Follow the money. Look at who funds these papers through advertising revenue: the car industry, the pharmaceutical industry and the petrochemical industry. What do these sectors have in common? They all have problems recruiting skilled labour. That's why they have an interest in cheaper labour from the East.

This is a nothing but a corporate recruitment campaign. Those Western corporations want to induce wage dumping, a race to the bottom. That's why they try to lure our workers with false promises of a better life.

The job of the press should be to help people make an informed choice, through balanced reporting – not to do the bidding of a corporate paymaster.

The GDR Solidarity Campaign in the UK agrees with the minister's assessment. According to their press statement on the subject:

West Germany's corporate media barons are desperate to undermine the East German Workers' State because they see it as a threat by example. They hate it because it is a source of hope for working people in West Germany and beyond. They hate it because it demonstrates that a better world is possible. And so, it must be destroyed, like every other example of an economy run for the benefit of working people before it.

We can no longer pretend the Western press in East Germany is impartial[3]
The Guardian, 3 October 1996

In the past, the greatest threat to freedom of expression in this country came from the government. State censorship of critical voices meant that our media was unable to do what it should: hold those in power to account, equip

---

3   With minor tweaks, large sections of this fictitious article are based on a real *Guardian* article by Owen Jones. See: We can no longer pretend the British press is impartial, *The Guardian*, 9 October 2017 (https://www.theguardian.com/commentisfree/2017/oct/09/no-longer-pretend-british-press-impartial-country-more-leftwing).

people with reliable and relevant information, and help them in forming a considered informed opinion.

Today, the greatest threat to freedom of expression comes not from the government, but from corporate dominance. Over the past few years, we had to learn that corporate control can be just as insidious as state control.

This statement from the East German Department of Media and Culture prefaces the new Media Diversification Bill (*Mediendiversifizierungsgesetz*), which will come into force next month. Its main element is the introduction of a maximum market share. From now on, no single newspaper, or media group, will be allowed to hold a combined market share of more than one eighth (12.5 per cent) of the national print market. The aim is to break up the cartel of the corporate West German media giants, to give small and medium-sized newspapers a chance, and to enable a wider range of voices to be heard.

Although critics denounced the Bill as the 'return of censorship' and 'the GDR's recidivation to its bad old ways', the truth is that it is hardly draconian. It will only affect three newspapers, namely the liberal-conservative *Frankfurter Allgemeine Zeitung* (FAZ), the liberal-conservative *Welt*, and the conservative *Bild*. Even then, the Bill's impact on the FAZ will be negligible, as the FAZ's current market share is only a few percentage points above the permitted maximum. The Bill will, however, have a major impact on the *Bild*, which has by far the widest circulation of all newspapers. It currently sells over 1.8 million copies every day; from now on, it will only be allowed to sell up to about

600,000. The *Welt*'s market share is about a third below the permitted maximum, but since the *Welt* and the *Bild* are owned by the same company, they will have to divide their permitted market share between them. Thus, the *Welt* could disappear completely from East Germany.

One can debate the fine print of the Media Diversification Bill, but the need for some reform is undisputed. Before 1990, the GDR did not really have a non-state media sector. So once the Berlin Wall was gone, East Germans more or less just copied West German reading habits.

This has led to a number of problems. There is a substantial body of opinion in East Germany which feels marginalised, unheard and attacked by the broader media.

The reason for that is this: the West German press is not an impartial disseminator of news and information. It is, by and large, a highly sophisticated and aggressive form of political campaigning and lobbying. It uses its extensive muscle to defend West Germany's current economic order which, after all, directly benefits the rich moguls who own almost the entire West German press. Whether it's *Bild*, *Welt* or the *Frankfurter Allgemeine Zeitung*, that means promoting capitalism and denigrating socialism. The press has been instrumental in upholding the political consensus established by the coalition in Bonn: deregulation, privatisation, low taxes on the rich and weak trade unions. It has traditionally defined what is politically acceptable and palatable in West Germany, and ignored, demonised and humiliated individuals and movements which challenge this consensus. It is now doing the same in East Germany.

Rather than challenging powerful interests, the press is more interested in punching down, disseminating myths and outright lies in the process, especially about the alleged shortcomings of socialism. Polling shows widespread acceptance of myths on everything from the true extent of shortages in the GDR to how well East German emigrants in West Germany are doing, and media coverage plays a critical role in spreading these dangerous misconceptions.

The distinction between 'news' and 'opinion' throughout much of the West German press is blurred. The press abounds with writers who use their 'news' writing as a means to advance political aims and causes, even if they pretend otherwise.

Pundits do play, at least in theory, an important role in democracy. The problem is that the West German commentariat is by and large a cartel. Its members are mostly there because of their views, their backgrounds, and – to varying degrees – their connections. People from working-class backgrounds, for example, are consistently underrepresented. Our backgrounds inevitably play an important role in forming our worldviews, determining our priorities and creating our blind spots.

The spectrum of opinion represented in the commentariat is limited indeed. There is a broad consensus on economic issues – a defence of the market, a rejection of socialist alternatives – and contempt for ideas that challenge this consensus.

In addition, there are prominent broadcast journalists who have outright partisan backgrounds (some used to be prominent conservative or liberal activists, others worked for industry associations). The priorities of broadcast news are in large part determined by those of the right-wing press: their headlines and angles often frame debate on TV and radio each day. The problem with broadcast news coverage is that it treats the status quo as 'neutrality'. The voices that depart from the consensus are to be checked for bias.

A media so weighted in favour of capitalism makes progressive, campaigning journalism a necessity. Much of modern journalism exists – often aggressively so – to defend the way West German society is currently structured. And the most common form of doing this is to attack the most obvious counterexample: East Germany.

Granted, a sales cap on West German newspapers cannot be more than a makeshift solution to these problems, as the Secretary of State for Media and Culture, Lars Becker, has readily acknowledged. The GDR will have to do better than that. It will have to find ways of building up an independent media landscape of its own – where 'independent' refers to independence both from the state *and* from corporate interests. It will have to find ways of encouraging working-class kids to take up journalism as a career. It will have to develop a media culture which is better suited to the GDR's specific social and economic environment.

None of this will happen overnight. But nobody in East Berlin is under any illusions about the scale of the challenge ahead. On the contrary, East Berlin is positively brimming with exciting, innovative ideas for progressive change. The Media Diversification Bill is no more than a clumsy first step. The important lesson for now is this: an economic model based on satisfying the needs of the people, and a corporate media model based on promoting the economic self-interest of its owners, do not mix well.

East German government plans introduction of minimum notice period for emigrants
The Guardian, 1 April 1997

Of all the hard-earned rights that East Germans won for themselves in the peaceful revolution of 1989/90, the right to emigrate is the one that has acquired the most sacred and the most iconic status. Surveys show that freedom of movement is almost universally seen as one of the most precious achievements of the renewal period. It enjoys high levels of approval even among those who have the most positive view of the 'old' (i.e. pre-1990) GDR, and among those who have no desire to emigrate themselves.

Is the East German government's introduction of a six-month 'qualifying period' for emigrants a serious infringement of that right? Of course not. Organising a move from one country to another can easily take several months anyway, and it is not a decision that many people will make overnight. But given the country's history, it is easy to see why the announcement has made emotions run high.

In the future, East Germans who wish to emigrate will be required to notify their local record section six months in advance. Contrary to the way it has been presented in parts of the West German and British media, this does not mean that they will require a 'permit' to emigrate. Once they have handed in their notification, the record section will acknowledge the receipt, in written form. With effect from six months from then on, this receipt entitles the holder to emigrate. It is not a permit as such, because a permit can be refused. A receipt cannot. This new measure, while no doubt inconvenient for many, cannot prevent anyone from emigrating. It can, at best, delay their emigration by a few weeks or months.

Sven Holtermann, the Home Secretary of the GDR, explains:

> The freedom to choose where we want to live is one of the most fundamental and unnegotiable of human rights. Nobody knows this better than I do. Back in the bad old days, I spent a year in prison for assisting a friend to escape. He committed no crime. He never harmed anyone. All he wanted to do was live together with his West German girlfriend.
>
> During this year in prison, I learned that there was something fundamentally morally wrong with a country which denies its citizens such a basic human right. I am immensely proud of being a member of a government under which the right to emigrate became set in stone.
>
> And so it will remain.
>
> But we need to strike a balance here. To our would-be emigrants, we say this: you are valued members of our communities and we are sad to see you leave. But the decision is yours. No one on earth has a right to stop you.

What we expect from you, however, is that you give us a chance to adjust. Your decision to leave has an impact on other people around you. There is a Five-Year Plan in place, which counts on your contribution. If a lot of people in a particular industry are suddenly no longer available, production in that industry falls behind its schedule. This has knock-on effects on complementary sectors of the economy, which then affects other sectors. And so on. In the worst case, this can jumble our Five-Year Plan as a whole.

Our opponents have long asserted that socialism is incompatible with individual liberty. They are obviously wrong, and in fact the reasonable compromise we have just found proves them wrong yet again. But their assertion contains a small grain of truth: there is a tension between personal autonomy on the one hand and the demands of a close-knit community on the other hand. It is a tension that can be resolved – and resolving it is precisely what we're doing right now. But it is a tension that exists and that requires imaginative solutions.

The big difference between a capitalist economy and ours is that ours is a *collective* endeavour. Once you are part of a collective endeavour, you can no longer automatically just do whatever you like.

We all know this from our personal lives. If you have a spouse and children, you no longer have the flexibility that you had when you were single. If you work with a team, you need to behave like a team player; you need to coordinate your actions with other people and accept that you won't always get your way. If you live on your own, you can turn up the music late at night as loud as you like, but if you share a flat with other people, you can no longer do that. And so on.

In our personal lives, we all know this, and most of us act accordingly without even thinking about it. It's just what you do. But the same principle applies to whole economies. Unlike the West German economy, our economy is a team effort. Our socialist economy turns our society into a large community, a much more close-knit community than West Germany will ever be. This has many advantages. But it does impose certain constraints upon us as individuals.

None of this means that we cannot have personal autonomy. Of course we can. And we do. But unlike in West Germany, it needs careful management. And that's what we're doing with these changes. You have a right to live wherever you like. But we, as a community, have a right to know in advance, so that we can amend our plans and make alternative arrangements. That's all we ask of you.

We think the current solution strikes a reasonable balance between the rights of the individual and the rights of the community.

A number of practical problems still need sorting out. It is not clear how the new system will deal with people who simply leave without notifying the record sections in advance. A complementary tightening of border controls might also become necessary.

East Germany shows that protest can be a reassertion of privilege[4]

The Guardian, 6 November 1997

The feeling of déjà vu is overwhelming. Streets filled with protesters marching in lockstep. Crowds chanting 'We are the people!' GDR flags with the national emblem – the hammer and compass symbol – cut out. Haven't we been here before? This looks like 1989 all over again.

But this outward semblance is extremely deceptive. East Germany's new protest movement could not be any more different from the protest movements of the late 1980s.

Let's take a step back and look at the bigger picture. The upsurge in global protest in the past couple of years has driven home the lesson that mass demonstrations can have entirely different social and political meanings. Just because they wear bandannas and build barricades doesn't automatically mean protesters are fighting for democracy or social justice.

In some countries, mass protests have been led by working-class organisations, targeting neoliberalism, privatisation and corporate power. In others, predominantly middle-class unrest has been the lever to restore ousted elites. Yet on TV, they look similar.

---

4   With minor tweaks, large sections of this fictitious article are based on a real *Guardian* article by Seumas Milne. See: Venezuela shows that protest can be a defence of privilege, *The Guardian*, 9 April 2014 (https://www.theguardian.com/commentisfree/2014/apr/09/venezuela-protest-defence-privilege-maduro-elites).

From the overthrow of the elected Mossadegh government in Iran in the 1950s, when the CIA and MI6 paid anti-government demonstrators, the US and its allies have led the field: sponsoring 'colour revolutions', funding client NGOs and training student activists, fuelling street protest and denouncing – or ignoring – violent police crackdowns as it suits them.

And after a period when they preened themselves on promoting democracy, they are reverting to their anti-democratic ways. This is what is happening in East Germany, which, for the past two months, has been racked by anti-government protests aimed at overthrowing the socialist VL/PDS government re-elected two years ago.

The right-wing East German opposition seems to have a problem with the democracy business, having lost both elections since the country's return to democracy in 1990. So the opposition leaders – who are closely linked to American and West German corporations, and receive substantial support from them – have now launched a campaign to oust the coalition. They have called on their supporters to take to the streets. And they responded.

For eight weeks, they have organised street protests, marches and sit-ins, bringing parts of the GDR's major cities to an almost complete standstill. At least 53 people have been injured. Despite claims by the West German Foreign Minister, Klaus Kinkel, that the GDR is 'returning to its bad old ways', the evidence suggests a majority have been injured by opposition supporters, including eight members of the People's Police and seven soldiers of the National People's Army.

What are portrayed as peaceful protests have all the hallmarks of an anti-democratic rebellion, shot through with class privilege and contempt for ordinary people. Supposedly, these protests are about ongoing shortages and renewed restrictions on personal freedoms, but don't be fooled.

In order to understand where these protests suddenly came from, we need to understand the GDR's peculiar class structure. In theory, the GDR has been a classless society from its inception. In the Soviet Zone of Occupation, the Soviet interim government dismantled the old class structure in Eastern Germany by expropriating all the large landowners and industrialists. The SED then tried to build a society without classes on the 'clean slate' they inherited from the Soviets.

But even though the material *basis* of the old class society had disappeared, the mindset, the attitudes and the social practices associated with a class society still lingered. In subtle ways, class privilege was preserved and passed on to the next generation. It was as if East German society had an 'institutional memory' of class structure, even if that class structure itself had long gone. And this institutional memory is now being used to attempt to rebuild the old class structure. What we currently see, albeit cloaked in the hood of 'progressive' street protest, is nothing short of the reassertion of class privilege.

The protests are dominated by the closest thing that a socialist society can have to a privileged class. These are people in the kind of comfortable, cushy jobs which are relatively safe even in capitalist countries. They are the ones who would most obviously stand to gain from a restoration of capitalism. And they know it.

Listen to the protesters when they are being interviewed by TV news crews. You will not hear many working-class accents. You will not hear the uncouth dialects that are so common in the Berlin/Brandenburg area, or in the region of Saxony. But you will hear posh accents. You will come across family names that smack of old money, the equivalents of surnames like 'Montgomery' or 'Bartholomew' in the UK. Even names with a 'von' are making a comeback.

We should not pretend that these protesters speak for the wider public. What we see here is not a popular protest, but a return of the old elites trying to reclaim their former class privileges. Support for the government, meanwhile, remains solid in working-class areas.

But even if we ignore the classist elements, this is not a movement which has sprung up spontaneously. It is not really an East German protest movement at all. It is a movement which has been systematically created from outside, with Western money, Western support and Western encouragement. It is hardly surprising in the circumstances that the East German government regards what has been going on as a destabilisation backed by West Germany and the US. Evidence for the US/West German subversion of the GDR – especially the large-scale funding of opposition groups and the provision of logistical support – is voluminous.

That is partly because from the perspective of Western corporations, the GDR represents vast untapped potential: industries to asset-strip, a workforce to exploit, consumers to hoodwink. And so on. They cannot bear the fact that there is a country which escapes their clutches, because its people have the audacity to do things differently.

But it is also because the GDR has spearheaded the progressive tide that has swept Western Europe over the past decade: challenging US and EU domination, taking back resources from corporate control, and redistributing wealth and power. Despite its current economic problems, revolutionary East Germany's achievements are indisputable.

It has massively expanded public health, housing, education and women's rights, boosted pensions and the minimum wage, established tens of thousands of People-Owned Enterprises, put resources in the hands of a grassroots participatory democracy, and funded health and social development programmes.

So it is not surprising that the VL and the PDS still have majority support. To maintain that, the government will have to get a grip on shortages and inflation – it has the means to do so. For all its problems, the economy has continued to grow, if at a slower rate than West Germany's. There is no unemployment and no poverty. East Germany is very far from being the basket case of its enemies' hopes. But the risk is that as the protests run out of steam, sections of the opposition turn to greater violence to compensate for their failure at the ballot box.

East Germany and its progressive allies matter to the rest of the region because they have demonstrated that there is a social and economic alternative to the failed neoliberal system that still has the West and its allies in its grip.

Their opponents hope that the impetus for change has exhausted itself. They are wrong. The tide is still flowing. But powerful interests at home and abroad are determined that it fails – which means there will be more GDR-style protests to come.

Opinion: Socialism has not failed in East Germany – it hasn't been tried[5]
The Guardian, 7 December 1998

Last night's election result has brutally choked off the experiment of socialist renewal in East Germany. The main governing party, the United Left (VL), has suffered a crushing defeat, dropping to just 0.2 per cent of the vote. Its coalition partner, the PDS, has stabilised at 21.6 per cent, but since all the major parties have ruled out a coalition with the PDS, this means that their days in government are numbered.

---

5   Large sections of this fictitious article are a mashup, with minor tweaks, of actual articles by Slavoj Žižek, Mary Dejevsky, Ryan Beitler and Owen Jones. See: The problem with Venezuela's revolution is that it didn't go far enough, *Independent*, 9 August 2017 (http://www.independent.co.uk/voic es/venezuela-socialism-communism-left-didnt-go-far-enough-a7884021 .html); Most politicians decrying the crisis in Venezuela don't care about its people – they care about a stick to beat Corbyn with, *Independent*, 10 August 2017 (http://www.independent.co.uk/voices/venezuela-jeremy -corbyn-why-wont-he-condemn-chavez-general-election-a7886931.html); What's the matter with Venezuela?: It's not socialism, it's corruption, *Paste Magazine*, 19 June 2017 (https://www.pastemagazine.com/artic les/2017/06/whats-the-matter-with-venezuela-its-not-socialism.html). My thoughts on Cuba, *Medium*, 29 November 2016 (https://medium.com/@ OwenJones84/my-thoughts-on-cuba-32280774222f).

All of the parties that could realistically form a government now have made it abundantly clear that they would immediately enter into reunification negotiations with the Federal Republic. It is therefore safe to say that by the end of next year, Germany will be reunited and the GDR will be no more. All the achievements of the past eight years will be swept away. The same neoliberal agenda which has wreaked havoc in Britain, the US, Ireland, New Zealand, Chile and, to a lesser extent, West Germany, will now be let loose in East Germany as well.

Predictably, many on the right are now crowing about how, allegedly, 'socialism' has failed. The glee and the we-told-you-so attitude of certain commentators has been unbearable. But blaming all of the GDR's problems on 'socialism' is woefully simplistic and one-dimensional. It betrays a basic lack of understanding of the GDR's complicated history, its unique geopolitical situation, its special relationship with the Soviet Union and the Federal Republic, and the long-term structural problems of its economy. To claim that 'socialism has failed' may be a convenient (and cheap) way to score political points, but the situation is infinitely more complex than that.

The reasons why the GDR is now in the perilous state it is cannot be ascribed only, or even largely, to dogma – Marxist, socialist, populist or whatever. The dominance of one party always carries dangers; corruption, incompetence, the decline in global markets for manufactured goods, the country's social structures all played their part.

There can be no doubt about the East German government's failure to diversify the economy. But this is a long-term structural problem, which predates socialism by at least a generation. Back in the 1920s, an expert commission warned that the economy of the state of Saxony (which later became part of the GDR) was dangerously overreliant on heavy industry. Was that also the fault of 'socialism'? Did socialism create that problem retroactively?

After 1990, political turmoil in Eastern Europe and the Soviet Union meant that the GDR's traditional export markets suddenly became a lot less reliable. Was that also the VL/PDS coalition's fault? Is the East German government responsible for the geopolitical situation of the entire continent?

As far as the GDR's poor productivity performance is concerned, mismanagement explains a lot more of the current problems than 'socialism'. Talk to any VEB manager in the GDR. They will tell you about vital supplies that have not arrived on time, of unrealistic production quotas, of a misallocation of productive resources, of SPK planners unwilling to listen to people on the ground, of a lack of coordination between SPK departments, etc. This has nothing to do with socialism. It has everything to do with sheer incompetence and a lack of joined-up thinking.

In addition, there were the constant attempts by West Germany and the US to undermine socialism in the GDR, which the government did not know how to fend off. If socialism always 'fails', one wonders why its enemies always do everything in their power to undermine it. Why not just lean back and wait for it to fail, if failure is 'inevitable'?

The truth, of course, is that socialism's failure is far from inevitable. It 'fails' because powerful vested interests desperately *want* it to fail. Socialism *must* fail, because a successful socialist model would become a threat by example to the established order in the West. It would prove, merely by existing, that there is an alternative. No wonder the Western elites are so keen to ensure its failure. They simply cannot allow it to succeed.

West German and American corporations will now be the biggest winners from German reunification. For them, it will mean new markets to colonise, new assets to strip and a new labour force to exploit. The losers will be the millions of ordinary workers in the GDR, whose hopes for a better life have been so cynically exploited by the West German elites.

Nonetheless, those of us on the democratic left must not turn a blind eye to the fact that East Germany was already slipping back into its old, Stalinist ways. Almost immediately after securing their re-election in 1994, the VL/PDS coalition began to erode the hard-won gains of the November 1989 revolution. Had the coalition won a third term, it would probably have finished the job. The GDR was already well on its way to turning, once again, into the authoritarian police state it used to be for the first forty years of its history.

The VL/PDS government was initially on the right track. But it was never really willing to see its reforms through. As soon as it became clear that the ride would be a bit bumpier than it expected, it lost confidence in its own project.

This was the moment when the old Stalinist bureaucracy saw its opportunity to reassert itself. The VL lacked the courage and the wherewithal to stand up to them. The PDS probably never really wanted to; their change of heart after November 1989 was only skin-deep. It has often been pointed out that the PDS is the successor of the SED. What has less often been pointed out is that the SED itself was the successor of the Weimar-era Communist Party of Germany (KPD), a party which was 'Stalinist' not in the sense of 'authoritarian' but in the literal sense: in the 1920s and early 1930s, the KPD used to be Stalin's most reliable supporters in Europe. Stalinism was in their DNA. Parties can change, but they cannot become the polar opposite of what they have always been.

And so the coalition heeded the siren calls of the old Soviet-inspired elites, who told them: 'Never mind this whole democracy business. Give us back some of our old powers, and we will sort things out for you.' This techno-cratic elitism is directly at odds with everything socialism represents and everything the people of East Germany long for. Socialist ideas are not what has led the country to shortages, low productivity and shoddy products.

From a long history of Red Scare brainwashing, so-cialism is equated with tyranny in the UK, despite the central goal of the ideology being an equitable, classless society. Elitism and disdain for democracy is widespread and widely known in the GDR, so why do we blame so-cialism? It is not the ideology that is at work here, just like socialism wasn't practised in the Soviet Union. If the VL/PDS government had truly fulfilled the stated values of egalitarian democratic socialism, people wouldn't be emigrating, there wouldn't be queues, there wouldn't be shortages, there wouldn't be inflation, and there wouldn't be protests.

Why was there no East German left to provide an authentic radical alternative to the VL and the PDS? Why did the initiative in the opposition come from the neoliberal right, which triumphantly hegemonised the oppositional struggle, imposing itself as the voice of the ordinary people who suffer the consequences of the VL/PDS mismanagement of economy?

The only future for socialism – and the only possibility for socialism to win mass support – is through democracy. That doesn't just mean standing in elections, although that's a big part of it. It means organising a movement rooted in people's communities and workplaces. It means arguing for a system that extends democracy to the workplace and the economy. That's socialism: the democratisation of every aspect of society.

Championing East Germany in its current form will certainly resonate with a chunk of the radical left, but it just won't with the mass of the population who will simply think, 'Aha, that's really the sort of system you would like to impose on us!' Which it isn't.

'There is only one hope for mankind – and that is democratic socialism', said Nye Bevan. That's my own firm belief, whether it be for Britain, West Germany, East Germany or anywhere else. If you're a socialist, you believe all people deserve the same economic and political rights. That can't be achieved without democracy – not the limited democracy the West currently has, but a full democracy that we should aspire to. A socialist society doesn't exist yet. But one day it must.

And maybe it soon will. Venezuela is preparing for an election later this year. The most recent polls show a surge in support for a candidate of the radical democratic left. This hitherto virtually unknown outsider, Hugo Chávez, stands for a platform of democratic socialism. He has learned the lessons that the East German government refused to learn. He understands that socialism cannot be imposed from above, but must be rooted in a mass movement, in the lived experience of ordinary working people. Unless the polls change dramatically, he will soon get a chance to put his vision of democratic, participatory socialism into practice.

We might be witnessing the beginning of a remarkable experiment.

REFERENCES

Alexander, S. (2013) Noisy poll results and reptilian Muslim climatologists from Mars, 12 April (http://slatestarcodex.com/2013/04/12/noisy-poll-results-and-reptilian-muslim-climatologists-from-mars/).

Aly, G. (2012) *Unser Kampf: 1968 – ein irritierter Blick zurück*. Frankfurt am Main: Fischer Verlag.

Bade, K. and Oltmer, J. (2005) Migration, Ausländerbeschäftigung und Asylpolitik in der DDR. Bundeszentrale für politische Bildung (http://www.bpb.de/gesellschaft/migration/dossier-migration/56368/migrationspolitik-in-der-ddr?p=all).

Bandow, D. (2006) *Foreign Follies: America's New Global Empire*. Longwood, FL: Xulon Press.

Barro, R. (1994) Democracy and growth. Working Paper 4909. Cambridge, MA: National Bureau of Economic Research.

BBC News (n.d.) Brits abroad. World overview (http://news.bbc.co.uk/1/shared/spl/hi/in_depth/brits_abroad/html/s_america.stm and http://news.bbc.co.uk/1/shared/spl/hi/in_depth/brits_abroad/html/caribbean.stm).

Benton, G. and Chun, L. (2010) *Was Mao Really a Monster? The Academic Response to Chang and Halliday's Mao: The Unknown Story*. New York: Routledge.

Berger, S. and LaPorte, N. (2008) In search of anti-fascism: the British left's response to the GDR during the Cold War. *German History* 26(4): 536–52.

Berger, S. and LaPorte, N. (2010) *Friendly Enemies: Britain and the GDR, 1949–1990*. New York and Oxford: Berghahn Books.

Bergström, G. (1978) Kampuchea. Trip report by Gunnar Bergström.

Berkman, A. (1925) *The Bolshevik Myth (Diary 1920–1922)*. New York: Boni and Liveright.

BPB (2014) 18. März 1990: erste freie Volkskammerwahl (http://www.bpb.de/izpb/195467/18-maerz-1990?p=all).

Borbe, A. (2010) *Die Zahl der Opfer des SED-Regimes*. Erfurt: Landeszentrale für politische Bildung Thüringen.

Burda, M. and Weder, M. (2017) The economics of German unification after twenty-five years: Lessons for Korea. Working Paper 2017-07. University of Adelaide. School of Economics.

Caplan, B. (2006) *The Myth of the Rational Voter. Why Democracies Choose Bad Policies*. Princeton University Press.

Caplan, B. (2009) Is socialism really 'impossible'? *Critical Review* 16(1): 33–52.

Carrier, F. (1975) *North Korean Journey: The Revolution Against Colonialism*. New York: International Publishers.

Caute, D. (1988) *The Fellow Travellers: Intellectual Friends of Communism*. New Haven: Yale University Press.

Cheremukhin, A., Golosov, M., Guriev, S. and Tsyvinski, A. (2013) Was Stalin necessary for Russia's economic development? NBER Working Paper 19425. National Bureau of Economic Research.

Chomsky, N. (1986) The Soviet Union versus Socialism. *Our Generation*, Spring/Summer Issue (https://chomsky.info/1986____/).

Chomsky, N. and Herman, E. (1977) Distortions at fourth hand. *The Nation*, June edition (https://chomsky.info/19770625/).

Chomsky, N. and Herman, E. (1979) *After the Cataclysm: Postwar Indochina and the Reconstruction of Imperial Ideology.* Boston: South End Press.

CIA World Factbook (2017) Country comparison: GDP per capita (PPP) (https://www.cia.gov/library/publications/the-world-factbook/rankorder/2004rank.html).

Cleaver, E. (1970) Statement from the US peoples' anti-imperialist delegation to Korea. History and Public Policy Program Digital Archive, University of California, Berkeley (http://digitalarchive.wilsoncenter.org/document/114495).

Cleaver, E. (1971) Message to Kim Il Sung from Eldridge Cleaver. 9 September 1971. History and Public Policy Program Digital Archive, University of California, Berkeley (http://digitalarchive.wilsoncenter.org/document/114497).

Conway, D. (1987) *A Farewell to Marx: An Outline and Appraisal of his Theories.* Harmondsworth: Penguin Books.

Corrales, J. (1999) Venezuela in the 1980s, the 1990s and beyond: why citizen-detached parties imperil economic governance. ReVista Harvard Review of Latin America.

Courtois, S., Werth, N., Panné, L., Paczkowski, A., Bartošek, K. and Margolin, J. (1999) *The Black Book of Communism: Crimes, Terror, Repression.* Harvard University Press.

Cumings, B. (2004) *North Korea: Another Country.* New York and London: The New Press.

De La Motte, B. and Green, J. (2015) *Stasi State or Socialist Paradise? The German Democratic Republic and What Became of It.* London: Artery Publications.

Deutsche Botschaft Budapest (n.d.) Chronik der Geschichte der Grenzöffnung in Ungarn.

Deutscher Bundestag (2006) Bertolt Brecht und sein Verhältnis zur Politik. WD 1 – 119/06, Wissenschaftliche Dienste des Deutschen Bundestages. Berlin: Deutscher Bundestag.

Dieterich, H. (1996) *Der Sozialismus des 21. Jahrhunderts: Wirtschaft, Gesellschaft und Demokratie nach dem globalen Kapitalismus.* Werder an der Havel: Homilius Verlag.

Dowty, A. (1988) The assault on freedom of emigration. *World Affairs* 151(2): 85–92.

Dowty, A. (1989) *Closed Borders: The Contemporary Assault on Freedom of Movement.* Yale University Press.

Duany, J. (2017) Cuban migration: a postrevolution exodus ebbs and flows. Migration Policy Institute (https://www.migration-policy.org/article/cuban-migration-postrevolution-exodus -ebbs-and-flows).

Dunt, I. (2015) The questions Corbyn's critics must answer, 15 September (http://www.politics.co.uk/comment-analysis/ 2015/09/15/the-questions-corbyn-s-critics-must-answer).

Ear, S. (1995) The Khmer Rouge canon 1975–1979: the standard total academic view on Cambodia. Dissertation, Department of Political Science, University of California, Berkeley.

European Commission (2017) European Union, trade in goods with Cuba (http://trade.ec.europa.eu/doclib/docs/2006/sept ember/tradoc_122460.pdf).

Fleischhauer, J. (2009) *Unter Linken. Von einem, der aus Versehen konservativ wurde.* Reinbek bei Hamburg: Rowohlt Verlag.

Foster, P. (2014) *Why We Bite the Invisible Hand. The Psychology of Anti-Capitalism.* Toronto: Pleasaunce Press.

Fraser Institute (2017) Economic Freedom of the World: 2017 Annual Report. Dataset (https://www.fraserinstitute.org/res ource-file?nid=11606&fid=7542).

Fröberg Idling, P. (2006) *Pol Pots leende*. Stockholm: Bokförlaget Atlas (http://www.wordswithoutborders.org/article/from-po l-pots-smile).

Gallacher, W. (1953) Tribute to Stalin. *Labour Monthly* 35(4) (https://www.marxists.org/archive/gallacher/1953/04/stalin .htm).

Graff, H. (1991) *The Legacies of Literacy: Continuities and Contradictions in Western Culture*. Bloomington and Indianapolis: Indiana University Press.

Griffiths, R. (2011) *Fellow Travellers of the Right: British Enthusiasts for Nazi Germany*. London: Faber and Faber.

Habermann, G. (1994) *Der Wohlfahrtsstaat. Die Geschichte eines Irrwegs*. Berlin: Propyläen Verlag.

Haggerty, R. (ed.) (1990) Venezuela: a country study. Federal Research Division. Washington: GPO for the Library of Congress (http://www.country-data.com/frd/cs/vetoc.html#ve0000).

Haidt, J. (2012) *The Righteous Mind. Why Good People Are Divided by Politics and Religion*. London: Allen Lane.

Hansard (1949) Germany and Eastern Europe. House of Commons Debate, 23 March 1949, vol. 463 cc430-512 (http://han sard.millbanksystems.com/commons/1949/mar/23/germa ny-and-eastern-europe-1#S5CV0463P0_19490323_HOC_394).

Hansard (1986) Enterprise and deregulation. House of Commons Debates, 13 June 1986, vol. 99 cc665-731 (https://api.parlia ment.uk/historic-hansard/commons/1986/jun/13/enter prise-and-deregulation).

Hayek, F. A. (1945) The use of knowledge in society. *American Economic Review* 35(4): 519–30.

Hayek, F. A. (1988) *The Fatal Conceit: The Errors of Socialism*. Abingdon-on-Thames: Routledge.

Hayek, F. A. (1993) [1945] *The Road to Serfdom*. London: Routledge.

Hayek, F. A. (2002) [1968] Competition as a discovery procedure. *The Quarterly Journal of Austrian Economics* 5(3): 9–23.

Heath, A. (2017) There is no more political debate in Britain – just an endless series of surrenders to the Left. *Daily Telegraph*, 6 September (http://www.telegraph.co.uk/news/2017/09/06/no-political-debate-britain-just-endless-series-surrenders/).

Hollander, P. (1990) *Political Pilgrims. Travels of Western Intellectuals to the Soviet Union, China, and Cuba 1928–1978*. Lanham: University Press of America.

IMF (2017) GDP per capita, current prices. Purchasing power parity, international dollars per capita. Dataset (http://www.imf.org/external/datamapper/PPPPC@WEO/THA).

Jones, O. (2016) My thoughts on Cuba. Medium (https://medium.com/@OwenJones84/my-thoughts-on-cuba-32280774222f#.e1r6b7vus).

KPD (1922) *Programm-Entwurf der KPD*. Berlin: Kommunistische Partei Deutschlands.

KPD (1930) Programmerklärung zur nationalen und sozialen Befreiung des deutschen Volkes. Proklamation des ZK der KPD. Berlin: Kommunistische Partei Deutschlands.

Laski, H. (1946) *Reflections on the Revolution of Our Time*. Allahabat: Central Book Depot.

Legatum Institute (2017) *Public Opinion in the Post-Brexit Era: Economic Attitudes in Modern Britain*. London: Legatum Institute.

Locard, H. (2015) The myth of Angkor as an essential component of the Khmer Rouge Utopia. In *Cultural Heritage as Civilising Mission: From Decay to Recovery* (ed. M. Falser). Heidelberg: Springer Verlag.

Macrotrends (2018) Crude oil prices – 70 year historical chart. Dataset (https://www.macrotrends.net/1369/crude-oil-price -history-chart).

Maddison, A. (2008) Statistics on world population, GDP and per capita GDP, 1–2008 AD. Dataset, University of Groningen.

Makovi, M. (2015) Two opposing literary critiques of socialism: George Orwell versus Eugen Richter and Henry Hazlitt. *International Journal of Pluralism and Economics Education* 7(2): 116–34.

Milne, S. (2015) Foreword. In *Stasi State or Socialist Paradise? The German Democratic Republic and What Became of It* (ed. B. De La Motte and J. Green). London: Artery Publications.

Mises, L. (1922) *Die Gemeinwirtschaft. Untersuchungen über den Sozialismus.* Jena: Gustav Fischer Verlag.

Mosbacher, M. (2004) British anti-Americanism. London: The Social Affairs Unit (http://socialaffairsunit.org.uk/digipub/in dex2.php?option=content&do_pdf=1&id=12).

Myrdal, J. (1978) Kampuchea and the war – speeches and polemics. Skriftställning 11, Oktoberförlaget.

Myrdal, J. and Kessle. G. (1976) *Albania Defiant.* London/New York: Monthly Review Press.

NatCen Social Research (2017) British social attitudes (http://www.bsa.natcen.ac.uk/media/39145/bsa34_role-of-govt_fin al.pdf).

Niemietz, K. (2011) *A New Understanding of Poverty: Poverty Measurement and Policy Implications.* London: Institute of Economic Affairs.

Niemietz, K. (2013) De-politicising airport expansion. IEA Discussion Paper 51. London: Institute of Economic Affairs (https://

iea.org.uk/publications/research/de-politicising-airport
-expansion).

Niemietz, K. (2015) Reducing poverty through policies to cut
the cost of living. London/York: Joseph Rowntree Foundation
(https://www.jrf.org.uk/file/47498/download?token=dkBct
xBK&filetype=summary).

Norberg, J. (2008) The Klein Doctrine: The rise of disaster polemics. Briefing Paper 102, Cato Institute (https://www.cato.org/
publications/briefing-paper/klein-doctrine-rise-disaster
-polemics).

OECD (n.d.) Fiscal decentralisation database (http://www.oecd
.org/tax/federalism/fiscal-decentralisation-database.htm).

Our World in Data (2013/2017) Global extreme poverty (https://
ourworldindata.org/extreme-poverty/).

Our World in Data (2017) Life expectancy (https://ourworldin
data.org/life-expectancy/).

Piñeiro Harnecker, C. (2009) Workplace democracy and social
consciousness: a study of Venezuelan cooperatives. *Science
and Society* 73(3): 309–39.

Przeworski, A. (2002) Democracy and economic development.
In *Political Science and the Public Interest* (ed. E. Mansfield
and R. Sisson). Columbus Ohio State University Press.

Przeworski, A. and Limongi, F. (1997) Modernization: theories
and facts. *World Politics* 49(2): 155–83.

Quandl (2018) Venezuela general government total expenditure,
% of GDP. Dataset (https://www.quandl.com/data/ODA/VEN
_GGX_NGDP-Venezuela-General-Government-Total-Expen
diture-of-GDP).

RCPGB-ML (1995) *Draft Programme for the Working Class*. London:
Revolutionary Communist Party of Britain (Marxist-Leninist)

(http://www.rcpbml.org.uk/articles/DRAFT_PROGRAM ME.pdf).

Restuccia, D. (2010) The monetary and fiscal history of Venezuela 1960–2005. Working Paper. University of Toronto.

Revel, J. (1978) *The Totalitarian Temptation*. Harmondsworth: Penguin Books.

Rinser, L. (1986) *Nordkoreanisches Reisetagebuch*. Frankfurt am Main: Fischer Taschenbuch Verlag (https://web.archive.org/web/20100831053645/http://www.kdvr.de/reiseberichte/luise/luise.html).

Robinson, J. (1965) Korean Miracle. *Monthly Review* 16(9): 541–49.

Röhl, K. (2009) *Strukturelle Konvergenz der ostdeutschen Wirtschaft*. Cologne: Institute for Economic Research.

Roser, M. (2017) Working hours (https://ourworldindata.org/working-hours/).

Roser, M. (2018) Life expectancy (https://ourworldindata.org/life-expectancy).

Roser, M. and Ortiz-Ospina, E. (2013) Global extreme poverty (https://ourworldindata.org/extreme-poverty).

Roser, M. and Ortiz-Ospina, E. (2017) Literacy (https://ourworldindata.org/literacy/).

Russell, B. (1920) *The Practice and Theory of Bolshevism*. London: Allen and Unwin.

Schumpeter, J. (1976) *Capitalism, Socialism and Democracy*. London: George Allen and Unwin.

Searle, J. (2011) The depiction of the GDR in prominent British texts published between official recognition of the 'other' German State in 1973 and the fall of the Berlin Wall in 1989. *eTransfers*, A Postgraduate eJournal for Comparative Literature and Cultural Studies, Issue 1.

Seldon, A. (2004) *The Virtues of Capitalism. The Collected Works of Arthur Seldon.* Indianapolis: Liberty Fund (http://oll.liberty fund.org/titles/seldon-the-collected-works-of-arthur-seldon -vol-1-the-virtues-of-capitalism).

Snowdon, C. (2017) *Killjoys: A Critique of Paternalism.* London: Institute of Economic Affairs.

SPGB (n.d.) Russia was never socialist – and why... what we said over the years (https://www.worldsocialism.org/spgb/educa tion/depth-articles/history/russia-was-never-socialist).

Stalin, J. (1921) Our disagreements. *Pravda*, No 12 (https://www .marxists.org/reference/archive/stalin/works/1921/jan/05 .htm).

Steiner, A. (2010) *The Plans That Failed: An Economic History of the GDR.* Oxford and New York: Berghahn Books.

Stöcker, R. (2016) *Das Parteiensystem Sachsen-Anhalts. Eine An- alyse der Ursachen seiner Entwicklung hin zur Stabilisierung.* Wiesbaden: Springer Fachmedien.

Trotsky, L. (1936) *The Revolution Betrayed. What Is the Soviet Union and Where Is It Going?* (https://www.marxists.org/arch ive/trotsky/1936/revbet/index.htm).

Tullock, G. (2006) [1976] *The Vote Motive.* London: Institute of Economic Affairs.

Tupy, M. (2016) Castro's 'accomplishments' in Cuba a load of nonsense. *Reason*, 29 November (https://reason.com/arch ives/2016/11/29/castros-accomplishments-in-cuba-a-load-o).

Udy, G. (2017) *Labour and the Gulag: Russia and the Seduction of the British Left.* London: Biteback Publishing.

Venezuela Solidarity Campaign (2012) *Viva Venezuela! Magazine* 2(2) (https://issuu.com/venezuelasolidaritycampaign/docs/ viva_venezuela_volume_2_issue_2).

Venezuela Solidarity Campaign (2013) *Viva Venezuela! Magazine* 3(1) (https://issuu.com/venezuelasolidaritycampaign/docs/venezuela_solidarity_campaign_magaz).

Venezuela Solidarity Campaign (2014) *Viva Venezuela! Magazine* 4(1) (https://issuu.com/venezuelasolidaritycampaign/docs/vsc_magazine_volume_4_issue_1).

Venezuela Solidarity Campaign (2016) *Viva Venezuela! Magazine* 6(1) (https://issuu.com/venezuelasolidaritycampaign/docs/vscnews_v6_issue1_5).

Vereinigte Linke (1990) Vorläufiges Programm zu den Volkskammerwahlen am 18. März 1990 (http://www.ddr89.de/vl/VL 38.html).

Webb, S. (1933) Is Soviet Russia a democracy? *Current History*, February.

Webb, S. and Webb, B. (1936) *Is Soviet Communism a New Civilisation?* London: The Left Review.

Werner, A. (2015) Convenient partnerships? African American civil rights leaders and the East German dictatorship. In *Anywhere But Here: Black Intellectuals in the Atlantic World and Beyond* (ed. K. Radcliffe, J. Scott and A. Werner). University Press of Mississippi.

Wilson Center (2013) 'Our common struggle against our common enemy': North Korea and the American Radical left. E-Dossier No. 14, North Korea International Documentation Project, Woodrow Wilson Center for International Scholars (https://www.wilsoncenter.org/sites/default/files/NKIDP_eDossier_14_North_Korea_and_the_American_Radical_Left.pdf).

Wolin, R. (2010) *The Wind from the East: French Intellectuals, the Cultural Revolution, and the Legacy of the 1960s.* Princeton University Press.

World Bank (2017) Ease of doing business index. Dataset (https://data.worldbank.org/indicator/IC.BUS.EASE.XQ).

Wunschik, T. (1997) ‚Die maoistische KPD/ML und die Zerschlagung ihrer „Sektion DDR" durch das MfS', BF informiert 18/1997, Berlin: Bundesbeauftragte für die Unterlagen des Staatssicherheitsdienstes der ehemaligen Deutschen Demokratischen Republik, Abteilung Bildung und Forschung.

YouGov (2013) Nationalise energy and rail companies, say public (http://d25d2506sfb94s.cloudfront.net/cumulus_uploads/document/tu07589ap6/YG-Archive-131028-Class.pdf).

YouGov (2015a) Majority support for rail nationalisation – but also policies from the 'radical' right (https://d25d2506sfb94s.cloudfront.net/cumulus_uploads/document/537apwugsy/InternalResults_150805_left_right_policies_W.pdf).

YouGov (2015b) Nationalisation debate: it's not about 'whatever works' (http://cdn.yougov.com/cumulus_uploads/document/0877rs0qlh/Results_150310_PublicSector_Wesbite.pdf).

YouGov (2016a) Socialism and capitalism results (https://yougov.co.uk/opi/surveys/results#/survey/94978480-d625-11e5-a405-005056900127/question/a3ee8500-d625-11e5-a405-005056900127/toplines).

YouGov (2016b) 62% of British people support nationalising Port Talbot Steelworks (https://yougov.co.uk/news/2016/04/01/support-nationalising-port-talbot/).

YouGov (2017a) What if we had a socialist government (https://yougov.co.uk/news/2017/06/16/what-if-we-had-socialist-government-owning-signed-/).

YouGov (2017b) [no title] (http://d25d2506sfb94s.cloudfront.net/cumulus_uploads/document/4b0fz1wav2/PeterKellnerResults_171121_IdeologyStatements_w.pdf).

YouGov (2017c) Nationalisation vs privatisation: the public view (https://d25d2506sfb94s.cloudfront.net/cumulus_uploads/document/uufxmyd8qm/InternalResults_170518_nationalisation_privatisation_W.pdf).

Young, N. (1995) A comparative study on North and South Korean economic capability. *Journal of East Asian Affairs* 9(1): 1–43.

ABOUT THE IEA

The Institute is a research and educational charity (No. CC 235 351), limited by guarantee. Its mission is to improve understanding of the fundamental institutions of a free society by analysing and expounding the role of markets in solving economic and social problems.

The IEA achieves its mission by:

- a high-quality publishing programme
- conferences, seminars, lectures and other events
- outreach to school and college students
- brokering media introductions and appearances

The IEA, which was established in 1955 by the late Sir Antony Fisher, is an educational charity, not a political organisation. It is independent of any political party or group and does not carry on activities intended to affect support for any political party or candidate in any election or referendum, or at any other time. It is financed by sales of publications, conference fees and voluntary donations.

In addition to its main series of publications, the IEA also publishes (jointly with the University of Buckingham), *Economic Affairs*.

The IEA is aided in its work by a distinguished international Academic Advisory Council and an eminent panel of Honorary Fellows. Together with other academics, they review prospective IEA publications, their comments being passed on anonymously to authors. All IEA papers are therefore subject to the same rigorous independent refereeing process as used by leading academic journals.

IEA publications enjoy widespread classroom use and course adoptions in schools and universities. They are also sold throughout the world and often translated/reprinted.

Since 1974 the IEA has helped to create a worldwide network of 100 similar institutions in over 70 countries. They are all independent but share the IEA's mission.

Views expressed in the IEA's publications are those of the authors, not those of the Institute (which has no corporate view), its Managing Trustees, Academic Advisory Council members or senior staff.

Members of the Institute's Academic Advisory Council, Honorary Fellows, Trustees and Staff are listed on the following page.

The Institute gratefully acknowledges financial support for its publications programme and other work from a generous benefaction by the late Professor Ronald Coase.

Other books recently published by the IEA include:

Scandinavian Unexceptionalism: Culture, Markets and the Failure of Third-Way Socialism
Nima Sanandaji
Readings in Political Economy 1; ISBN 978-0-255-36704-2; £10.00

Classical Liberalism – A Primer
Eamonn Butler
Readings in Political Economy 2; ISBN 978-0-255-36707-3; £10.00

Federal Britain: The Case for Decentralisation
Philip Booth
Readings in Political Economy 3; ISBN 978-0-255-36713-4; £10.00

Forever Contemporary: The Economics of Ronald Coase
Edited by Cento Veljanovski
Readings in Political Economy 4; ISBN 978-0-255-36710-3; £15.00

Power Cut? How the EU Is Pulling the Plug on Electricity Markets
Carlo Stagnaro
Hobart Paperback 180; ISBN 978-0-255-36716-5; £10.00

Policy Stability and Economic Growth – Lessons from the Great Recession
John B. Taylor
Readings in Political Economy 5; ISBN 978-0-255-36719-6; £7.50

Breaking Up Is Hard To Do: Britain and Europe's Dysfunctional Relationship
Edited by Patrick Minford and J. R. Shackleton
Hobart Paperback 181; ISBN 978-0-255-36722-6; £15.00

In Focus: The Case for Privatising the BBC
Edited by Philip Booth
Hobart Paperback 182; ISBN 978-0-255-36725-7; £12.50

Islamic Foundations of a Free Society
Edited by Nouh El Harmouzi and Linda Whetstone
Hobart Paperback 183; ISBN 978-0-255-36728-8; £12.50

The Economics of International Development: Foreign Aid versus Freedom for the World's Poor
William Easterly
Readings in Political Economy 6; ISBN 978-0-255-36731-8; £7.50

Taxation, Government Spending and Economic Growth
Edited by Philip Booth
Hobart Paperback 184; ISBN 978-0-255-36734-9; £15.00

Universal Healthcare without the NHS: Towards a Patient-Centred Health System
Kristian Niemietz
Hobart Paperback 185; ISBN 978-0-255-36737-0; £10.00

Sea Change: How Markets and Property Rights Could Transform the Fishing Industry
Edited by Richard Wellings
Readings in Political Economy 7; ISBN 978-0-255-36740-0; £10.00

Working to Rule: The Damaging Economics of UK Employment Regulation
J. R. Shackleton
Hobart Paperback 186; ISBN 978-0-255-36743-1; £15.00

Education, War and Peace: The Surprising Success of Private Schools in War-Torn Countries
James Tooley and David Longfield
ISBN 978-0-255-36746-2; £10.00

Killjoys: A Critique of Paternalism
Christopher Snowdon
ISBN 978-0-255-36749-3; £12.50

Financial Stability without Central Banks
George Selgin, Kevin Dowd and Mathieu Bédard
ISBN 978-0-255-36752-3; £10.00

Against the Grain: Insights from an Economic Contrarian
Paul Ormerod
ISBN 978-0-255-36755-4; £15.00

Ayn Rand: An Introduction
Eamonn Butler
ISBN 978-0-255-36764-6; £12.50

Capitalism: An Introduction
Eamonn Butler
ISBN 978-0-255-36758-5; £12.50

Opting Out: Conscience and Cooperation in a Pluralistic Society
David S. Oderberg
ISBN 978-0-255-36761-5; £12.50

Getting the Measure of Money: A Critical Assessment of UK Monetary Indicators
Anthony J. Evans
ISBN 978-0-255-36767-7; £12.50

Other IEA publications

Comprehensive information on other publications and the wider work of the IEA can be found at www.iea.org.uk. To order any publication please see below.

Personal customers

Orders from personal customers should be directed to the IEA:

Clare Rusbridge
IEA
2 Lord North Street
FREEPOST LON10168
London SW1P 3YZ
Tel: 020 7799 8907. Fax: 020 7799 2137
Email: sales@iea.org.uk

Trade customers

All orders from the book trade should be directed to the IEA's distributor:

NBN International (IEA Orders)
Orders Dept.
NBN International
10 Thornbury Road
Plymouth PL6 7PP
Tel: 01752 202301, Fax: 01752 202333
Email: orders@nbninternational.com

IEA subscriptions

The IEA also offers a subscription service to its publications. For a single annual payment (currently £42.00 in the UK), subscribers receive every monograph the IEA publishes. For more information please contact:

Clare Rusbridge
Subscriptions
IEA
2 Lord North Street
FREEPOST LON10168
London SW1P 3YZ
Tel: 020 7799 8907, Fax: 020 7799 2137
Email: crusbridge@iea.org.uk